Cat
Wrangling
Made
Easy

Cat
Wrangling
Made
Easy

maintaining
peace & sanity
in your
multicat home

Dusty Rainbolt

THE LYONS PRESS

Guilford, Connecticut

AN IMPRINT OF THE GLOBE PEQUOT PRESS

Copyright © 2008 by Dusty Rainbolt

ALL RIGHTS RESERVED. No part of this book may be reproduced or transmitted in any form by any means, electronic or mechanical, including photocopying and recording, or by any information storage and retrieval system, except as may be expressly permitted in writing from the publisher. Requests for permission should be addressed to The Lyons Press, Attn: Rights and Permissions Department, P.O. Box 480, Guilford, CT 06437.

The Lyons Press is an imprint of The Globe Pequot Press.

10 9 8 7 6 5 4 3 2 1

Printed in the United States of America

Designed by Claire Zoghb

Illustrations by Nelle Davis

ISBN 978-1-59921-224-1

Library of Congress Cataloging-in-Publication Data is available on file.

Dedication

JIM RICHARDS—

You left this world
a happier, healthier
place for cats.
People too.

Contents

Acknowledgments

WRITING A BOOK IS LIKE acting in a movie. The star may get the glory, but a huge team of people made her look brilliant on the screen. *Cat Wrangling Made Easy* had a great team.

My deepest thanks go to my editor, Holly Rubino, and my agent, Kate Epstein. You're both the best! Thank you to my eternally patient husband, Weems Hutto, and the hardworking and ever wise Rainbolt Test Kitties. I love y'all! I really appreciate Beth Adelman and Dr. Cindy Rigoni for being the world's most thorough tech editors, Mary Anne Miller for her suggestions, and Rhonda and Jimmy Simpson for the title.

I also want to acknowledge the veterinarians and behaviorists who generously shared their expertise—especially Jim Richards, who was my medical consultant before he was tragically killed in a motorcycle accident in April 2007. I'm grateful to the following people for kindly sharing their knowledge: Karen Overall, Nick Dodman, Alice Moon-Fanelli, Kathryn Kollmeyer, Pam Johnson-Bennett, Susan Little, Patricia Hague, Jean Hofve, Julia Mandala, J. R. "Bert" Dodd, Peter Borchelt, Neils Pedersen, Michael Dryden, Granville C. Wright, Jill A. Richardson, Bonnie Shope and Linda A. Ross. Thank you also to Peggy Atkerson and Barn Cats Inc., Linda Gorsuch, Pat Chapman, Sondra York, Debbie and Bobb Waller, Joan Miller, Jacque Schultz, Nancy Peterson, Elaine Gardner-Morales, Marion Lane, Donna Dickey, Dorothy Wilkinson, Ali Aldaz, Anne Leighton, Don Aslett, Lauren Bond, Serena Fusek, Linda Kay Hardie, Art Rainbolt, Susan Hamil. I can't forget Ellen Urban, Diana Nuhn, Chris Mongillo, and Rose Marye Boudreaux at The Lyons Press. I couldn't have done it without you.

And a special thanks to you, dear reader, for wanting to improve your cats' lives.

Cats are like greatness: Some people are born into cat-loving families, some achieve cats, and some have cats thrust upon them.
—**William H. A. Carr**

WHEN I WAS A KID, I knew I wanted to be a writer, but I had no desire to be a cat writer. As a matter of fact, I didn't care for cats. My parents never permitted me to touch them for fear I would contract a wide variety of "incurable" diseases, including ringworm. In my senior year of high school, my sister moved back home and brought with her a black-and-white cat named Mista Peo. It was the end of the world as I knew it. Really!

As it turned out, Mista was a sweet, gentle creature. So when I left home, I found myself living with another cat. And another. Then I rescued a pregnant queen. I ran up the white flag and I surrendered to two of the kittens who turned me into a card-carrying ailurophile. Who'd have thought? Now I find myself surrounded by my little friends and can't imagine my life without at least a handful of them.

Because you're reading this book, I assume we share a love of cats. You either already have multiple cats or you're planning on adding kitties to your household. Welcome to my world, the wonderful world of multicat and megacat living. I consider any home with more than one cat a multicat home. Those of you who have the good fortune to live with ten or more cats are megacat families.

I'm also going to assume that you have more than two cats and you're starting to have problems. Or maybe you're getting a new kitty or you're moving in with someone who has kitties and you want to avoid trouble. Are you considering fostering abandoned cats for your local rescue group? Either way, this book is for you. *Cat Wrangling Made Easy* will help you avoid the pitfalls most multicat cat owners have fallen into. If you're already in the pit, it will send you a lifeline and help you pull yourself out. I've only included information I feel is practical from personal experience or from other people who have truly been there, done that.

When I first started writing this book, I debated whether to write it from a serious perspective or with a humorous point of view. I recalled the crazy things that happened to me and decided that most cats seem to have a sense of humor. And the chaos that engulfs those in a multicat home is often funny . . . in retrospect. So here's to our cats. And the way they can always cut our dignity down to size. May they always keep me in my place.

Now before we go any further, I know you want to do what's best for your cats. Whether you have three or thirteen, it's easy to get smothered when you smell the litter boxes, hear those nails shredding your leather chair, or, ugh, you step on a hairball in bare feet. Take a deep breath. We'll get through it together.

This book is also a great resource for working people who want to make life more interesting for their tabby twins. Or you and your cats already live a harmonious life together, but the carpet is a hazardous waste site. For those of you who feel hopeless and trapped, the house stinks, or the cats fight constantly, I'll help you make changes that will make everyone happy.

I make a promise too. I'll cut right through the cat poop. I'm not going to tell you to do anything I wouldn't do myself. For example, while I was writing an article on leash training your cat I interviewed a behaviorist who explained, "Leave the harness in the middle of the room and give your cat a treat. Later put it closer to the cat and give him a treat. Then, lay the harness next to him and hand him another treat. Next, rub the harness against the cat and reward him. Finally, put the harness on him loosely. Don't forget the reward. Later, tighten the harness. Later, —"

I stopped her in midsentence. "You expect people to do all that?" Yes she did! I asked her how she leash trained her cat. She paused. "I put the harness on him and rewarded him." "Then why would you expect the readers to do something you're not willing to do yourself?" Because that's the proper way to train them, she said.

So, I'll tell you the *practical* way from real people who have been in your place.

You're probably wondering what makes me think I'm qualified to tell you how to care for all of your kitties. My husband, Weems, and I have had as many as twenty cats under our roof at one time. Granted, some of those were foster cats or kittens. But having twenty cats at a time certainly was an eye-opener. I've been fostering kittens and cats for more than twenty years and have bottle-raised more than two hundred fifty orphan kittens. Maybe you've read my book, *Kittens for Dummies*. I'm a member of the International Association of Animal Behavior Consultants and must constantly upgrade my knowledge to stay current. For over ten years, I've been the product reviewer for *Catnip*, the newsletter published by the Cummings School of Veterinary Medicine at Tufts University. To give my readers an unbiased evaluation of the various cat products available on the market, I've enlisted the help of the Rainbolt Test Kitties, basically, my little product testers. They've tried stuff for every aspect of cat life—everything from cat fences to cat litter. They were my little guinea pigs. (By the way, no cats were hurt in the testing of these products. But on occasion their dignity might have been a little bruised.) You wouldn't believe the wonderful products I've run across. I've also tried some stinkers.

When you're building a cat tree (like the one you can build from plans you'll find in "Happy Habitats"), it helps to have the right tools. You can't build a scratching post with a car jack. It's the same thing when you're trying to manage a home full of cats. Having the right tool for the job and using a product that works is critical. So as you read through these pages, you'll occasionally see a product mentioned. These products have received the Rainbolt Test Kitties Paw Print of Approval. You can also refer to the Shopping Guide section for the complete list of useful products mentioned throughout *Cat Wrangling Made Easy.*

Because of my connection with Tufts, I've had the privilege to interview and associate with some of the best cat-loving minds in the industry—the best feline behaviorists, the best vets, the best rescuers, the best cat breeders, and the top product designers. Not only are you learning from my experience, you're benefiting from theirs, and without all the long distance calls.

As you read these pages, I'd like you to keep a few things in mind. To make it easier for you to read, as well as for me to write, unless I'm talking about a specific kitty or person, I'll be referring to all the cats in the book as "he" and the people as "she." "Kilroy" is the name of my generic dominant cat throughout the book. So please don't be insulted by all my cats being boys and my people women. Also, for the record a group of cats is a clowder, but I'll be talking about a "herd" of cats. After all, we are cat wranglers.

I'll be sharing with you a few of my experiences. You'll see that much of what I know, I learned at the School of Hard Knocks. Hopefully, you can bypass my screwups.

You are special and different from all other human beings on the planet, as are your cats. While everything I discuss has been proven successful by myself and other experts, not every technique or remedy will work in your particular situation or for your specific cats. Keep experimenting. You'll find what works for you.

The following sidebars appear throughout the book:

Reality Bites: these tips break an overwhelming problem into manageable baby steps. They help you give the best care without killing yourself and they provide suggestions to make possible cat care you might not otherwise be able to afford. Sometimes it's going to be tough love.

Tails from the Trenches: these stories detail the experiences of different multicat and megacat owners. Some have successful outcomes. Others fall on their tails. After all, we also learn from failure, preferably someone else's.

Feline Fact or Fiction: here I take fun facts or myths and either make or break them.

While you and your cats would benefit if you read the book cover to cover, you probably had specific problems in mind when you picked up *Cat Wrangling Made Easy*. Feel free to dive right into the chapters that will address the troubles you're currently experiencing. To avoid repetition, I'll give concepts a thorough explanation in the most appropriate chapter and cursory explanations throughout with a cross reference.

Now, grab someone furry and something to drink. Get your highlighter out so you can make notes. It's time to learn how to wrangle cats.

CHAPTER ONE

I May Be the Cat Lady/Guy, But I'm Not Crazy

Most beds sleep up to six cats.
Ten cats without the owner.
—Stephen Baker

SAY THERE, FRIEND, IS YOUR corral full of felines? Are you spending all your time rounding up strays and not enjoying them? If so, then it sounds like you might need some lessons in cat wrangling. I believe I can help you. People call me the Cat Wrangler.

My parents owned a ranch in south Texas that we worked on the weekends. Those Black Angus could wear you out, run you down, or break your leg with a well-placed kick, but that was nothin' compared to herding cats.

Like most people I started with one cat. Houston came into my life when I was nineteen. Twelve years later I rescued a pregnant cat abandoned in the snow. I found homes for all but two kittens. Before long a starving stray wandered up. *He* stayed for more than twenty years. Suddenly, I became the accidental head of a multicat household. I was no more prepared to care for multiple cats than I was to perform brain surgery.

Herding cattle, a challenge for any greenhorn working only on the weekends, doesn't even compare to the challenge of wrangling four cats. Frustrated, I looked inside their collars but couldn't find any care instructions.

I finally married a great guy who owned more cats than I did. Suddenly I went from a multicat home to a megacat family. I wouldn't say we were up to our eyeballs in cats. But cat wrangling became a full-time occupation.

Friends began to call me "the Crazy Cat Lady," as they dropped off the cat they plucked off the expressway medium. Sometimes I wondered, "Am I a crazy cat lady?" I may be a cat lady, but I not crazy, or am I? We had a lot of kitties, but we didn't live like those people you see on the ten o'clock news. I'll wager neither do you.

Where Are You on the Cat Lady/Guy Scale?

- The cat furniture has a leopard-spot motif. So do your car upholstery, your house key, and your bra or boxer shorts.

- The closest emergency animal clinic is programmed into General Motors' OnStar system's computer for you.

- You have your vet on speed dial.

- Your vet has you on her speed dial.

- You have as many cat sculptures in your yard as you have live cats.

- People always give you cat stuff for your birthday and Christmas, but you'd really rather have a gift card for your vet clinic.

- You don't have an ophthalmologist, but your cat does.

- Your cell phone's ring tone is "Mr. Mistoffelees" from the musical *Cats*.

- You're divorced because the cat was allergic to your ex.

- You know every word to the Meow Mix theme song.

There's nothing charming about being the crazy cat lady.

- You spend more on cat food than on your own food, medicine, and school supplies combined.
- The photos in your purse are of Fluffy, Kilroy, and Tabby, not your spouse or grandchildren.
- A friend gave you the Crazy Cat Lady Action Figure—and you have more cats than she does.
- You get a personal birthday card from the president of the Iams Company.
- You have more boxes than U-Haul.
- There are more dishes on the floor than in the cupboards.
- The new checkout clerk always asks, "How many cats *do* you have?"
- You have tennis elbow. But you got it from scooping the boxes.
- You coordinate your wardrobe with the color of your cats' fur.
- You've added a room or floor to your house just for the cats.
- Total strangers call you from another state asking you to take a rescued kitten.
- Your house has a designated "cat-free zone."
- You have more cat carriers than the local pet store.
- Animal control officers leave cats with you rather than pick them up.
- You buy human allergy medicine in bulk.
- All of your friends have adopted kittens that you rescued.

If you answered yes to one to five of these statements, you're a cat lover.

Six to ten: Neighbors wonder if you might be a cat lady/guy.

Eleven to twenty: You're a confirmed cat fancier.

Twenty-one to thirty: Some people are sure you're a crazy cat lady.

Anything, no matter how wonderful and loving, when taken to extremes can cause problems in your life. Do you have too much of a good thing? You might. Do you:

- let the cats have the bed while you sleep on the recliner?

- look for flea collars with rhinestones to go with your black dress?
- always make sure the cats get shots, but can't afford a doctor visit for your sinus infection?
- automatically lie when someone asks, "How many cats do you have?"
- have teary eyes even when you aren't watching *Titanic*?
- regularly miss Jay Leno's punch lines because the cats are fighting?
- own stock in the company that makes lint rollers?
- look around you and feel overwhelmed?

If you answered yes to any of these questions, you either have too many cats, or you need to make changes around your home to give everyone a little more breathing room. Don't worry. The Cat-valry is riding over the hill.

You may not have huge problems in your home. You may just want to learn how to juggle your "cat time" more efficiently and make cat care easier. This book will make you and your cats' lives much easier and more fun. Your kitties will stop fighting like cats and dogs. You'll learn about the down and dirty truth in your cats' litter box habits and how to keep everyone out of the doghouse. Dinnertime will be a time of bonding not conflict. When something's rotten in the state of your carpet, you'll know the way to properly clean your rug and which products really work. To keep everyone from declaring war with their housemates you'll increase territory and make sure everyone is healthier and happier with games and exercise. And when kitty illness and parasites raise their ugly rear, you'll be armed with the latest on health care in a multicat home.

How Many Is Too Many Cats?

How many kitties are too many? Only you can say. For some people three is two too many. Other people manage twenty happy cats effortlessly. A friend of mine who is a cat vet recommended keeping your numbers under ten. She said cats prefer a relationship more like a marriage.

Here are some guidelines on whether or not you should increase your ranks. You have too many if:

- You can't afford to keep everyone current on their vaccinations, get annual exams by a vet, and have cash left over for routine care and emergencies. Don't forget day-to-day expenses like food and litter and city licenses ($500 to $700 per kitty per year).
- You don't have cuddle and play time with everyone every day.
- You can't afford to have everyone fixed.
- The fur flies more than just occasionally.
- Scooping all the cat boxes every day is too much trouble.
- Everything in the house has been marked with cat pee.

Even though you feel oppressed, your situation isn't hopeless. As with any twelve-step program, you have to take it a day at a time. With good advice (found within these pages), work, and perseverance you'll be pleasantly surprised at the progress you can make in taking control of your house and your life again. Inside this book, you'll find kitty boot camp for both you and your cats.

Evaluate your possible overpopulation situation with this rule of thumb: you need at least one litter box per cat in the house plus one extra. And at least one box on every floor of your home. If you have three cats, you need four boxes. A family with twenty cats needs twenty-one boxes scooped once or twice a day. Do you have the time and energy plus the space for that many litter boxes? If you don't, you have too many cats.

Before you bring in any new kitties, consider this: an inside cat lives an average of fourteen to eighteen years. Are you still going to be able to care for these kitties in twelve or eighteen years? Another formula: if you're thinking about adopting a kitten, take your age (I know, you're twenty-one—just like me) and add eighteen. If you're twenty, the kitten may live until you're thirty-eight years old. If you're sixty now, you'll be seventy-eight. Does that change anything? Do you have friends or family who will help you take care of your kitties if you're sick or hurt?

Think carefully before adding another set of whiskers to your realm. After all, these aren't stuffed animals; they need love and attention just like you do.

Consider what's best for your current kitties. If you don't feel you're giving everyone all the one-on-one time and attention they need now, you certainly don't need more cats!

Just Say No (More)!

Everyone knows you have cats. Whether you have two or twenty, the neighbors call you the Crazy Cat Lady or Crazy Cat Guy. A lot of us got the reputation of Crazy Cat Lady because other people won't take responsibility for their own actions or their cats. A neighbor's cat has kittens; can you help them find homes? When a kid finds a stray cat, his mom sends him straight to your door. After all, you have a magical bank account that regenerates for charity cases. Right?

When people find out you have more than one cat, you suddenly become a lightning rod for everyone in the hemisphere who wants to dump a pet. I suspect that my name and phone number are written on the bathroom wall at Petco.

The neighbors feel self-righteous because they save a kitten, and you're saddled with vet bills and months of nursing. Hopefully, you'll be able to find a home, but sometimes kittens are unadoptable. It's very difficult to find homes for kitties who are unsocialized, fearful, abused, and infected with lifelong diseases—basically, cats that no one else will want. Do you have the ability to euthanize an unadoptable cat? I can't. Keep saying yes, and it won't take long before you're up to your eyebrows in whiskers. Even if you got stuck with only one unadoptable kitty a year, in ten years that's ten cats, in addition to the ones you have now.

Even if the spirit is willing, other factors may keep you from taking in a(nother) needy cat. Not the least is the needs of your own cats. Don't forget city ordinances restricting the number of pets you can have or even your home-owner's association's restrictions. Not to mention your ability to clean up after your cats and the greater chance that your kitties are going to start marking your home.

It's no sin to say no. It's a word you need to learn to say. You know how to say no, don't you? Just put your lips together and blow. Or was that "whistle?"

There are two kinds of people. Those who really want help finding a home for a cat and those who just want to dump their pet and their problems on you. For the people who suddenly find themselves in a difficult situation, any information you can give them about rescue groups and potential homes will be a godsend. They'll work earnestly to find the kitty a home. The other kind of person will expect you to do everything. Emotional blackmail is their primary tool.

One woman called me about a two-week-old kitten she found. She knew that animal control would euthanize him because it didn't have the staff to care for orphans. When I told her I'd raise the kitten if she would bring it to me she became abusive. In addition to the two o'clock feedings, vet bills, cost of formula, and other expenses I'd incur, she also wanted to me to drive an hour each way to pick up the kitten.

"I thought that's what you people did. If you don't pick it up, I'll take it to the pound."

That was her decision. Not mine. She tried to saddle me with the guilt of her own choice. This is a common tool. Unless you have unlimited finances, you're going to have to turn some of them down. But you can offer the resources to help the cat and the person. If you don't want to take the cat, the best and least antagonistic thing I have found to say that shifts the blame to where it belongs is, "That's your choice." The guilt is theirs, not yours.

You can help people, maintain your sanity, and keep your cat numbers stable by taking some preemptive preparation.

- Have a prepared list of area shelters, rescue groups, behaviorists, vets, feral cat assistance, allergy options, info on finding pet-friendly housing and a low/no cost spay/neuter clinic. I'll give you sources for all these in the following section. If people truly want your help, they'll be glad for the referral.

- To maintain your sanity and a stable cat population, team up with an established rescue group in your area. This gives you an opportunity to find homes for the adoptable rescues who have found themselves on your doorstep.

- Never name foster cats or kittens. That opens a level of intimacy and bonding that's hard to give up. Yes, you need to differentiate between the foster boy and girl. Rather than giving names that match the personality, like Bogie or Lyra, I give descriptive names, like BK (black kitty or boy kitty), Tabby, Spot, or Tiger. If the rescue group needs a more endearing name before the cat can be placed for adoption, ask the vet tech to hang a moniker on the little guy. I can't tell you how much easier it is to let them move on when you haven't named them personally!

- Require people whose cats you accept to have the cats fixed and vaccinated. A donation is not unreasonable. After all, you're going to feed and care for this cat until he is adopted (if he finds a home).

Resources for People Who Don't Want to Be a Crazy Cat Lady/Guy

Anticipate what people are going to ask you. Keep a list of resources that you can refer them to.

For information on a wide variety of subjects:

Humane Society of the United States (HSUS)

Our Pets for Life Program

www.hsus.org/

Allergies

http://stickypaws.com/askEinstein2005_0815.cfm

www.petsforlife.com

Behavior Consultants

International Association of Animal Behavior Consultants (IAABC)

http://iaabc.org

PETFAX

PETFAX is a remote consulting service for the behavior clinic at Tufts University Cummings School of Veterinary Medicine. They can provide behavior help worldwide. www.tufts.edu/vet/petfax/index.html

Feral Cat Issues

Locate a group that is involved in Trap-Neuter-Return (TNR) in your area. The groups below can provide information about TNR and alert you to resources in your area.

Alley Cat Allies
1-240-482-1980
www.alleycat.org

Alley Cat Rescue
1-301-277-5595
www.saveacat.org

Neighborhood Cats
www.neighborhoodcats.org

Lost and Found
Pet Resources
www.petfinder.com
www.missingpet.net
www.pets911.com
www.carlwashington-petdetective.com
www.1888pets911.org
www.hsus.org/pets/pet_care/finding_a_lost_pet.html

Orphan Kittens and Bottle Babies
Kittens for Dummies by Dusty Rainbolt (Wiley, 2004)
www.acfacats.com/orphan_kittens.htm
www.kitten-rescue.com

Pregnancy Issues
www.cdc.gov/ncidod/dpd/parasites/toxoplasmosis/toxoplasmosis
_brochure_8.2004.pdf
www.hsus.org/pets/pet_care/introducing_your_pet_and_new
_baby.html
www.cdc.gov/ncidod/dpd/parasites/toxoplasmosis/factsht
_toxoplasmosis.htm#8

Home Rental Issues

hsus.org/pets/pet_care/renting_with_pets_the_online_resource
_for_rental_managers_and_pet_owners

www.peoplewithpets.com

www.rentnet.com/apartments/mme/pets/;$sessionid$GEVDTUKMUY
HYWCQAQUCCFFA

www.rentwithpets.org

www.petsforlife.org

Shelters

For a complete list of rescue organizations, go to www.petfinder.com. Locate one in your area by zip code. Many of these groups are grass roots, fostering cats in private homes until kitty's forever home comes along. Unless there are extenuating circumstances, cats will probably need to be fixed and current on shots. Providing the cat is healthy and socialized, most groups are willing to accept them into the program if the owner is willing to keep the cat and transport him to and from adopt-a-pet events.

http://worldanimal.net

www.1888pets911.org

http://hsus.org/pets/animal_shelters

Or you can get less comprehensive information from your city animal control, local Petco and PetSmart, and vet clinics. Differentiate between shelters that are no-kill and those that take all animals and are forced to euthanize.

Low-Cost/No-Cost Spay/Neuter Clinics

A few hints about some of the low-cost spay/neuter certificates. Some vets will give you a good deal on the surgery, but they'll require presurgery blood work, proof of all vaccinations, and other nickel-and-dime services at full price. Call before you book the surgery and ask what these required services cost. While in a perfect world blood work would be performed before any operation, it may not be affordable when you're helping a stray.

Your local animal control or local rescue society may know who offers a low-cost or even free spay/neuter program in your community.

FELINE FACT OR FICTION

Two Unaltered Cats and Their Kittens Can Produce 420,000 Kittens in Just Seven Years

That's true and false. If each litter had six kittens and all of them survived and reproduced, theoretically your two cats could produce that unbelievable number of progeny. But Dr. Christine Wilford did the math—or rather had the University of Washington's Math Department do it—using figures from population studies of feral cat colonies in North Carolina that took into account the mortality rate due to sickness, predators, and accidents. Those slide-rule geniuses figured out that a single female cat and her offspring could produce between one hundred and four hundred cats by the end of seven years. That's still a box load of kitties. Even within a year, if no one is fixed, you can be swimming in kittens, an excellent reason to fix your own cats and help maintain feral colonies through a little surgical birth control.

Low-Cost Spay/Neuter Resource Database

neuterspay.org

This is an online database of locations across the country that offer low-cost sterilization for pets and ferals.

Low-Cost Spay/Neuter Certificates

Friends of Animals

1-800-321-7387

1-203-656-1522

www.friendsofanimals.org

Friends of Animals will send you an order form and a directory of participating veterinarians nationwide. You pay Friends of Animals for a certificate, which you then take to a participating vet.

Spay/USA

1-800-248-SPAY

1-516-883-7575

www.spayusa.org

Call Spay/USA to get the names, phone numbers, and prices of services of groups that have agreed to provide lower-cost spaying/neutering for pets in your area. Private veterinarians, community programs, and special clinics participate nationwide.

www.lovethatcat.com/spayneuter.html

www.friendsofanimals.org/programs/spay-neuter/signup.html

CHAPTER TWO

Felinese as a Second Language

My cat speaks sign language with her tail.
—**Robert A. Stern**

YOUR CATS MAY NOT BE able to speak to you with human words, but they certainly have a way of getting their point across. They communicate using a combination of

1. scent

2. body language

3. vocalizations

Learning how to recognize some common signs will help you understand your cats better and will allow you to respond to what they're trying to tell you.

The Importance of Scent

The most important mode in the feline linguistic repertoire is scent. From the cat's perspective, you and I are considered olfactorily challenged. While we don't get cats' scented communiqués, depositing their own essence and sniffing out other cats' scents forms a rich stealth language all their own. They can leave messages using scent or pheromones from glands located on the paw pads, on the chin, temples, the corner of the lips, and from anal sacs at the base of their tail. The smell of the pheromones produced by these glands is unique to each individual cat—like Chat-nel No. 5, it's a signature scent. When cats give themselves a spit bath, they transfer that signature scent to their fur. They may also leave their scented message by spraying pee, scratching an object, or by rubbing against a person, other cat, or object. It's their way of saying, "This is mine," or "I was here."

In the wild, scent is the most vital mode of communication because cats can send each other messages by proxy. Although it's not long distance in the traditional sense, scent is long lasting. It reveals information from one cat to another without having an actual confrontation. Cats have two hundred million odor-sensitive cells in their noses compared to about five million in yours and mine. You'd be amazed by the amount of information cats can glean from pee or other marks on a tree. It's much safer than waiting to see if another cat is willing to take you on. By sniffing the pee on tree bark, a cat can learn if the marker is a familiar cat or an intruder, if he or she is looking for love, or if the cat is sick. The pattern of a natural cat's marked trees delineates territory much like surveyor's stakes. It's a warning to other cats to keep out. He might spray a challenge to see if other cats are actually willing to rumble.

Wild cats use their sense of smell like humans use the newspaper. Your kitties smell the latest news, traffic reports (which cats have traveled through his territory), food ads (any mice in the area?), war report (that tom from down the street has crossed the line and wants to kick tail), and even the personal columns (Woohoo, Fluffy's in heat again!).

In a recent interview, Dr. Karen L. Overall, a board certified applied animal behaviorist at the Center for Neurobiology and Behavior at the University of Pennsylvania School of Veterinary Medicine, said that "Urine contains all the metabolic by-products of anything that goes through the blood. It contains hormones, including things like cortisol, a hormone indicative of a stress state and a particular molecular process. So, cats can learn a lot about the internal state of other cats and what is going on in their heads by sniffing urine. Feces contain the breakdown products of eating. So . . . you can find out what was eaten when, and may be able to track it back to its source. Also, you can tell if an animal is ill or well based on digestion. Finally, because neurochemical patterns can be signatures, urine IDs an individual whose internal state, health and food you can now follow."

When an unneutered male cat becomes sexually mature (between six and nine months of age), he'll start marking territory with pee. And not just any old pee. No, he'll be hosing down the place with that pungent pheromone-rich tomcat piss that can sear off your nose hairs from twenty feet away. If he becomes the dominant tomcat, he'll crank it up a notch and mark his territory by leaving his poop uncovered for all the other cats to find, while less-dominant cats and kittens carefully cover their stools, leaving themselves in protective anonymity.

FELINE FACT OR FICTION

Cats Can Not Only Smell Odors, They Taste Them

That's true—it's something like a sixth sense. Felines have been blessed with an additional scent mechanism that people don't have. It's called the vomeronasal organ or Jacobson's organ. The cat appears to grimace, opening his mouth slightly and sucking air up into the organ located in the roof of the mouth just behind the incisors (this is called *flehmen*). How convenient that he carries along his own lab that allows him to analyze odor molecules!

In the wild, an interested male marks his territory with pee, and a receptive female will likewise leave a message that she's looking for love. It's basically the feline version of writing a phone number on the public bathroom wall.

An easy rule of paw: starting at the cat's head and moving down his body, the pheromones become more antagonistic. Pheromones produced by the face are calming, friendly pheromones that say, "Wanna be my friend?" Paw pads give off "alarm pheromones" warning other cats to avoid dangerous areas. Messages sent by the rear part of the cat literally say, "Piss off." And while those "love me" pheromones females exude when they're in heat aren't angry themselves, they certainly inspire their share of cat fights.

So in the wild when a cat sprays a tree or leaves a stool uncovered, he's warning other cats that this is his territory. Instead of "Kilroy *was* here," he's saying, "Kilroy *is* here," with a little postscript that says, "Keep out." Or it could say, "This belongs to Kilroy."

Like people who want to avoid that intimate talk about what's bothering them, the cat sprays a tree or other vertical object (in your house it's a wall or a piece of furniture) to reveal this vital information without having to confront other cats. In a multicat environment, marking objects around the house helps create and renew your clowder's communal smell. When a strange cat enters a home (or an old friend returns from the vet, or even a new piece of furniture appears in the living room), it changes and confuses the communal scent. The resident cats panic and they start a round of spraying, scratching, and face marking to try to return their territory to its preintruder aroma. If it's permitted, the new cat will rub against the dominant resident cats to blend in his scent. Like a right of initiation, a cat has to do this before the others will accept him as one of their clowder, or for cat wrangling purposes, herd. Before the new cat's arrival, the home had its own unique smell.

When your cat weaves in and out of your legs or gives you those flattering head butts, he's marking you with those friendly pheromones, claiming you as his own property. It must be very frustrating for cats to deal with the pesky human habit of shedding that communal scent whenever we change clothes, take a shower, or put on cologne. Our poor cats have to constantly tag us to make us smell right.

Nixie, my Tonkinese wannabe, waits next to the bathtub every evening. The second I get out of the shower she rubs her head on my legs and weaves around my ankles. Apparently she doesn't want me leaving the bathroom without wearing her "special perfume."

Other than spraying, our least favorite feline behavior is usually the costly habit of scratching the furniture. The cat is marking the location with scent from glands in his paw pads. He's also leaving a visual sign that Kilroy was there. Long after he has walked away, that tattered sofa will not only wear the physical scars, it will continue (for a while) to wear the scent left behind from the glands in his paw pads. Just as the pee contains a full array of information, so do scratch marks on a tree or chair. By the height of the marks, a competitor can tell how big a cat is and whether he should hang around to issue a challenge. It's also believed scratch marks can reveal gender and maybe even the cat's age.

Other Scented Greetings

In close-contact olfactory communication, cats who are friendly will often approach each other with their tails held high. They greet each other by touching noses, rubbing up against each other, or giving a head butt to exchange scent. The greeting ends with an offer from one cat to allow the other cat to sniff his bottom.

So it's not surprising that your cat would also approach you, turn around, and present his rear end to you as if to say, "Wanna smell my butt?" Offering his behind is something he'd only invite his friends to do, whether the friend is human, feline, or even canine. Kitties don't let just any old Tom, Dick, or Hairy sniff their bottoms.

Scents play an important role throughout life. So since our cats—I'm sure to their constant frustration—can't use scents to pass messages to us, they resort to less efficient body language and voice.

Body Language

Welcome to "Introduction to Felinese as a Second Language," in which we'll examine the unique vocabulary of cats. Your cats' body language works like grammar. Most languages use different parts of speech to convey a total message. Your cats use different parts of the body in combination with their voices to get their messages across. In English, you must catch the entire sentence to understand whether the person meant the word "there," "their," or "they're." Likewise, you must look at the whole cat, his eyes, ears, tail, and body posture, to comprehend what he's trying to tell you.

If you focus on a single aspect of kitty communication, you may miss the point.

Not every cat speaks exactly the same language. As with human languages there are different dialects; you'll see variations from cat to cat. But you have to look at everything before jumping to a conclusion.

My Siamese-mix, Cosmo, flattens his ears against his head and closes his eyes whenever I stroke his head. On the surface those flat ears give the impression that he's going to take my hand off. But if I stop petting, he grabs my hand gently with his claws and pulls it next to him.

Taking a Stance

When you were a kid, your mom probably bugged you about your posture. "Don't slouch. Stand up straight." You, too, should be concerned about your cats' posture, but for a different reason. His stance is another key to unlocking what he's thinking at any particular moment.

Cats use body language and bluff in order to avoid an actual tooth and nail battle or to show a dominant cat that he's not a threat. Neither the aggressor nor the passive puss is spoiling for a fight. After all, Kilroy has fearsome weapons at his command, but so does his more timid adversary. An injury from a brawl could leave him either defenseless or unable to hunt. Better to win through intimidation rather than win a battle but lose the war and his life. Most disputes are resolved with a stare down and some cat calls. When they engage in full-contact combat, the confrontation rarely lasts for more than a few seconds.

A rule of paw is, the more defensive a cat feels, the bigger he looks. A cat frightened by a predator or a more dominant cat will stand on his toes, arch his back, stick out his tail, and bristle his fur to make himself appear bigger and more ominous. The frightened cat typically responds to scary situations by yowling, trying to escape, and as a last resort, showing teeth and claws. Sometimes he'll curl his tail tightly around his body. When the bully continues to intimidate, and if he can't escape, the victim will fall to his side bringing all weapons to bear (teeth and four sets of claws) just in case he's pushed into a fight. He showing his tormentor he has weapons and he's prepared to use them.

A submissive cat tries to look as small as possible to prove he's not a threat. He'll hold his whiskers flat against his face and shrink into a crouch.

Bottom line, unless you need your own blood drawn for a medical procedure, stop messing with your cat if you notice he's acting restless, the tail starts to thrash, his ears are either turned back or twitching back and forth, or he's moving his head toward your hand. His message is clear. He doesn't like what you're doing.

It's a Matter of Approach

The way your cats approach you indicates their intentions. A cat who walks toward you with his tail high and the end curled forward like a question mark, and rubs against your leg, obviously wants affection. You can watch kittens do this with their mothers, or cats with their owners. "Whaddaya got to eat?"

If he retreats as you move toward him, he wants to be left alone. Stop walking toward him, squat down, and offer your hand. Often he'll be drawn to you because you stopped pursuing him. When he sits down he is signaling you to stop approaching him. When he sits with a raised paw, he's apprehensive and preparing to get outta there.

A Tail of Two Kitties

Your cat's tail is one of his most effective communication tools. The cat's tail works a lot like a semaphore flag, the signaling system used by ships before the advent of electricity. Signalmen positioned small hand-held flags in a sequence to visually convey messages to ships within their line of sight. In semaphore,

"I don't understand a thing she says. She speaks with an accent."

each hand position has a particular meaning, usually an individual letter. Cats use their tails like semaphore flags to relay vital information about their moods.

TAILS FROM THE TRENCHES

Several years ago my Aunt Dot got her first cat. For her first seventy-eight years she owned dogs and understood fluent canine. She was so excited that her new Turkish Van mix loved to be groomed. She explained that Miss Kitty wagged her tail like crazy every time she started brushing her. Dot was interpreting Miss Kitty's tail wagging the same way she would a dog's, when what the cat really was telling Dot was, "If you don't put that comb down, I'm going to nail you." Fortunately, Dot kept her skin intact and took a short course in Felinese. Now she translates with the best of them.

Today's cats are likely descendents of the African wild cat, a large cat who used his tabby coloration to blend into the desert environment. So when cats feel relaxed, they'll hold their tails up. This shows that they're unafraid to be seen.

Flying his tail at half mast, he may not be observing a tragedy, but he's certainly showing much less enthusiasm about the situation. This is the tail's normal position.

A sitting cat with his tail wrapped around his front legs says he'd just as soon you keep your distance. In this submissive posture he may be thinking,

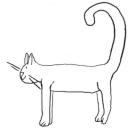

A tail with a question mark means he's curious and happy. "Whacha got for me?" "Wanna pet me?"

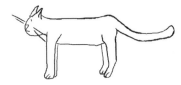

Relaxed tail flowing at half mast is normal carriage, friendly rather than aggressive or defensive.

"Busted again." Or he may just feel cold. This is where you have to look at the entire body to determine the message.

The lowered tail twitching at just the tip shows interest in something provocative. He might be saying, "Woohoo! Mouse—the other white meat." Or he may hold his bristling tail in an inverted U to indicate he's ready to take you on. This is a good time for you to stand down.

An offensive cat ready to start something will be found in a low crouch, the tail low with the tip fidgeting from side to side. When he thumps or twitches his tail, he's annoyed. Stop petting, brushing, trimming nails—you fill in the blank. In a further escalation on the pissed-ometer, thrashing like a cat-o'-one-tail shows that your kitty is rapidly losing his patience. The intensity with which he thumps his tail is directly proportional to how likely he is to open your veins.

Never play poker with your cats, for they are sneaky and the master of the bluff. Cats aren't interested in a face-to-face confrontation. When frightened or threatened, they'll arch their backs, hold up their tails, and puff up their fur like a bottlebrush. This defensive posture gives the illusion of something huge and scary. Add to that a banshee scream, which would give any tormentor pause for thought. In that hesitant moment, kitty sidles away like a crab maintaining his intimidating profile in full view of his potential attacker. This slow retreat hopefully keeps from triggering the attacker's prey response and provoking a sudden attack.

A cat with an arched tail sporting big hair should be given wide berth.

We've often heard the old phrase, "like a dog with his tail tucked between his legs." Well, I don't want to hit this one too hard, but when frightened and submissive, cats tuck their tails too, and for the same reason.

Ears Lookin' at You, Kid

Your cat's ears not only hear, but their position speaks volumes. They work like two miniature satellite dishes. With thirty-two muscles each controlling them,

Kitty number one wants to know what you have to eat. The kitty with airplane ears is getting ready to take off . . . and swat someone.

the ears can independently swivel up to one hundred eighty degrees in different directions at the same time.

Like the tail, these auditory semaphores are vital to interpreting Felinese. A relaxed cat will hold his ears facing forward, but tilted slightly backward. When a sound catches his attention, his ears perk upright or swivel in any direction to locate the source. A cat with erect ears is alert even if he appears relaxed. Ears pointed forward indicate he's curious about something. The squeak of a mouse should bring him to full attention with both ears tracking the source of the sound in any direction. A fearful, defensive, or a submissive cat will usually lay his ears flat against his head to protect them from being scratched or bitten in case the disagreement escalates into a full-contact skirmish. Airplane ears mean leave him alone! A cat on the offensive folds his ears so the insides are facing behind him like wings. Twitching ears indicate that he feels agitated or nervous.

More Than Meets the Eye

Eye contact, like tail activity, is subject to human misinterpretation. The classic case is when several people are in a room for a social occasion and the host's cat walks in. The cat unerringly attaches himself to the person who doesn't like cats. Is kitty simply being perverse? No. The answer is in eye contact. For the cat, the penetrating eye contact made by cat lovers is a display of dominance—even a hostile signal. He avoids his ogling admirers and seeks out the poor lady who would rather have a root canal than suffer the adoration of a cat. Unfortunately the ailurophobe—a person who hates or fears cats—is the only person in the room showing proper feline etiquette by avoiding eye contact.

Much cat-to-cat communication occurs below our human radar. To them, it's as plain as the whiskers on their face. In a showdown, rival cats get into a staring competition. Cats in a staring match look equally aggressive, but look at the body language to see who's who. The pupils of the cat on the defensive will dilate to give him broader peripheral vision just in case he has to protect himself. (Dilated pupils could also indicate low light conditions.)

While the victim carries on vocally, the aggressive cat calmly fixes an unblinking laser stare on his victim. The bully's ears generally point forward or are flattened sideways (airplane ears). During the aggressive cat's covertly hostile display, his pupils constrict to provide greater depth perception. It's almost the same as a human staring contest when the first one to blink loses. With cats, the first one to look away loses. The victor walks away. The loser takes a bath.

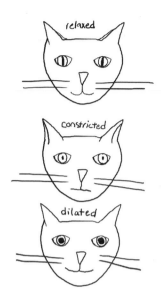

The pupils of the cat on the defensive will dilate to give him broader peripheral vision just in case he has to protect himself. During the aggressive cat's covertly hostile display, his pupils constrict to provide greater depth perception.

When you see two cats in an obvious conflict you can usually figure that the cat who hisses is the victim, not the aggressor. He's responding to the one who's giving him "The Look," an intimidating expression that could freeze engine coolant. (Husbands and boyfriends know The Look well.) I've heard men complain (including my own husband) that they are eternally fearful of The Look from their wives and girlfriends. It's a look so searing, it could melt the polar icecaps, yet so frigid it could ice up antifreeze. Some men fear it more than death.

The feline recipient of the look is just as intimidated. Subtle aggression doesn't stop at The Look. The aggressor may be lying on his side. It looks innocent enough, but a cat who is alert but casually lying on his side at the end of a hallway is threatening the other cat. The Look can bar a shy cat from his favorite place on the couch, the litter box, and even food. Keep your own eyes open for a stare that can bore a hole in diamonds. The victim knows exactly what the other cat is saying, but most cat owners are clueless.

If your cat mistakes your admiring gaze for a laser stare, give him a slow blink, which translates to a kitty kiss. Or show him an even more reassuring gesture: a yawn, which is a signal of trust and affection. Often your cat will return the tender expression.

During those lazy moments when your cat is relaxed, his eyes will remain half opened. When a cat feels curious and happy he'll walk around with wide open eyes.

Instead of just two eyelids per eye, cats have three: the upper, lower, and the *nictitating membrane,* or third eyelid, located at the inside corner of the eye. It protects his eyes from grass and other foreign objects and helps him produce tears. Don't expect to see it except when he's suffering from parasites, running a fever, or otherwise feels sick. If it doesn't go away in a day or two, take him to the vet.

The Whisper of the Whiskers

On each side of his nose your cat has twelve flexible, moveable whiskers called vibrissae. They're twice as thick as ordinary cat hair and the roots go three times deeper into the cheek than other hairs, anchoring into nerve endings. The tips are extremely sensitive to pressure. Whiskers can detect subtle vibrations that help the cat locate prey and potential dangers. Using air currents, he can sense the size and shape of objects or navigate tight places even on a moonless night. You'll also find vibrissae on the eyebrows, chin, and the backs of the front legs.

Though they serve as information sensors, the whiskers can help you translate Felinese into English. They will extend forward when your cat is interested and curious. But when he's frightened or prepared to fight, they lie flat against his face to protect them. When he's relaxed, they'll angle out sideways.

Meow Y'all

Now we come to the part of kitty communication that most humans can get their ears around: kitty talk. Cats understand that humans suffer from communication handicaps. Through trial and error they figure out what their particular people respond to and what goes over our heads. Scent obviously doesn't work. Body language is moderately successful depending on how observant a person is. For many cats the only direct way to get what they want is to have a conversation. Studies have found that cats vocalize more to us than they do to each other because they learn that we respond to vocal communication.

A 2002 Cornell University study presented at the June 5, 2002 143rd meeting of the Acoustical Society of America, in Pittsburgh documented hundreds of different cat vocalizations that ranged from soft purrs to tomcat battle yowls. Each noise has a meaning. Although we can guess, no human knows what every one means. Some sounds appear to mean the same thing to most cats, while other sounds vary from cat to cat.

Researcher Nicholas Nicastro doesn't believe that kitty vocalizations are a true language; he thinks cats have become very skilled in getting what they want from their humans, especially when it comes to food, shelter, and a little human affection. He believes that cats have learned what sounds to make to manage our emotions. Since we respond to their demands, the question becomes, who domesticated whom?

In conversations with your cats you'll hear chatter, chirps, murmurs, hisses, growls, spits, caterwauls—and our favorites—the purrs and, of course, meows.

Like aloha, meow can have a variety of meanings. It could mean, "Feed me," "I wanna kill something," "Wake up!" or "Timmy's in the well." You can figure out the definition by the way the cat says it. The more disturbed the cat, the lower the pitch. A high-pitched meow says, "I'm hungry." Just like a human, volume conveys urgency.

In a cat world without people, adult cats seldom meow to each other. Meow, and vowel variations of it, are reserved for that special relationship between kitten and his human mom. After all, you do all the things a queen would do by feeding them and protecting them. When we pet them, our hands running across their fur feels a lot like Mom's tongue giving her kittens a bath. Since we effectively fill their mother's role, our cats respond to us as they would to their mom. Meow is a universal word, but whatever it means, it usually starts out, "Mom!"

Then there's the endearing, silent meow. While the meow comes across as demanding, the silent meow is a polite request similar to, "Please, sir, may I have some more?" The cat makes eye contact, then opens his mouth in the shape of the meow, but you hear nothing. The truth is, he is making a sound, but it's so high it's out of our range of hearing. It certainly inspires me to get the treats out.

Neils Pedersen, director of the Center for Companion Animal Health and the Veterinary Genetics Laboratory of the School of Veterinary Medicine at University of California-Davis, said in his book *Feline Husbandry Diseases and Management in the Multiple Cat Environment* (Mosby-Year Book, 1991), that soft sounds, such as purring, usually reflect contentment, while more shrill sounds are usually reserved for mating and wanting to scratch each other's eyes out. We assume whenever we hear a cat purr that a cat feels happy or content. Often that's true. But not all the time. A cat purring with a relaxed body and partially closed eyes feels very contented. However, a cat who's anxious, fearful, hurting, or even dying will purr, but his body will be tense. Just as a cat's purring comforts you when you're feeling sad, fearful, or nervous, it comforts your cats too. Studies have shown that the vibrational frequency of a cat's purr speeds up the healing of broken bones and injured tissue and also helps relieve pain.

Each kitty may speak a different dialect of Felinese, but here's some basic vocabulary you can expect to hear from your kitties.

Feline Phrase Book

- Chatter—An excited cat chatters when he has spotted prey he can't get through the window. He'll also chatter in frustration when his prey escapes. He makes the "ack-ack" machine-gun sound by clicking his teeth together rapidly.

- Chirp—This is a friendly greeting that sounds like a cross between a meow and a purr. Kitty is happy to see you.
- Growl—This is a challenge, threat, or a warning. Go away. Leave him alone or you're going to get hurt.
- Hiss—It sounds similar to a snake's hiss prior to striking. This is also warning from a fearful or defensive cat. It's best to let hissing cats lie.
- Spit—This is more serious than a hiss. He's not bluffing. Do you have a good medical plan? Is your tetanus shot current?

For years cat owners have expected their pets to understand human language but didn't understand a thing their cats were trying to get across. Learning any language takes practice, and Felinese is no exception. With some time and effort you'll be able to better understand what your cats are trying to tell you with their bodies and their voices. You'll find the more you attempt to translate their language, the closer your relationship with all of your cats will be. You'll also be able to channel destructive behaviors early on and keep everyone happier and healthier.

CHAPTER THREE

Cat Psychology 101

If you yell at a cat, you're the one
who is making a fool of yourself.
—**Unknown**

"HOW DO I LOVE THEE? Let me count the ways." Maybe Elizabeth Barrett Browning should have changed this to, "Let me count the cats." Cats remind me of potato chips; you can't stop at just one. Every time you say, "That's the last one," another kitty in a desperate situation shows up.

The human-kitty love affair started eight thousand years ago on the island of Cyprus, where archeologists discovered the bones of cats, mice, and humans together. An intact cat skeleton was found with the remains of a Cyprus resident. No one knows whether that cat was simply a mouser or a beloved pet. In another four thousand years Egyptians would elevate the predator to pet, and then finally to a god.

Four thousand years after they first became common household pets, cats left canines behind in the dog park. They are now the most popular air-breathing pet in the United States. There are more fish, but try to cuddle with a guppy. Many experts think that dogs became domesticated some twenty thousand years ago. That makes the cat a relative newcomer on the domestication scene.

While kitties seem perfectly happy eating our food and sleeping on our soft beds, they're not entirely domesticated. This is where the misunderstanding between people and cats arise.

There's a yin and yang about the human/feline relationship. For every trait that makes them the perfect pet, there's a behavior that makes them "bad cats."

What if I told you there's no such thing as a "bad cat?" Well, there isn't. Most of the things that drive us crazy about cats are just normal cat behaviors. These behaviors are not just perfectly normal, in the wild they serve a useful, even life-saving, purpose. They only become bad behaviors when they come into conflict with humans and our anal-retentive lifestyles.

As humans, we tend to anthropomorphize animals and look at our cats as little people with human emotions and sensibilities. We expect them to join our household and become our little children with whiskers. But they're not. They look at life through mouse-colored glasses. We want a playmate; cats want a preymate.

To understand a cat, any cat, let's hunt for a few minutes with his whiskers. Originally they were solitary desert hunters, usually coming together to mate. After a few moments of passion the tomcat heads off in search of more passion. The queen would then raise her kittens alone. Of course, in the desert, food is quite limited, and mice and rats weren't big enough prey to inspire cooperative hunting, so natural cats lived an isolated existence. But in recent years researchers have learned when food is plentiful, such as within a managed colony or multicat home, cats can function well in a social group (as long as they aren't packed into a house liked smoked oysters in a can). In many multi-cat situations, cats enjoy the company of other felines.

Think about what cats eat, how and when they play, where they hang out, the amount of time they spend sleeping, and their bathroom habits. All these things are driven by a cat's predatory instincts. The yang of the feline predator is that a cat is also prey. Siamese is on the menu of a good many larger animals.

Even as they sit in front of the television watching kitty videos, you can see that cats are sophisticated hunting machines. Despite man's need to tamper with the genes of animals, the cat's appearance and behavior still remains much the same as his wild ancestor.

Look at the cat's design, starting with his eyes. A cat's pupils can dilate to 90 percent of the eye and can also narrow to a mere slit. This permits him to comfortably hunt in low light and then bask in the sun a few hours later. Cats' eyes appear to glow in the dark because they have a special layer of cells behind the retina called the *tapetum lucidum* (meaning bright carpet). These cells act like mirrors, reflecting light back onto the retina, doubly exposing the photoreceptors. It's this reflective process, plus the large number of rods in the retina, that is responsible for the cat's exceptional night vision. Very few animals can hold a candle to a cat's nighttime sight. Consider the lowest light you can see with. Cats can see with seven times less light—not in complete darkness, but close to it.

Those miniature satellite dishes atop his head can detect sounds that are a full octave and a half higher than humans hear. This allows him to hear a can opener during a sound sleep or to pinpoint the high-pitched squeak of a potential meal scurrying nearby when it's nearly pitch-dark. His four fangs or *canine teeth*, are tools for seizing and killing prey. Cats who must hunt for his groceries use those canines to sever the prey's spinal cord. The fangs have special nerves in their roots that allow the cat to slide them between the bones of the prey's vertebrae when delivering the killing bite. The fangs are also fearsome defensive weapons, as virtually any creature on the receiving end of that bite will receive some nasty bacteria.

And let us not sell short those magnificent claws. Claws are so much a part of his essence that a cat living in the wild simply couldn't survive without them. A cat named Descartes might tell you, "I scratch, therefore I am." After all, he uses his claws as a defensive weapon and as a tool to capture prey for food. He also uses them to stretch and tone his muscles as well as to mark his territory with scent from glands in his paws.

In the wild, cats are such efficient predators that they only need to hunt eight hours a day. Nature permits wild cats to do what many humans wish we could do and that's sleep for the other sixteen hours. Likewise, our housecats keep the same schedule as their free ranging counterparts. But during their eight waking hours they don't have hunger driving them to go out and work for their living. They wander over to the food bowl, eat their fill, and then, fully fueled, they look around for something to do for the next seven hours and fifty minutes. To fill this time they scratch furniture, stalk human feet, and climb the drapes—activities similar to what they would be doing in the wild.

While the antics of our cats may seem mysterious to us, they often arise from very mundane origins. Let's start with one of the most annoying and destructive behaviors—scratching the furniture.

Cats mark with pheromones from glands all over his body. When he scratches an object he's depositing his scent *and* leaving visual marks—kind of like street art.

Street gangs spray paint graffiti as a visible sign of their presence. Like rival gangs, you and your cats may be fighting a similar turf war. Your "bad" cat shreds your Cindy Crawford couch, because it's the closest thing to a tree he can find around the house. If he were a wild cat those scented scratches on that tree and the torn bark would be visual signs that he was there. Sometimes tree scratching is a warning of danger to other cats.

I can understand your frustration that the Dijon-colored recliner you bought a month ago now looks like a deranged haystack. You could call the new artsy appearance of your furniture Early Italian or even Spaghetti Decor.

While scratching is a natural behavior, it doesn't have to rule (or ruin) your life. You don't have to put up with chaos at the paws of the Great Destroyer. Using a multifaceted approach to the problem, you can put a stop to your cats' applying their own war-torn version of custom decorating to your furniture.

1. Give your cats satisfying things to scratch.

2. Make scratching the furniture unpleasant.

3. Keep their nails clipped.

Some cats destroy furniture because of stress or boredom. Since you haven't had the courtesy to plant any twenty-foot oaks in your living room, he scratches the next best thing—the sofa. He insists on using the furniture because it's the most stable scratching surface in the house. No matter how hard he pulls, it doesn't move. It's perfect. Rechannel this natural cat behavior into an acceptable venue by giving your cats what they want: a reasonable substitute for an old oak tree—like a good, sturdy scratching post.

You may protest that they have a scratching post they never use. That twelve-dollar scratching post won't do the trick because cats aren't just sharpening their claws when they set to work on the settee. They're toning and strengthening their muscles. A lot of people buy an unstable, short, inexpensive scratching post and expect the cats to throw themselves at it. Scratch that one off. Short, flimsy scratchers aren't worth dog spit to a cat who wants to scratch. You need to get or build them a scratcher that will stand up to a good rip-and-tear session. (If you're the handy type, you can find the plans for a first rate scratching tree at www.dustyrainbolt.com) Even a stout log could provide the cat with a more enjoyable option than your heirloom Queen Anne couch.

The most important thing to consider when buying cat furniture is it must be heavy enough to support climbing and stretching. If your cat sinks his claws into a post and it tips over, he'll go elsewhere. Next time you invest in cat furniture, don't waste your money unless it stands at least thirty inches high with a broad, stable base. (Slanted scratchers don't have to be nearly that high.) Make sure the scratcher doesn't wobble when you push against the top.

A post worth scratching should be tall enough for the cat to stand on his hind legs and completely stretch his forelegs, because cats scratch to stretch and limber up, said Alice Moon-Fanelli in an interview. She's a clinical assistant professor and a certified applied animal behaviorist with the Animal Behavior Clinic at Cummings School of Veterinary Medicine at Tufts University. She says cats want a really stable surface so they can throw their body (and weight) into it.

If you've given them a sturdy scratcher and they're still giving it the cold shoulder, they may not like the way it feels. Cats also have texture preferences. Some like sisal (rope); others prefer wood and bark; others prefer a knobby, looser-weave fabric; still others go after cardboard or carpet. Keep trying till you find posts they like. If your cat is attracted to catnip, rub some into the post to get his attention and inspire him to scratch it. Once he's claimed it, he'll keep going back to it.

The Rainbolt Test Kitties gave a paws-up to the 😺 **SmartCat Ultimate Scratching Post** and the 😺 **Scratch Away Cat Scratcher.**

FELINE FACT OR FICTION

Declawing Is Just a Nail Trim

False. Not so long ago, declawing a cat was a matter of course. Get a new cat and have him declawed when you neuter him. However, today, as owners are armed with a better understanding of cat behavior and new and better thought-out scratchers along with products that deter inappropriate scratching, declawing is going the path of the saber-toothed tiger. Whether or not to declaw a cat is a highly emotional and controversial subject.

Routine as it may be, declawing is still major surgery. It's not just an extreme nail cut; it is the amputation of the first joint of each digit. Declawing a cat would be the human equivalent of removing the fingers at the first joint. But it's not a single amputation—it's ten different, painful amputations with medical risks.

Even properly done and with pain meds, the cat will experience discomfort from mild to significant pain for the first week. Improperly performed, it can cause pain from nerve damage that can haunt the cat for life. Infection and irritation are other concerns. Many people involved in humane work swear that behavior problems, such as inappropriate elimination, nervousness, and aggression, crop up in cats who have been declawed. The American Veterinary Medical Association doesn't acknowledge any behavioral problems as a result of declawing because no documented studies have been done to confirm the change in personality of declawed cats.

I hope that you'll make every effort to retrain your cats before having them declawed. Under no circumstances should you declaw your kitten as a preventive measure, or because you're afraid he *might* scratch the kids. If you feel you must have your cat declawed, please seek out a vet who uses the more humane methods: by dissection or laser and not using a Resco guillotine.

> ## REALITY BITES
>
> C ardboard scratching pads are inexpensive options that give cats a satisfying scratch. When given a choice, the Rainbolt Test Kitties preferred larger pads. Sometimes they even liked to nap on them. When the mood hit them, they would go in for some vigorous scratching at the same place they slept. Even the declawed rescue cats seem to enjoy the feel of cardboard pads beneath their feet. They preferred ✿ **Scratch Lounge** and ✿ **WorldWise Wide Body Cat Scratcher.**

As any real estate agent will tell you, one of the most important selling features of any property is location. In an interview with Nicholas Dodman, professor of behavioral pharmacology at the Cummings School of Veterinary Medicine at Tufts University and director of the Tufts Behavior Clinic, he suggested placing a scratching post immediately next to the cat's favorite point of destruction.

Once he begins using the scratching post on a regular basis, move it a five feet at a time closer to the spot where you would like to keep it, preferably in a high-profile location.

Protecting Your Furniture

Now, that your cats have a cat tree that's satisfying to rip into, take the pleasure out of scratching the furniture. Dr. Dodman said there are other deterrents people should try before ever considering anything as extreme as declawing. A wide variety of products are available to do this. Of all the products and schemes to outwit your razor-footed roommate, no single product or training aid works for every cat in every case. You may have to experiment. Here are the ones I have found to be the most successful.

✿ **Sticky Paws for Furniture** is a nontoxic, water-soluble, double-sided tape applied directly to the furniture or drapes that deters cats from scratching because they don't like the tacky feel.

⊛ **Soft Paws Nail Caps for Cats** are vinyl nail caps that are placed over the claws to protect surfaces from the cat's claws. You must be able to trim your cat's nails in order to apply them.

⊛ **Comfort Zone with Feliway** is a synthetic feline facial pheromone that helps with stress-related marking and scratching.

Whether you decide to buy an adhesive barrier or claw covers, retraining is an important part of the process. A deterrent working in tandem with a scratching post your cat enjoys and positive reinforcement, such as praise and treats for good behavior, will be a winning combination for you and your furniture.

Jumping on Counters and Stoves

Your cats want to be where the action is. The action is where you are and, of course, where you're preparing dinner. Not only do your cats want to stand in the middle of your chicken enchiladas, they want to be high up. Outside they would spend much of the day way up in trees watching the activity below. Instinctively they seek out the highest point they can reach to still supervise the cooking of the evening meal (and steal a snack or two).

Even if you don't mind a little cat hair spicing up your casserole, there's a long list of injuries your cats can suffer aloft. He could impale himself on a knife when jumping up on the counter or he could land on a hot stove, and that's just for starters. You have to give him options that appeal to his normal need to be high up. Provide a tall cat tree in the kitchen. Give him treats only when he's sitting on his perch, nowhere else in the kitchen.

TAILS FROM THE TRENCHES

Cat rescuer Mary Anne Miller of Sweet Home, Oregon, said her cats lost their desire to hang out on the stove and counter after she started scrubbing down the surfaces with baking soda and a damp sponge to remove the smell of food.

Two surefire deterrents for high jumpers are 🐾 **Sticky Paws XL** (an extra-large version of **Sticky Paws for Furniture**) and 🐾 **Ssscat**. Sticky Paws XL comes in large sheets of double-sided tape. Stick the sheets to cardboard so you can easily remove them when you need the counter. Arrange the sheets side-by-side. When the cat jumps up on the counter and lands on the adhesive, he should jump right back down. Keep your countertop covered for several weeks until the cats get out of the habit of jumping up.

🐾 **Ssscat** is the ultimate weapon in the human-feline territory dispute. This is almost the perfect cat repellent. It's an aerosol spray triggered by a battery-activated motion detector. When it senses the cat's movement it shoots a blast of air. Cats never get used to it. The downside is that it might take several units to fully protect your counters.

REALITY BITES

You could try some low-tech but less-reliable booby traps, including penny-filled soft drink cans or water-filled plastic soft drink bottles lined up precariously on the edge of the counter. When a kitty jumps up, some of them should fall to the floor with a bone-jarring crash. Or fill aluminum trays with water and line them up at the edge of the counter. It's a mess, but often gets the point across. You can use bubble wrap, aluminum foil, carpet runners or car floor mats with the pointy side turned up. Other options include taping inflated balloons to the edge of the counter. When the cat jumps on the counter, he'll pop one. Run away! How long it takes to catch on varies. Some cats catch on the very first time. Some cats take a day, a week, even a month. If they later become curious again, you may have to give them a refresher course.

Generosity, Kitty Style

Your cat's ancestors were deadly predators programmed to catch and kill prey. And while your couch potatoes spend most of their day snoozing, that efficient killer still lurks just beneath the surface. Unfortunately, indoor cats seldom have mice running around on the floor to challenge their mental and physical energies. Since they still have that innate need to hunt, they chase flies and other crawly things. Disgusting as it is, the roach or cicada captured so skillfully permits the cat to fulfill that predatory instinct that drives him.

And who among us hasn't been blessed with a half-dead bird (for the occasionally

"That wasn't the kind of birdie I had in mind."

lucky inside cat), a disemboweled mouse, or even the fluttering cockroach? Don't scold him. It is a gift of affection, regardless of how distasteful it is. Say, "Good kitty." Then distract him and discreetly throw his gift away. Don't forget to give him a treat.

Late-Night Hunting Expeditions

Your cats' predatory nature presents another problem for you. Remember a little earlier I talked about how your cats' eyes allow him to hunt in what we would call dark? That's because his most likely meal, the mouse, likes to scurry around late at night. Naturally, it makes sense that our little predator would hunt while meals-on-paws is out and about. Once again, bad behavior is just normal behavior. And since kitty is up protecting the house from rogue rodents, he occasionally wants you to join him on a hunting expedition. Lucky kitties get to sleep all day while you're trying to keep your eyes open at work. Unless you work the night shift too, you don't want to be dealing with an overly enthusiastic cat at two in the morning. Don't give in to him. The worst thing you can do is get up and feed him or play with him. That way, he's training you to get what he wants.

You can get a good night's rest if you:

- Have a rigorous play session before your bedtime—ten to fifteen minutes with irresistible interactive toys that let them hunt, leap, and run. (I talk about the best toys and how to make them come alive in "Happy Habitats".)

- Since a cat's natural activity cycle is to hunt, kill, eat, groom, and then after a full evening, take a nap, you can tap into this cycle to help your cat sleep at night. If you free-feed, pick up the food in the early evening so he will be ready for a meal before bed. In the evening, exercise kitty with an interactive toy that has him running and jumping, then gradually wind down the game so there is a calm-down period at the end that mimics the prey being killed and becoming still. Then feed the cat. A grooming session should be followed by a long nap, and hopefully a good night's sleep for you.

- Instead of leaving food in a bowl, set up treasure hunts. A treat ball will allow your cats to hunt all night long. You'll read about all kinds of cool stay-busy activities and toys in "Happy Habitats."

- Don't feed your cats as soon as you get up. It's like opening the presents first thing on Christmas morning. If that's your tradition, the kids are going to wake you up at four in the morning. "Is it time yet?" Cats do the same thing. Waiting until right before you leave for work to feed changes your waking-up ritual to a less anticipated event.

If he tries to wake you up, drop a penny can, zap him with a water pistol, or spray compressed air in his direction. For persistent night owls, you may have to just lock the cat(s) with the nighttime naughties out of your room. I know. Bummer.

If he ignores your Do Not Disturb sign, discourage him by parking your vacuum cleaner outside your door. Run the cord under the door near a plug next to your bed. Turn the machine on, but don't plug it in until kitty's persistent crying or clawing wakes you. Then plug in the machine only for a second, and unplug. Bless the dirt beast that causes cats to scatter.

Crime and Punishment

While cats aren't really bad, there's a lot of "bad" information out there about how to discipline your cats. You may even hear some bizarre recommendations from your vet.

- The number one rule of paws in dealing with a "bad" cat is to remember that he's not bad. His actions are logical to him even if you don't like them.

- Rule two: discipline is only effective when you catch him in the act.

- Rule three: hitting never teaches him anything except you're a mean, scary person who is to be avoided.

- Rule four: make the action unpleasant and offer him an acceptable alternative, and everyone gets what they want.

Dr. Dodman said that most people try to change a cat's behavior by punishing or yelling at him. That approach doesn't work.

When an owner corrects the cat with a slap, she assumes the cat understands he did something bad. But in the cat's mind, whatever he did was logical. Kitties don't mentally go back in time like we do. So he doesn't understand that that finger to the nose is because he scaled the curtains. Curtain climbing is actually a lot of fun. He's getting exercise and when he reaches the top he can see everything that happens in the room (like climbing a tree outside). "So what's the problem, here?" he thinks. The real problem is now he's scared of you. That will stress him into marking territory with pee and claw marks. And thus begins the vicious cycle of crime and punishment that can't have a good ending.

Spanking, thunking on the nose, scruffing (grabbing by the scruff of the neck), hitting him with a newspaper, pinning him down, or rubbing his nose in poop or pee only convinces him that you suffer from occasional bouts of madness and that he should avoid you like the plague. He'll become afraid of your hands. He might cringe whenever you try to pet him. Worse than that, fearing a pop on the nose or to the butt, he might turn the tables and bite or scratch you. Fear aggression occurs when he feels threatened and backed into a corner.

When you come home from work and find toilet paper all over the bathroom (I call it "the Aspen look"), it does no good at all to grab Kilroy, drag him into the bathroom and swat the fire out of him. He'll hide from you. Then tomorrow, when he's bored and you're gone, he'll do it all over again. Besides, remember how fun it was when you toilet papered the principal's front yard?

Instead of punishing him you can try distraction, distraction, and distraction. This could take the form of a favorite toy thrown nearby to divert his attention to something appropriate.

When that doesn't work, try some remote punishment. You have to catch him while he's scratching furniture, jumping on the counter, stalking to attack ankles, playing with the toilet paper, and so on. When you see in the cat's body language that he's getting ready to do something, let the hand of God come out of nowhere. It's most effective when he gets the correction while he contemplating the action. Keep a close eye on his posture, as well as his ears and tail.

As a deterrent you could try

- squirting him with water
- throwing a magazine a few feet away (Don't hit him.)
- popping a balloon
- dropping a soda can containing pennies
- dropping a heavy book flat on the floor

Of course you have to be around to operate the water pistol and toss the magazine. Consistency is important in truly changing behavior. Remote punishment doesn't work if it happens only when you're there. He'll eventually figure out that somehow, you're responsible and stop doing the action when you're nearby.

When you need a full-time sentinel that can protect your property, consider the following:

- **Ssscat**, which shoots compressed air when it detects movement
- motion detector with a loud alarm
- **Sticky Paws** with its annoying tacky surface

- ⊛ **Sticky Paws for Plants** that makes digging in dirt impractical
- citrus solid air fresheners or lemon-scented car mirror deodorizers that smell unpleasant to the cats
- bitter apple that tastes bad

In our homes multiple cats mean multiplied mischief. With some imagination and ingenuity, you can channel those "bad" tendencies into more acceptable venues.

CHAPTER FOUR

Family Feud

Ignorant people think it's the noise which fighting cats make that is so aggravating,
but it ain't so; it's the sickening grammar they use.
—**Mark Twain**

AMERICANS LOVE THEIR CATS. MORE than ninety million feline family members live in thirty-seven million homes. That's a lot of multicat and megacat situations.

Actress Mae West, once said, "Too much of a good thing can be wonderful." Obviously she was referring to the human tendency to overdo things we find pleasurable. And while a house full of felines is pleasurable to us, the cats themselves are probably less than enamored with the situation. The more cats you have in a home, the more likely you are to experience behavior problems.

When our cats' ancestors lived in the Egyptian desert with its sparse prey, they had no choice but to defend their territory against newcomers. A desert feline couldn't afford to be generous with his food sources, not even with the females who carried his kittens.

Feline fortune changed when they joined the human community. The lunchroom opened—all the mice they could catch, no limit. With a perpetual fountain of prey, their territory shrank. When prey's aplenty, natural cats can live in small groups quite amicably, as they first did around the Egyptian granaries. During lean times, they divided into smaller groups or even went it alone. Since today's cat need only walk to the food bowl to satisfy his hunger, he doesn't need the vast acreage his forefathers did. Although housecats have an endless source of prehunted, prekilled prey in the food bowls, the need to maintain their own territory stems from their ancestors' less plentiful days . . . just in case. Each cat has a well-defined territory, built around a safe place called *home base*. A cat's home base doesn't have to be a single location in the home. It could be a series of spots.

An outside cat's home base is probably his yard and the adjoining yards. It's where he hangs out most of the time and is willing to defend. So there's no mistaking in the minds of other cats who the territory belongs to. A cat will mark strategic spots by spraying pee on it, leaving poop next to it, and scratching upright surfaces with his claws. This lets the other cats know that this spot is "Mine, mine, mine!" Inside cats have much smaller home bases than their outdoor counterparts. Most solo indoor cats claim their entire house as their territory. As with any house, some areas are more desirable than others. In a multicat home, an individual cat's home base may be smaller still—a window perch, a level on a cat tree, or a specific place on the couch.

The cat's *actual territory* or *home range* expands out from his home base. How much turf a cat claims for actual territory also depends on gender, whether the cat is altered, and on age. Intact males, those that haven't been neutered, need the most space to roam so they can hunt and mate; their territory is larger and less defined than either females or neutered males. The size of a domestic cat's home range, as well as his wild relatives', is always determined by the availability of food, shelter, and water, says Dr. Pedersen.

When prey abounds, the tomcat doesn't need as much territory. In lean times, he'll broaden his turf, undoubtedly to the chagrin of neighboring cats. While the size of a cat's home range varies, an intact male will have about ten times more room than an intact female. In some backcountry cases, intact females may have fifteen acres of home range, while intact males' home range can reach a whopping one hundred fifty acres, which they travel via regularly used paths. Intact females, neutered males, and spayed females seem satisfied with a smaller area close to home that they will passionately defend. Speaking of passionately defending, you may own a deed to your home and the yard, but that doesn't ensure that your cats will have the right to use it in the eyes of the neighborhood cats. Your outdoor cats may find themselves having to defend your property against cats that have established their territory in your backyard.

At times a cat may choose to hang out with other friendly cats who share his home range. In more private moments, he may go into restricted areas of his home base where he doesn't have to contend with other kitties.

Cats share a common communication style with some humans. They dread those face-to-face, heart-to-heart talks with each other, and they don't want to get into a fight. So instead, free-ranging felines leave messages by spraying trees. It's similar to a guy leaving a tie on the door for his roommate to find ("Don't bother me, I got lucky."). Or in the case of the sprayed tree, "I wanna get lucky." Preferring to avoid conflict, the cat often picks winding, out-of-the-way routes to avoid the home ranges of other cats. Since cats are somewhat anal-retentive when it comes to arranging their days, they also schedule their walks through shared territory carefully so they don't have to meet other kitties.

When the males do come to blows, it's usually the biggest and baddest who fight for the fair maiden's paw. That doesn't mean that the females are obliged to roll in the hay with the victor. Sometimes while the tough guys are duking it out, the females get it on with a less assertive, but luckier, male.

FELINE FACT OR FICTION

Cats Don't Get Along with Other Cats

When cats live together, they set up a flexible hierarchy, unlike dogs, who have a rigid social structure. Rather than a single alpha who's large and in charge, cats have a "relative rank order"—sort of a first-come, first-served arrangement. Usually cats recognize subtle territorial rules and respect specific territories even within a micro home range, like a room.

Another trait cats have in common with humans is that they have a real interest in real estate. They seem to have invented the concept of the time-share. Just like their free-ranging counterparts, inside kitties who live with other cats have overlapping territories that they occupy at different times to avoid clashing with housemates.

Feline Higher-Archy

While the U.S. Constitution says we are all created equal, it's not in the Kitty Constitution. They aren't equal. Personalities in cat culture range from your *dominant* or *alpha* cats, to the outcast (the *pariah*) and a lot of variations in between. The alphas are the most confident, aggressive cats—the rulers. We humans have a sense of fairness and we want our cats to all be happy and equal just like our kids. You may not want the dominant cat to be one of the alphas. However, it's not your choice. Trying to change the natural order of dominance frustrates the cat who should be an alpha. If you go against their system, the cat piss is really going to hit the fan. Your alpha cats will act up and may become more aggressive in an attempt to regain their role.

When it comes to dominance, testosterone rules; at least it does in the world of cats. You can expect to see the intact male asserting his authority from the top. When a cat is neutered his rank falls along with his testosterone levels.

Pam Johnson-Bennett, a nationally renowned certified cat behaviorist, said in a recent interview that the pecking order is dynamic and always subtly shifting. A couple of cats may hang out at the top of the totem pole or the cat tree. However, different totem poles may exist all over your home. Which cat is dominant depends on which rooms they're in and which cats are around. One may be dominant around the food bowls and litter box. The dominant kitty in that room is the one who eats first and uses the clean litter box before anyone else. Another cat stakes out the window perch or the cat tree. The alpha cat roosts on the highest vantage point in the room because in cat society height translates to respect. The rest of the cats rest at heights relative to their status.

When everyone has all four of their feet on the ground, you can still tell who's who by the way they act. The alpha or dominant cats will walk confidently through the middle of a room. A lower-ranking cat, or a cat walking through another cat's territory will walk next to the walls or furniture.

Not only do they claim the high ground, the dominant cats in the group will plant their scent all over the house to make sure it's well distributed and that the house smells like them. After a lower-ranking cat tries to scent up an area a little, the dominant cat will come up behind and refresh. You may even see mounting behavior in altered cats, whether between males or females. It's often a display of dominance.

The biggest, most strapping cat doesn't necessarily get the penthouse suite and the job title Alpha Cat of the Hour. It's the one who can keep his head about him when all others are losing theirs. It's the top cat's job to check out visitors to see if they're dangerous. In addition to gender and whether the cat has been fixed, other factors determining dominance include the availability of food, health, age, sexual and social maturity, and the number of cats, says Pam Johnson-Bennett. Think of John Wayne. With all that strength he didn't have to pick a fight (but he sure could finish it if he had to). Much of the time he could back a challenger down with just a look. Some cats are the Duke, others are Jim Carrey.

After our supremely alpha Turkish Van named Winkie died suddenly, there was some turmoil in the clowder. A couple of months later, we noticed that Winkie's companion Groucho assumed guard duty. Groucho took possession of the living room and the spare bedroom. Instead of running away when the doorbell rang (as he had in the past), he now stands in the center of the room to see who's coming in. It amazes me that a feline coward could rise to become the herd's brave protector. When he was lower in the hierarchy, he was more of a bully, constantly intimidating the subordinate cats, but now he neither has the time nor the desire to push other cats around.

According to Dr. Pedersen, overlapping home ranges can be times-hared by a small group of cats simultaneously, or different cats may dominate a place at different times throughout the day. He says, "Some cats use an area in the morning and others use the same area later in the day. Cats within a region of overlapping territories are well aware of the paths of movement and timetables of other cats in the same region, thus, further avoiding conflict."

And since the time of day makes a piece of real estate more desirable, the bed next to the east-facing window is likely to be claimed by a higher-ranking cat at ten in the morning because that's when it's drenched in sunlight. Later the next tenant shows up. Shift change! That same piece of real estate may change ownership two or three times throughout the day.

Since cats depend on predictability to avoid confrontations with other cats, changes around the house (like new furniture or carpeting) or deviation from their dinner or box-cleaning schedules can blow up their whole day, maybe even their week.

Since it's an opportunistic hierarchy and dominance is situational, a dominant Kilroy may allow a lower-ranking cat to keep the window perch when he got there first. This is where time-sharing comes in.

The dominant cat or cats (at that particular moment in that particular room) will perch where he has the best vantage point, watching for encroaching cats and other dangers. He's the first one to eat, play with the favorite toys, and seek attention from you.

Among a community of cats, unneutered males are usually the ones who are the most competitive and territorial; neutered males can be as sociable as females. In a colony where one or two fat cats rise to the top of the totem, they manage all aspects of feline business under your roof. You also have your mid-level managers, who want to stay out of the social and political turmoil. There are the low-ranking cats, who try to stay out of everyone's way and occasionally get beaten up.

Dr. Overall, says intercat aggression is extremely complex, often subtle, and underappreciated.

Inside territorial aggression is often a status issue. A top cat will act aggressive when he is concerned that the maturing cat will knock him from the top of the totem pole, or when a new a cat is thrown to the wolves, or rather cats, rather than afforded a proper introduction (see "New Kit in Town").

Finally, in extremely rare cases one cat is so far down the totem pole, he's almost buried beneath it—he's the pariah. In an interview with Pam Johnson-Bennett, she explains that this poor creature is everyone's whipping cat. He's so tormented and bullied that he finds a hiding place (often behind the refrigerator where the other cats can't get to him), only coming out to eat when the others aren't around. This cat tries to keep a low profile, walking low to the ground. For him, there's no positive interaction with other cats. No one knows why the pariah allows the other cats to pick on him. Dr. Overall believes it may be genetic, just as the alpha position often is. Others believe that he's shunned because he may suffer from health problems.

Some more dominant cats may stake out a large territory, even an entire floor, while other less-dominant cats claim a smaller area, such as a chair or bookshelf. The entire clowder has communal areas where they can all hang out together. They seldom get into brawls in the kitty community center. In most cases high-ranking cats assert their authority over subordinates the same way high school seniors pronounce authority over underclassman. That's way different from the school bully who beats up smaller kids for their lunch money.

Just because he's the top cat doesn't mean he's cruising for a fight. The peons, with their equally sharp teeth and nails, will defend themselves and their territory. Real cat fights are rare in established clowders. So instead of risking serious injury, cats resort to menace and threats. Cats would much rather bluff out their opponent with The Look. (For a full explanation of The Look, see the chapter "Felinese as a Second Language.") When confrontations happen, it's usually because an upwardly mobile cat or newcomer wants to climb up to a higher place on the totem pole. Unlike people, when two cats have settled their differences or challenges, they usually drop the issue until someone's status changes. When Kilroy grows older and weaker or the younger cat becomes mature and strong, they may revisit their territorial dispute.

Because cats are solitary hunters they developed a bum reputation as antisocial animals. Many people believe that cats don't have a social structure because they don't have an undisputed pack leader as dogs do. Cat lovers know this is a load of Dingo's kidneys. Recent research and observation has shown that even though cats are independent, their societies and hierarchies are far more complex than the classic and rigid dog pack.

Even though cats don't hunt together to bring down that big rat, under the right circumstances (including plenty of food), today's cats frequently live in congenial groups. Often people will describe an affectionate, outgoing cat as being doglike, but it's really normal social behavior around cats, dogs, and people that the cat feels safe and comfortable with. Look around. You've got your buddy cats who nap together and give each other a bath. I bet you witness the occasional game of tag and the friendly wrestling matches. None of these are the actions of a confirmed loner.

There's even some cooperation among cats and especially moms. Veterinarian Sharon Crowell-Davis, professor of behavior at University of Georgia at Athens, has found in her research that queens who have kittens close together, trade off babysitting and nursemaid duties. They feed and groom each others' kittens as needed, and even defend them against marauding tomcats since intact males will kill the kittens of other toms so the queens will come back into heat.

Every cat's an individual. Some cats are like Greta Garbo who wants to be alone (in much the same way some people are gregarious and others are loners).

Cat High Society

Add or subtract a new cat, and it throws the whole hierarchy into chaos. So could any change that cause cats stress, such as moving to another home, a kitten becoming sexually mature, or the illness, death, or disappearance of either a feline or human family member.

Johnson-Bennett says when a cat becomes sick, he loses his social status and drops to the bottom of the totem pole beneath all the healthy cats. This brings on the same stress issues for the other cats as a dominant cat dying.

When one of the dominant cats loses his place in the hierarchy or dies, the midlevel managers start jockeying for position. With the turmoil in the house, aggression and whizzing become the order of the day. Eventually they'll sort their positions out, but in the meantime the bullies will bully, the wimps get beat up, and the carpet gets hosed.

When Good Cats Go "Bad"

Your cat lives in a world that you've set up—an arranged marriage with numerous spouses. Unlike odd assemblies in reality TV, he can't vote annoying cats out of the house. He's stuck.

When more cats join the herd (and you haven't added more litter boxes), he has to wait in line longer to use a dirtier bathroom. After all, the cat ahead of him never flushes. He may feel like Goldilocks' bears. Someone's always eating from his bowls and sleeping in his bed. And even worse, there's not a moment's privacy. No wonder some cats get stressed and grumpy.

Any time you have more than two animals of any species in an environment, there's going to be the occasional butting of heads. Every so often in the 1970s sitcom *The Brady Bunch*, members of the blended family lobbed cross words at each other. The occasional hiss or swat is no problem. Rough play and chasing is fine, but sometimes the rough play stops being fun to the victim cat, and it's no longer a game.

There's more to overcrowding than a lot of litter boxes to scoop and bowls to wash. The more cats who live under one roof, the more likely they are to flip a whisker. Just as people in crowded conditions often become testy and violent, cats in homes with other cats often become aggressive to their feline housemates.

Even the stablest and happiest multicat home will suffer increasing fights and scuffles as your population increases and stress mounts. There's more competition for dominance, more kitties to kick the subordinate cats around, and the guys in the middle just want to hang on to the status they have.

Since no two cat families are alike, there's no concrete rule on how many cats are too many. Sometimes adding a second or third cat will start the kitty equivalent of World War III. Other homes run smoothly with twenty cats. Much of it has to do with the personality of your cats, the space you have available, whether you've provided adequate territory, the kinds of activities your cats have, and how well you keep up with the litter boxes.

According to his article "Fighting Tooth and Nail: A look at some common types of feline aggression" by Wayne L. Hunthausen, a member of the Veterinary Medicine Practitioner Advisory Board, aggression can vary from a cat who hisses simply because he wants to be alone to the cat who attacks other cats and even people. Aggression among cats is one of the most common complaints in multicat homes, right behind spraying and peeing outside the box.

Cats aren't just losing their temper; different forms of aggression are sparked by different catalysts. Some of the main forms of aggression are status related, dominance, fear, territorial, redirected play, and health related.

An easy-going cat who suddenly attacks other cats or even you, may be telling you he's not feeling well. Just like you, cats get cranky when they hurt or feel sick. The first step to dealing with any aggression problem is to take the cat to the vet.

In a disagreement, the loudest cat is usually the defensive cat. I explain this posturing completely in the chapter "Felinese as a Second Language."

Most of these encounters are just territorial disputes, which are none of your business. If you're only observing *occasional* mutual staring and hissing and a quick swat or two, let them work it out. Remember, the day-to-day running of the cats is their affair, unless you see corporate shenanigans going on. However, if it looks as if you've got a hit man getting ready to take out an adversary, separate them.

Territorial or Social Aggression

Although your cats have a steady supply of food and water, protection from predators, and a really good medical plan, their brains are stuck in a more primal mind-set. What if the bowl isn't full in the morning? What if that predator shows up in the middle of the night? Because of that, territory is just as important to each of them as it is to the cat who lives in the country.

Territorial aggression occurs when your cat thinks that another cat has invaded his territory. Sometimes this gradually happens to cats who were once buddies. It begins with some harassment, usually staring, hissing, and growling, then progresses to swatting and chasing and finally escalating into attack.

Even if they've been fixed, cats mature socially sometime between their second and fourth birthday. Like a teenage kid, the youngster may start to challenge the more dominant cats in the home. The mature cat can react to the challenges with a passive-aggressive response that includes The Look and posturing, fighting, or spraying. A dominant cat who fears for his territory will chase or ambush the interloper and spray his signature scent all over your home. Expect the gratuitous hissing and swatting when they're near one another. Territorial issues usually crop up when new cats join the herd.

The target cat often hides until his tormentor is gone, coming out of his cranny to eat and use the potty. When Kilroy blocks the litter box, the new cat has to make other arrangements, such as using the potted plant or the corner behind the television. This isn't just a guy thing; when it comes to their little corner of the couch, females can act as territorial as the males.

According to Dr. Overall, cats who consider each other as equals are less likely to be become physically aggressive toward each other. Instead they'll opt for catlike subtlety and intimidation. Watch for covert aggression, such as pushing others away from food bowls, litter pan ambushes, hiding under the stairs to attack, bluff charges, and swiping favorite toys. But dominant Kilroy can be even subtler. Sitting or lying on his side at the end of a long hallway with his back claws unsheathed and a focused look, Kilroy is covertly threatening his housemate. (This causes a lot of problems if Kilroy plants himself in front of the litter box, even if no physical move is made.) He's using body language to block access, waiting for a cat to approach the litter box.

The dominant cat can make life impossible for his target—attacking him at every opportunity, but still get along merrily with the other cats in the home.

Redirected Aggression

Have you ever had a boss or a significant other who was upset with someone else, but yelled at you? That's *redirected* or *misdirected aggression*. Cats aren't immune from it. In this kind of aggression, your cat, Kilroy, smacks or attacks another animal who had nothing to do with what upset him in the first place.

In redirected aggression Kilroy can't get to the animal, or even the person, who's thumbing his nose at his territory. For example, two cats are calmly sitting at the window watching the world go by. Suddenly, the tomcat from down the street strolls up on the porch and hoses the place down. The only problem is that pane of glass between him and the invading cat. Since Kilroy can't give the outside cat a piece of his claws, he does the next best thing (and figuratively what your boss sometimes does), he smacks the cat sitting next to him. The poor victim cat, licking a sore nose, wonders, "What'd I do?" But the recipient of redirected aggression may not be a cat. It could be the family dog or even you, if you happen to be in the wrong place at the wrong time.

The dominant cat sprays because he wants to tear up that stray tabby in the yard. And the poor victim, who unfortunately happened to be snoozing in the wrong place at the wrong time, sprays because he's frustrated and stressed. If the animal outside returns for an encore performance, it could trigger a whole new round of intercat aggression, territorial marking, and spraying. Opening windows further complicates matters. A fresh breeze could actually flood the home with threatening pheromones from the stray tomcat. Some neighborhood toms are so brazen they'll nap on the porch in full view of your herd.

Another version is *fear-induced aggression.* Two cats are sleeping together and a balloon pops nearby (or a dish crashes to the floor). Both startled cats assume defensive postures. Seeing that the other cat is ready to defend himself, the aggressor is convinced to launch a defensive but preemptive strike. A fight ensues. Suddenly, friendship is shattered. Unless you can help them, the friends will remain fearful of each other from then on. You'll see yowling, growling, gnashing of teeth, the Halloween cat stance, pacing, tail lashing, and dilated pupils fixed toward the source of his ire. This aggression is more common in males, possibly because males are more territorial.

The cause doesn't necessarily have to be something scary; it can be annoying or unfamiliar, such as the scent of another animal, weird noises, strange people, and even different things in the environment, such as a new mattress.

Redirected aggression is difficult to spot because you're not usually around when the stuff hits the fan. You might see one cat attack the other, but miss the stray cat hosing down your front porch. If you or a human family member wears the redirected bull's-eye, it's important not to give your cat a whap on the nose. Your retaliation can change the relationship with your cat. In a single moment you can convert years of love and trust into fear and defensiveness.

A cat with frequent bouts of redirected aggression may have to go in for the latest in feline fashion—in this case, a harness and leash. That way you can safely grab the end of the leash and lead him to his dark room. You won't have to get close enough to risk getting bitten. You'll have to bar him from the source of his upset. Unfortunately, that may also mean barring the other cats from bird watching. Keep him away from doors and cover the windows where he may see, hear, or smell whatever sends him over the top. Do this with 🐾 **Ssscat**, or motion detectors that emit annoying sounds. 🐾 **Sticky Paws XL** will make standing on an area unappealing. If you only have problems at certain times of the day (like late afternoon when the neighbor kids walk through your yard on the way home from school) you can install vertical blinds, shades, or shutters and close them at the appointed hour.

At the same time keep the intruder off your property by using repellents or outdoor booby-traps, such as the 🐾 **Scarecrow,** which is a motion detector connected to a sprinkler. Unfortunately, the Scarecrow doesn't discriminate between someone coming home from work or the cat from down the street. 🐾 **CatScram** keeps cats away by emitting a high-pitched sound (outside the human range of hearing but annoying as heck to kitties).

If you can't stop what's bothering him, you might be able to lessen his anxiety with drug therapy, along with desensitizing and counterconditioning. It's certainly worth discussing with your veterinarian and a behaviorist.

Fear or Defensive Aggression

A cat will show *defensive aggression* when he's backed up against a wall (literally or figuratively) with no escape or feels he's being threatened. He'd prefer to move away from a threat unnoticed. When that doesn't work, he resorts to bluff and bluster with the Halloween kitty posture, growling, and hissing. But when bluff doesn't make an aggressive cat back off, the victim ceases to bluff. Those fangs and claws transform into bona fide promises of pain and doctor or vet bills if he's not left alone.

He may lash out at you if he's being punished or launch at another animal if he thinks attack is imminent. He'll hiss and spit, crouch with his legs safely tucked under his body, his tail tucked beneath or around him, his ears flattened against his head. If the other cat (or you) continues to approach him, he *will* attack. If the threatening cat or person moves away, he won't pursue.

Few people or cats really want to have a close encounter of the painful kind. So when kitty does his Clint Eastwood impression (with strong talk and showing his teeth) the smart thing to do is back down. Fear aggression is common in timid cats and kittens who haven't been socialized to other cats and humans. It's also a problem in cats who have been mistreated by people, dogs, or even other cats.

The first step in overcoming fear aggression is to ignore the cat altogether. Avoid eye contact. When kitty is calm, put down tasty food and walk away. I've found that tiny pea-size chunks of chicken or turkey breast tossed in the cat's direction goes a long way toward creating a casual friend. Allow the kitty to make all the first steps. It could take months, even years to win the trust of an unsocialized or abused kitty.

Nonrecognition Aggression

Kitties don't have great memories and they depend on their nose to tell them who's who. With *nonrecognition aggression*, a cat coming home from the vet or the groomer has a different smell, and he may be acting differently. After all, he had a thermometer stuck in his butt or a needle in his skin. Worse still, he's no longer wearing the communal smell of his housemates. Suddenly he's a stranger. Your other cats' response may be something like, "Yew ain't from around here, ere ya?" The cats become territorial because an "invader" wants to join the party and eat at their table. As with redirected and fear aggression, one fight could shatter a lifelong friendship.

Put the returning cat in a bathroom with his bed and give him time to take a spit bath before you let him out. For a little added insurance, rub your alpha cats down with a clean, dry cloth and then run it over the returning cat before allowing any family reunions. When you open the door watch to make sure no one is suffering from a temporary case of amnesia.

Intermale Aggression

This is the classic cat fight: two whole males fighting over the love of the fair maiden. As young males mature, they want to take on the world; they'll start with that strapping tomcat next door or in the bedroom. You'll see it in the posture: stalking, growling, howling, and yowling. Of course, there's The Look. If the intruding male continues to threaten and neither cat stands down, then it's time to rumble! The attacker goes for the throat, the neck really, while the cat on the defense goes belly up. He's not asking for a tummy rub. All those pointy teeth and razor claws are poised between him and the aggressor. The aggressor usually gets bit in the butt. Generally, the battle only lasts a few seconds. One cat gets the girl, the other is humiliated. Mostly it's "The End."

Except it might not be the end of the story. The cats may share more than a Kodak moment. Fighting puts them at risk of the feline leukemia virus (FeLV) and feline immunodeficiency virus (FIV), both fatal diseases. Even if they manage to avoid these viruses, puncture wounds can turn into abscesses. Snipping a kitten's family jewels before he reaches a year decreases or prevents fighting by 90 percent says Dr. Overall. Other studies show that kittens altered prepuberty are friendlier and develop fewer behavior and health problems later in life.

Breaking Up Is Hard to Do

Keep notes when you notice preludes to an attack. When do altercations happen? At the same time every day or throughout the day or evening? Where do they happen? Are other cats attacked or is it the same cat every time? Is he an ambush predator who hides in wait, or does he attack his victim right out in the open.

When tempers erupt like Mount Vesuvius, put a cork in it immediately. Don't fall for the old line "Let them work it out." That doesn't work any better than depending on compassion from an elementary school bully. The dominant cat will dominate and the low-ranking cat will get pounded.

When you notice that a full-contact brawl is taking place, break it up, but don't try to break them apart with your hands or legs. I did that once and wound up with a nasty cat bite, a butt full of powerful antibiotics, and an emergency bill that cost roughly the same as the Louisiana Purchase. Unless you are wearing Kevlar protective gear, you can break up a fight by doing any of the following:

- Scoop him up with a fishnet.

- Throw a thick towel or blanket over the aggressor.

- Distract them by tossing a magazine near them, not at them.

- Slide a broom or cookie sheet between them.

- Zap the attacker with H_2O from a water Uzi or squirt bottle (get the one with the twenty-foot range).

- Blow a whistle.

- Spray canned or compressed air from an office supply store in their direction.

- Air horns.

- Drop a soft drink can containing pennies.

- Clap your hands (not terribly effective, but worth a try if you have nothing else available).

- Turn on the vacuum. This will distract the aggressor long enough for the victim to make an urgent retreat.

Once they've broken apart, don't punish them. Hitting or screaming won't accomplish anything. Neither cat will have a clue why *you're* acting out of control. They'll simply start to fear you, which will only add to the stress and contribute to future full-contact fighting matches.

As soon as it's safe, usher them into separate rooms. If the aggressor is really worked up, turn off the lights to help him calm down. Wait until everyone is calm before trying to reintroduce them. It might take a few hours or even a couple of days. One of the signs that tempers have cooled is when they start grooming. To help them calm down, put some 😺 **Bach Rescue Remedy**, a flower essence that has a relaxing effect, in the cats' water (or if you can do it

---

Requesting Sanctuary

The Sanctuary is a multipurpose safe room with all the comforts of home: food, water, litter box, a scratching pad, and maybe even some toys. The aggressor can go there after a scuffle to compose himself. Or you may put the bullied kitty in the sanctuary so he can slowly get reacquainted with the other cats. It's also the first stop for new kitties who may be joining the herd. (I explain the use of a sanctuary in more detail in the next chapter, "New Kit in Town.") Don't think of it as a prison. Visit whoever lands within its walls frequently.

safely, on the top of each kitty's head) and plug in a ⊛ **Comfort Zone Diffuser with Feliway** in their rooms. Comfort Zone fills the air with calming pheromones.

When the fighters have gone to their corners and pulled themselves together, check them both for bites. If either or both cats growl at you or start thrashing their tails, turn off the light and leave them alone until you can safely touch them, otherwise you might be nursing a serious cat bite yourself. After an hour, turn on the lights and offer them a couple of bites of food. If they don't eat, turn out the lights and leave them alone. When everyone has calmed down, let the timid one out and feed them on opposite sides of Kilroy's door so they once again start to associate food with the scent of the "other guy." (See "New Kit in Town" for more about these strategies.) Try to reintroduce them later. Be patient and don't rush them. *If you try to bring them back together too soon you'll just make matters worse.* Reunite them the next day over a nice joint breakfast, each cat with his own bowl, ten feet away from each other. If this doesn't work, you will have to reintroduce them as if the victim were a new cat.

If reintroducing them doesn't work, you may need to permanently isolate the two cats in different parts of the home. A little later I'll talk about desensitizing the two cats to each other. This is a trick that may help with most forms of aggression. You have to teach them that good things happen when they are together.

If any of your cats could be eligible to receive Mother's Day or Father's Day presents from future generations, get them snipped. Bottom line, as long as hormones surge through their veins you'll continue to have territorial problems of all kinds. However, even when everyone is fixed some territorial conflicts in multicat households are virtually inevitable.

Can't We All Just Get Along?

If conflicts continue to escalate, you'll likely notice an increase in furniture scratching, and some of the cats will spray the house like a battalion of firefighters. They're just relieving tension and marking their territory visually with scratch marks and with their scent.

The best cure for territorial aggression is to prevent it from ever happening. When you see these warning signs, separate them immediately. Each attack reinforces their identities as bully and victim.

There's no single cure for all forms of aggression. But, unless I mention specific situations, many of the steps you have to take to overcome aggression are the same. You have to relieve overcrowding. Depending on your situation, finding new homes for some of your cats would probably cut down on feline friction. But I'm willing to bet you're going to say that's not an option.

When slow reintroductions don't work, try desensitization and working with a behaviorist. You may need to isolate the two cats in different parts of the home. Your vet or behaviorist may recommend drug therapy. I'll cover the latest and greatest in drugs at the end of this chapter. Read about which "Bach Flower Remedies" are best for your cats in the Shopping Guide section.

The next best way to reduce aggression is to increase territory. Remember the higher-archy? Think height. You can relieve stress by providing lounging spots on every conceivable level. With some imagination you can give upper management the higher offices they need. Simply remove the stuff from the top of the kitchen cabinet or the refrigerator. Or clear cat-sized spaces on several different shelves of bookcases throughout the house. Add cat trees and window perches. That will give your family room to move up and around without having to bump into one another. (I'll give you a lot of ideas in "Happy Habitats.")

Filing for Separation

In some cases, you may have to resort to a divorce. That doesn't necessarily mean you have to get rid of one of them. The victim cat needs a safe haven to protect him from harassment and injury. But you may need to invest in a screen door so you can keep them separate without seeming as if they have been placed in solitary confinement. Even without a screen, cats can live happily in completely different territories behind closed doors. You get to play border guard and keep them out of each other's countries.

After the cats have been separated for several days (or a week), you need to desensitize both cats to each other, slowly. You do that by exposing the cat to whatever is upsetting him, which could be another cat in the household or something outside. The key is to get him to reclassify the context of aggravation. At the same time you want to countercondition them by rewarding the cats for being in each other's presence.

If the mere smell of the wimp sends Kilroy into a rage, try rubbing a clean washcloth along the victim's back and put it under the grumpy cat's food bowl. Hmm. Even his food smells like the wimp. And while you're confusing him with scent, rub Kilroy down with the cloth containing the wimp's smell. Then swap cloths. Things no longer smell black and white, so to speak. Now the wimp smells a lot like Kilroy and vice versa.

Just before dinnertime, when everyone is hungry and inspired to work for food, wedge open the sanctuary door by an inch and toss pea-sized roast or deli turkey treats to both the cat inside the room and outside the door. It's important not to reinforce bad behavior, so don't reward the aggressor with anything when he's giving The Look, hissing, or intimidating the victim. Give him the treat the second he looks away. He'll eventually get the message. If either of the cats becomes aggressive or frightened, close the door to separate them. Later repeat the process. After doing this several times they will hopefully get the idea that "Mr. Hyde" may actually have some Dr. Jeckyll benefits (and both kitties believe the other cat is the evil Mr. or Ms. Hyde).

When your open-door policy appears to be leading toward a truce, put the victim cat in a carrier and treat the aggressor. Again, Kilroy gets his treats only when he's not threatening his nemesis.

When you let the kitty out of the carrier feed them at least ten feet apart. Very gradually, begin to feed them at closer distances. *Don't rush the process.* Remember, patience is a virtue.

To broaden their happy experiences, get some interactive playtime in. Lock the rest of the cats up and get 🐾 **Da Bird** out of the closet. It's an interactive birdlike toy on a string that looks and sounds like a flying bird. With you manning the wand you'll have your predators jumping and running and even occasionally snagging the toy—using up that predatory energy they'd otherwise use on you and the other cats. The two feuding cats only get to play with the fun toy in each other's presence. With each play session, increase their time together by a few minutes. Use two Da Birds, one in each hand, so there's no competition.

Keep the battered cat in his sanctuary and continue the gradual reintroductions until you are certain it's safe to leave them together. If something happens and they get into a tussle, go back to the last successful step.

Working It Out with a Workout

Kilroy may have too much time and energy on his paws. In an interview, Dr. Dodman told me, "We know if we exercise for twenty minutes a day, we are healthier. If our cats exercise, they're healthier, too. Exercise increases serotonin levels in both humans and cats. Serotonin is found in Prozac. Low serotonin in our furry friends produces irritability, increases aggression and causes depression. Higher serotonin levels promote feelings of well-being and self-confidence."

Dodman also explained that, "In nature, cats don't have to arrange to get exercise. Although they sleep seventy percent of the time, in the thirty percent they are awake, they are very active, chasing things and climbing trees. Indoor cats seldom have the benefit of rodents scurrying. They get cabin fever." And they beat up other cats.

Here are some things you can do to get your cats to sing "Kum Ba Yah" and smoke a catnip pipe together:

- Schedule desexing operations for everyone!
- Trim claws and put 🐾 **Soft Paws** on Kilroy's nails.
- Introduce all new cats slowly.
- Give your cats a reason to want to be with the bad guy. Make being around the other cat fun and profitable with treats.
- Provide rigorous interactive playtime for each cat ten minutes a day.
- Put a loud bell on the aggressor. This might help the victim cat keep track of his whereabouts, reducing the opportunity of an ambush. (This doesn't always work. Some ambushers have been to charm school and can walk smoothly without ringing the bell.)

- Use **Comfort Zone** plug ins, especially in the rooms where the most attacks occur.

- Every day massage the fighting cats with a cloth that contains the other cat's scent.

- Set up nooks and crannies throughout the house so your cats can hide if they want to. (See the chapter "Happy Habitats".) Create vertical space with cat trees or empty shelves on a bookcase. Cats are more comfortable living in groups if they can layer themselves.

- Place feeding stations and litter boxes (not right next to each other) in several different parts of the house so Kilroy can't guard them all.

- Make sure you give everyone individual attention.

- Try the appropriate 🐾 **Bach Flower Remedy** on Kilroy and the wimp. (See the Shopping Guide section.)

- Reward the aggressive cat with praise and treats for ignoring his victim. Don't forget to reward the subordinate cat for holding his ground and being brave. If a fight breaks out, always separate them.

- Consider antianxiety medication (along with behavior modification and enhancing the environment) if things don't improve.

Cats on the Couch

If you've tried everything I've suggested and your guys are still spray painting with yellow pigment, you should consider calling in a cat shrink. As previously mentioned, look for one who has experience in multicat dynamics. Your vet may be able to recommend a behaviorist. If she doesn't know of anyone, check out the International Association of Animal Behavior Consultants Web site (www.iaabc.org) for a consultant in your area. You can also ask any nearby veterinary colleges or universities if they have a behavior clinic.

Failing that, you can contact the Animal Behavior Clinic of the Cummings School of Veterinary Medicine at Tufts University, which offers remote behavior counseling via the PETFAX program.

A Round of Prozac on Me

When all else fails, drug therapy may become necessary to manage spraying and peeing outside the box when the cat doesn't respond to medical treatment, neutering, and environmental and behavioral enhancements you've made in your home.

"A little bit of Prozac for Mr. Whisker. A little bit of Prozac for Mommy."

Many of the drugs vets give to cats for spraying and aggression are meds developed for humans but given to cats off label. You may even be taking some of them yourself.

Several classes of drugs are commonly prescribed for stress, aggression, anxiety, and inappropriate elimination in cats. Some of them have been shown to be very effective. Others have proven deadly. Don't take the initiative and give these drugs to your cats on your own. Work with your vet to find the right drug for your cat's specific problem. These drugs only work in pets with anxiety-induced marking behavior and have little or no impact on the cat who is peeing outside the box unless some stress component is involved.

Unless your behaviorist is also a vet, she'll have to work with your own vet to come up with the drug treatment that's the safest and most effective for your particular case. In most cases, drug therapy is recommended to assist in behavioral modification and training but doesn't replace them. The purpose behind giving any or all of these medications is to stabilize the cat's mood and reduce anxiety.

Dr. Dodman says in refractory cases of urine-marking (which is most of them) medication can be used to decrease cats' arousal and thus the drive for territorial or anxious urine-marking. The most effective medication, he says, is fluoxetine (Prozac), which resolves the problem in some ninety-percent of cases. The next most effective medication is the tricyclic antidepressant clomipramine (Clomicalm), then buspirone (BuSpar), with a fifty or sixty percent efficacy rate and, finally, the trycyclic antidepressant, amitriptyline (Elavil), which is also sometimes effective. Sometimes these medications need to be given long-term but other times a short course of a few weeks can be enough to resolve an otherwise chronic problem.

Dr. Dodman warns if there's been no behavior modification, once cats are taken off the meds, they would go back to urine marking. Antianxiety meds should be used in addition to behavior modification techniques in cats who haven't responded to behavior modification alone.

He added that there is no perfect medication for use in treating urine marking, but with the various choices of medicines your vet can probably find a drug that will work for your cat without too many side affects. Because of the potential side affects, your vet will probably want to check your cats' blood before prescribing antianxiety medications.

All the drugs mentioned below require a weaning period. Cats should never be taken off them cold turkey. If you have problems giving your cat pills, a compounding pharmacist can place most of these drugs in a tastier form to ease the stress of medicating your cat. You can find a compounding pharmacist online at www.iacprx.org.

Here are the most common antianxiety drugs prescribed for cats. This is based on a datasheet compiled by Dr. Dodman and given to clients at the Animal Behavior Clinic at Cummings School of Veterinary Medicine at Tufts University:

- Prozac (fluoxetine) is a selective serotonin reuptake inhibitor commonly prescribed for social stress, obsessive-compulsive disorder aggression, anxiety, and depression. In studies conducted at the University of California-Davis, fluoxetine was 90 percent effective in controlling urine marking. It shouldn't be given to cats with a history of seizures or heart, liver, or kidney disease. While side effects are uncommon, they may include lethargy, decreased appetite, increased thirst, constipation, vomiting, or diarrhea. It may cause social withdrawal and/or sedation. A cat can continue to learn while he is on fluoxetine. It's given orally every twenty-four hours. For cats, capsules can be diluted in liquid (tuna juice or clam juice) to the appropriate concentration. Alternatively, specialty pharmacies can compound Prozac into capsules of the proper dose or in a liver-flavored liquid. It takes four to six weeks for the meds to kick in, and may take up to twelve weeks to achieve the full effect. Treatment should continue for a month after symptoms disappear or are reliably controlled.

- Clomicalm and Anafranil (clomipramine) are brands of this drug that is a tricyclic antidepressant, and according to the study is 80 percent effective in controlling urine marking. It treats obsessive-compulsive behaviors, anxiety (including separation anxiety, phobias), aggression, and depression. It may cause social withdrawal and/or sedation. Clomipramine shouldn't be given to cats with a history of seizures, or heart, liver, or kidney disease. Results won't be experienced until the cat has been on the meds for four to six weeks. It may take up to twelve weeks to achieve the full effect. Treatment should be continued for a month after symptoms disappear. Prices vary among pharmacies so it pays to comparison shop. There is a generic form that comes in tablets and capsules and only requires daily dosing. It can be compounded into palatable drops.

- BuSpar (buspirone) is an antianxiety drug that blocks the effect of serotonin (a brain chemical). Often vets use it to treat urine spraying, low-grade anxieties and fears, separation anxiety, and offensive and predatory aggression. Less potent than fluoxetine, BuSpar is 60 percent effective in controlling urine marking, according to a study from the UC Davis. This drug is used to boost confidence in fearful cats. Buspirone can cause excitement or nervousness. It's pricey and must be administered in tablet form twice daily. Since it has an extremely bitter taste, it can't be compounded.

The most likely side effects are dizziness, headache, nausea/anorexia, restlessness, nervousness, excitement, mood changes, increased aggression between household cats, and increased attention seeking. Less common side effects include sedation, and in rare cases cardiovascular symptoms, and restlessness can appear shortly after starting treatment. It can take up to four weeks to realize the full effects of this drug.

- Elavil (amitriptyline) is a tricyclic antidepressant and a neurotransmitter blocker. While uncommon, side effects include idiosyncratic reactions, decreased appetite, increased thirst, lethargy, constipation, vomiting, and diarrhea. Some cats become groggy and depressed. Cats taking this drug for a prolonged period could be susceptible to liver problems. It can also cause urinary retention, so it is not a good choice for cats with a history of lower urinary tract infections. Because of the serious side effects, vets at Tufts University Cummings School of Veterinary Medicine seldom use it. It is considered a last line of defense. The generic, amitriptyline, is relatively inexpensive. It is usually only given once a day but cannot be given in food because it is bitter.

- Xanax (alprazolam) is a Class IV controlled drug that can only be dispensed via written prescription. It is used off label for cats to reduce anxiety, for phobias and separation anxiety, and other situational fears (car travel, veterinary office visits). It is considered 60 percent effective. It should be used with caution in cats with liver disease. It should also be avoided in cats with myasthenia gravis or glaucoma. The most common side effects are excessive sedation and loss of muscle coordination. In some cats, it may actually cause or exacerbate aggression. Long-term treatment with alprazolam can lead to physical dependence. Elderly cats are prone to depression of the central nervous system, even at low doses. Alprazolam increases cats' appetites and can make them wobbly on their legs. In addition, it can be associated with a withdrawal syndrome of anxiety following treatment (perhaps causing a relapse).

The following drugs are not recommended for use in cats:

- Valium (diazepam) has been banned for use in cats by the Animal Behavior Clinic at Tufts University, even though some vets may still prescribe it for various behavior problems. Diazepam is moderately successful at relieving anxiety-inspired marking and elimination, but the problem returns when diazepam is discontinued. Also cats are unable to learn while on the drug. Some cats develop a life-threatening liver disorder. Other side affects include excessive appetites and drowsiness.

- Ovaban and Megace (megestrol acetate), and Depo-Provera (medroxyprogesterone acetate) are synthetic female hormones vets used in the past to control inappropriate elimination. They were not terribly successful and had devastating side affects, which include drug-induced diabetes mellitus and mammary cancer.

Sometimes disputes between housemates can be resolved as easily as adding a cat tree or engaging your cats in a couple of rounds of kitty calisthenics every day. Other times it takes some detective work and experimentation to find a solution. Hopefully, armed with a better understanding of kitty etiquette and feline health behavior, your kitties should be able to live in harmony, or in a worst case scenario, in at least harmless indifference.

CHAPTER FIVE

New Kit in Town

*There is no more important a decision than the decision to adopt
and assume the responsibility for another life. That decision carries
an obligation to nurture that life—to give it love—to care for it.*
—**Roger Caras**

YOU'RE GETTING A NEW CAT? Congratulations! Have you decided that
your cat needs some feline companionship? Sometimes you simply have to
adopt what fate has dropped in your lap or taken from the center lane of a busy
street. Or you, a cat lover, move in with
another cat lover. Perhaps out of kind-
ness you've decided to foster a cat or kitten for a shelter or rescue group. Voilà,
you have a new cat!

But let's be real here. If you already
have a cat who sprays and carries on
whenever the neighborhood stray wan-
ders into your yard, then perhaps a new
kitty—no matter how cute and compatible—might launch the beginning of the
Great Cat War.

*Without proper introductions, your
house could become a war zone.*

Before you permanently open your home to a new lifelong companion, turn to the chapter "I May Be a Cat Lady/Guy, but I'm Not Crazy" and ask yourself if you're really up to a new pet. Do you have the energy it takes to care for another feline family member? Will you be willing to take your cat with you if you move? Are you expecting turmoil in your life (a move, divorce)? Will you be able to continue to care for him in the midst of havoc?

Be honest with yourself. What kind of care are you giving the cats you already have? Is it already a struggle to scoop the litter boxes once a day? Additional pets will just make the job more arduous. If you're always caught up on the scooping and cat grooming, your cats get plenty of attention, and you can afford food and veterinary care for one more—then enjoy your new pet.

Picking Out a Cat-panion

If you're making the conscious decision to adopt a cat, I'm going to briefly tell you how to screen potential family members. Rather than tell you to pick the cat with the bright eyes and avoid the ones with the snotty noses, I'm going to tell you how to pick a cat that will best fit into your feline family from a personality standpoint.

When you interview potential mischief assistants, be respectful of your present cats' personalities and activity levels. Pick a companion who is compatible. Carefully consider the following about your current cat residents:

- Are your cats young, adults, senior citizens, or a mixed bag?

- Do they move at rocket speed 24/7 or prefer to watch *Animal Planet* between catnaps?

- Have your cats never met a stranger, or do they think everyone's a stranger?

- Do your cats get their tails in a kink when they smell other cats on you, or do they check your pockets for leftover treats when you return from volunteering at the animal shelter?

- Do they leave peepee graffiti around windows or doors?

- Is your cat's role model Mike Tyson or Mahatma Gandhi?

FELINE FACT OR FICTION

Adopt a Kitten and All Will Be Right with the World

Every cat will happily accept a bouncing wad of fur—right? Not necessarily! Don't get me wrong. I love kittens. I've been involved in kitten rescue for twenty years. But, I'll share a little secret with you. While they're irresistible, kittens are a royal pain in the tail. They're into everything and need lots of attention and training. If you don't spend time teaching your kitten boundaries, you're going to have an out-of-control hellion when he gets older. Worse than the aggravation a kitten will cause you is the distress he could cause your other cats. Your senior cat with achy joints probably wouldn't appreciate Tommy the Terror jumping on him and chewing on his ears.

In some cases, it might be wise to adopt a kitten over a kitty who has some miles under his paws. Some highly territorial cats will accept a kitten with less *Sturm und Drang* than they would a mature cat. Kittens aren't as threatening to the resident adults because they're small. A baby hasn't yet developed a sense of territory, so he's not interested in staking a claim to the window perch. Their hormones haven't kicked in either—another plus from your cats' perspective. That's why kittens under the age of five months have a greater chance of being accepted.

If your resident kitty is shy, don't bring home an aggressive, in-your-face type hoping to bring the wallflower out of his shell. Rather than making him more outgoing, Kilroy, the aggressive cat, will have the quiet cat setting up housekeeping under the bed or in the back of the closet.

On the other hand, if you have an assertive four-year-old with high energy and a strong personality, get a kitty with a similar personality. Don't bring home a shy ten-year-old to tone him down. He'll become territorial and turn the timid newcomer into a doormat.

Whatever your cats' ages, you should look for a sociable type who's friendly and not aggressive around other kitties. Shelter staff can tell you which kitty candidate gets along best with the other cats and who has lived happily in multicat homes. Watch the cats hang out with each other and try to find one with a personality similar to your cats. Some people think girl kitties get along better with boys, but as long as everyone has been fixed, I don't think it makes much difference. You and your resident cats will live happier and less stressful lives if everyone has been fixed. Adopt from a rescue group that will take the newcomer back if he and your resident cats don't make a love connection.

Age Over Beauty

When considering whether to get a youngster or an oldster think about these points:

Dr. Jekyll and Mr. Katz. Young kittens start out cute and affectionate, but as they get older their personalities may change. They may think you're cool when they're little fuzz balls, but once they hit four or five months, they're just like adolescent kids. "Don't hug me!" "Don't hold me!" Your lap kitten may develop into an independent cat who only wants to be petted when you have a cat food can in your hand. Or he might turn into a clingy kitty who constantly hovers underfoot. Sometime after they hit that two-year mark they settle down and may want to snuggle again, but like kids, there are no guarantees about their personality when they're grown.

Older cats have established personalities. What you see is what you get. His personality won't change later unless there's a medical issue or trauma. If he's a lap cat at the shelter, he'll probably be a lap cat next year. You won't be disappointed.

Older cats are less destructive and require less supervision. With a kitten in the house, you're not going to be able to display your expensive knickknacks on the coffee table. Kittens can turn today's treasures into Tuesday's trash faster than you can read this paragraph. Power cords are fair game. Although older cats can get into mischief, you're likely to have fewer headaches than you will with a kitten going through adolescence. Kittens need constant supervision, which may be difficult in busy families. He can't learn what's expected of him without you 'splaining it to him. It could take you months, or even years, before you reach the same comfortable relationship with Junior that you could have with an older cat in just a few days.

Senior citizens and small children are safer with adult cats. While everyone wants a cute little kitten, there's nothing cute about the way those sharp little claws penetrate the thin skin of the elderly as they scale a leg like Mount McKinley or bite arthritic fingers. Kittens also have a bad habit of getting underfoot. That's a broken hip waiting to happen for both the senior and the kitten. On the other end of life's spectrum, children under five can unintentionally hurt or kill a little kitten by dropping, squeezing, or falling on it. And since wee humans still need lessons in gentle handling, there's a good chance a toddler with a vise grip may end up nursing scratches or bites left by a kitten who just wants to get away. To protect the kid and the kit, many humane organizations have a six/six rule. They won't adopt a kitten under six months to a family with a child under six years.

Shelter workers should be able to tell you about the personalities and maybe the histories of the cats in their care. Their cages are filled with mature cats who are gentle and tolerant of small children and also kitties whose senior owners have passed away. Shelters frequently have a steady supply of declawed kitties that would be perfect pets for seniors.

Papers Please. If you're interested in a pedigreed cat, you can find a retired show cat by talking to breeders at cat shows. These guys are used to being handled by a lot of different people. They've been around other cats all their lives. They're also accustomed to traveling and being groomed. A pedigreed kitten could cost a fortune. But, in order to place cats in a good home, breeders may only charge a token adoption fee for a retired show cat. You could also contact a "purebred" cat rescue organization in your area. (Look for them at www.petfinder.com.)

Personally, if I was searching for a lifelong companion, I'd go straight to the adult cats. Older kitties often wind up in shelters because of a problem with the owner rather than with the cats. A couple gives up their eight-year-old tabby because the woman is pregnant or just had a baby. They fear the cat might hurt their child or they no longer have time for their kitty. Someone in the family is suddenly allergic. Ah, and an oldie but goodie: the family is moving and can't take their cat with them. So adult cats sit in shelters waiting for a new family that never comes. By adopting these cats, you can fill a void in your feline family *and* save a life. It doesn't get any better than that.

Remember, There's No Such Thing as a Free Cat

Most rescue groups charge an adoption fee of $100 or more for a cat. Don't balk. In most cases these cats have been fixed, tested for diseases, had shots, been wormed, and have recovered from whatever crud they caught in the pound. In some cases, they've even been microchipped. If you had all those things done yourself you could be looking at vet bills of more than $200, maybe $300.

Beware the kittens being given away in front of Wal-Mart. Inside a cardboard box you see eight or ten big, bright eyes peering back at you. The sign says, "Kitty—no charge." They look skinny. How can you say no? While you may want to take one of the little cuties home to get him out of the hot sun, think about what your "free cat" will cost you.

The kitty will need to be spayed or neutered, have three sets of shots, a feline leukemia/feline immunodeficiency virus test, worming, and flea treatments. Depending on the cost of veterinary care in your area, that free but healthy kitten could cost you $200. If he's got an upper respiratory infection, ringworm, or other health issues, he could cost you way more than that.

In 1996 I bought a dying, four-week-old Tonkinese mix at a garage sale for ten dollars. The woman wanted to keep her for a barn cat but realized she was too sick to survive without vet care. Starving and dehydrated, the kitten wouldn't have made it another day. To treat her for abscesses, parasites, ringworm, ear mites, diarrhea, an upper respiratory infection, and other problems ran another $258 (in 1996 dollars) from my personal vet. While I've been rewarded exponentially, it was a chunk of change I wasn't expecting to have to pay. I still had to pay for more testing, shots, and spaying. Remember, there's no such thing as a free cat.

Emily Scratching Post

You can't choose the members of your human family and sometimes you aren't given much choice in the cat that enters your life either. He might be the one eating out of the Dumpster at the school, or a kitty that a family down the street left when they moved away. Now he's yours. Regardless of where he came from, you can't just throw him in with your cats and let them work it out—at least not if you want your little family to be civil to each other. The secret to a new cat and a happy home is a proper introduction.

We humans are sticklers for etiquette and protocol. Just take a brief glance at the book by Emily Post from the 1920s, *Etiquette in Society, in Business, in Politics and at Home* (Funk & Wagnalls, 1922). Every aspect in the proper introduction of one stranger to another was crucial. The person giving the introductions must use the proper words. "Mrs. Smith, may I present Mr. Brown?" To avoid a huge faux "paw," you had to know whose name is presented first, use voice inflection at specific moments in the introduction and when to make eye contact and when it was proper for a lady to shake hands. There's so much to keep straight, but it was necessary to be accepted into social groups and to achieve status.

Cats have their own version of etiquette. And some of their rules of introduction may sound as silly and nitpicky as the early twentieth-century human formalities. But to cats, it's important.

To determine proper feline customs I'm going to refer to the "Emily Scratching-Post Book of Cat Etiquette."

The First Step: Health Checkup

In the Emily Scratching-Post world of puss protocol the new kit on the block needs to get some stylish body piercing for everyone's protection. Nothing ostentatious, like such as a nose or eyebrow ring, just current shots and blood testing for diseases like feline leukemia. A vet should check him out for upper respiratory infections and parasites so he doesn't bring your cats any unwanted housewarming gifts.

Regardless of where Newy the newbie came from, if you have time before bringing him home, offer your resident cats some comfort, or rather some ⊛ **Comfort Zone with Feliway**. It's a diffuser, like a plug-in air freshener. But instead of making the place smell like roses or ocean breezes, it smells like kitty cheeks—the cheeks in the front, not the back ones. (Don't worry. You won't smell a thing.)

The Second Step: Creating a Sanctuary for the New Arrival

Regardless of where your new cat comes from, don't just bring him into the lion's den. As the old adage goes, you never get a second chance to make a first impression. That's never been so true as when introducing cats. Some cats simply hate each other at first sight, and this can never be reversed. You can prevent territorial aggression altogether by introducing the new cat to your resident cats gradually—*very gradually*—and by plying your family cats with treats whenever they come in contact with Newy. Patience can make the difference between forever friends (or at least forever ambivalent) and lifelong foes.

Set up Newy's sanctuary in a quiet, small room, like a bathroom or a bedroom, for a week or so. While it may seem like a punishment to you, this room will become his own personal territory in a scary place full of strange cats and strange people, too. Provide him with his own food and water, a scratching pad, and a cardboard box with a towel or blanket where he can hide. Put his litter box in another part of the room. Spray the place down with Comfort Zone before you open the carrier. From his safe room, he can gradually adjust to the sights, sounds, and smells in his new home.

When you first bring him home, unceremoniously take Newy, carrier and all, straight to the sanctuary. Set down the carrier unopened and return to the herd.

Your resident cats immediately get special treats—small pieces of turkey, chicken, or tuna, or even turkey baby food. Rest assured, nothing has gotten past your cats. They already realize that the house is abuzz with that new cat smell. They're obligated to stare indignantly at the sanctuary door, adding an occasional growl or hiss. If you're smart, you'll ignore their carrying on. Let them know they're still large and in charge. They should get more personal attention from you, and their feeding and box-cleaning schedule should stay the same. (A couple of drops of the Bach Flower Remedy Holly massaged onto the crown of their heads will help your cats deal with the threat and jealousy of the newcomer.)

After they get their share of treats, return to the new cat's sanctuary, open the carrier door, and stand back. Newy may just wait until he's alone before venturing out; he'll eventually come ambling out when he's ready. Check on him every few hours and visit with him. Talk to him while you scoop his box.

When you can, put a few drops of Bach Rescue Remedy on Newy's head or a dropper full in his water to help keep him calm.

The Third Step: Letting Him Explore

The best way for your cats to get to know their future best friend is to check out each other's scent through the crack at the bottom of the door. Let them play footsie. Better still, let them share a meal on either side of the closed door. (See, your cats are associating Newy's scent with food, and so is Newy. Win-win.)

Visit him. If he's friendly, hold him while you read aloud to him. If he's hiding or shies away from you, be patient. Before dinner, read out loud to him and toss treats in his direction. When you leave, set a few more treats on the spot where you were sitting. Soon he'll figure out he's safe and you're the food person.

It won't be long before you'll see him rubbing his face against cabinets or furniture. That means he's beginning to feel at home and he's marking it as his own.

Newy will show you he's ready to go on a supervised walkabout of the house when he's strolling confidently around his sanctuary holding his tail up. For this big event the other cats should be locked away so they don't get their whiskers kinked up. However, when the door opens, if Newy stares out as if to say, "Have you lost your flea-bitten mind?"—let him be. Allow him to explore his new home at his own pace. Forcing a timid cat into the house will just make him more withdrawn—not a good state of mind to be in when you're thrown to the wolves, uh, other cats. When he goes out on those short excursions, the other kitties get to go into his room and eat. And not yucky dry stuff, but special treats—something they only get on important occasions like birthdays or when they bag an extra big rat. Once again, they're associating special treats with Newy's scent. It's like Pavlov's dog, except with cats. When they smell Newy they know something delicious is going to happen. Before you put them in there, spray the place down with Comfort Zone. Hopefully, while Newy's checking out the house, he's cheek marking and they will also hopefully cheek mark his sanctuary, blending their scents so your guys know that Kilroy—or rather Newy—was there. After Newy's been running around for a few minutes, switch everyone back to their original places. As Newy becomes more confident and knows where the litter box is, you two can swap stations for longer periods.

Next, wedge the sanctuary door open (about an inch) from the inside with doorstops. This way the kitties can safely check each other out. This is another good time to get the treats out. Don't open the door any wider until they can eyeball each other without fur flying.

A two-minute date is perfect for first introductions. That doesn't give them enough time to decide that they really loathe each other.

If one of the cats has an enduring problem with Newy, lock up everyone except him. With Newy safely inside the carrier, bring Kilroy over for formal introductions. Of course, once again, Kilroy is obligated to act appropriately indignant—from a cat's point of view—stare threateningly, hiss, and maybe even growl. Newy will probably return the honors. When Kilroy acts calm, tell him what a wonderful cat he is and give him some of those special treats. After a few minutes, sequester Newy back in the sanctuary. Later repeat the performance for a longer period (and more treats). Reward Kilroy only when he is relaxed. Don't treat him for staring because that's a threatening action to another cat. Soon Kilroy will decide that all these treats are a pretty good deal and accept the newcomer, but it might take several weeks.

Step Four: Making Introductions

When the time feels right, open the carrier or bathroom door and let everyone meet full on. Hissing's OK; spitting's OK, but if things turn ugly—your resident cats stalking Newy or ambushing him—the greenhorn should be sent back to his room. Kilroy should get no attention or treats until you try again later. Go back to the last successful stage, then start moving forward again.

Keep an eye on them until you feel that they are getting along well. Put the new cat up in his room when no one is there to ride herd.

Now it's possible that even after all your work, their first in-person meeting may get off on the wrong paw. If the very scent of the new cat sends anyone's hackles up, try stroking Newy's face with a clean cloth (to capture his scent), then put it under Kilroy's food bowl. After you've done that, rub Kilroy's head and Newy with separate cloths, then switch cloths and massage the other kitty's scent into the fur. In a sense you're creating a new communal scent. Do this every day. Or put vanilla extract in a small pump sprayer, and mist each cat with it. Make sure to mist the tail and hips, but not the bum directly. Everyone smells the same; there's no longer an olfactory outsider. You might need to do this for a few days.

Throughout this process, remember the needs of your older kitties. If your cats have favorite sleeping spaces, don't let the newcomer snooze there. Give him his own toys, bowls, and litter box so your other kitties don't feel threatened.

Yours, Mine, and Ours

When you bring more than one cat into your home simultaneously, the same rules apply, but they're just a bit more complicated. Let me warn you again, if you just throw all the cats together, the fur is going to fly. First the feline fur, then human hair. Your cats hate his cats and vice versa. Your home will be constantly disrupted by the mind-jarring screeches of cats locked in mortal combat. You know the screams—they sound like the evil killer cats that appear in Stephen King movies. Suddenly both people and cats have to wear clothespins on their noses because everyone's peeing everywhere. Most of this havoc can be avoided by taking Emily Scratching-Post's advice.

My hubby and I are living proof that making the effort before you make the move can result in a somewhat peaceful, albeit hectic, home. We merged two multicat households with a surprising scarcity of growling and gnashing of teeth. Our home looked like a feline version of the old Lucille Ball–Henry Fonda classic movie, *Yours, Mine and Ours* (or if you prefer, the more recent version starring Dennis Quaid and Rene Russo).

Chances are, with patience and persistence your cats will work out their differences and keep the pissing and cat fights down to a minimum. After an initial breaking-in period your kitties' relationship will probably fall somewhere between merely accepting each other from a safe distance to curling up together for a nap.

Getting Ready for the "Merge"

Make sure everyone's current on their shots and free of passengers like fleas, ear mites, and internal parasites. After they've passed their health tests, set aside a room or section of the house for the newly arriving pets. Put a 🐾 **Comfort**

Zone Diffuser in the new cats' area as well as in the rooms where your cats hang to get everyone in the mood for love instead of war.

Clean and vacuum the room. And check the whole area with an ultraviolet light for evidence of pee stains. (It works best when you let it warm up for fifteen minutes.) You'll want to make sure your own guys haven't already marked up the new cats' room. A pee spot on the walls or floor is a declaration of war. Maybe not all-out war with blood and biting, but it would certainly bring on a pissing match between old cats and new cats.

Since cleaning this area is so important, refer to the chapter "Cleanup on Aisle Two." I've included information there about getting all the odor out of a carpet. Once the pee is cleaned up, put the new cats' unwashed linens or bedding in the room with their toys. Don't forget their personal food and water dishes and litter boxes. Make sure they have cardboard boxes and shelves on bookcases where they can spread out and up in their new room. In cramped quarters even the best of friends may have disagreements.

When my husband and I merged homes, we piped air-conditioning into the garage and insulated the walls and doors so the kitties didn't bake in the Texas heat. His cats had the run of the garage with all the comforts of home including their cat trees to climb on and beds, bowls, and their litter boxes. We kept some of Weems' dirty T-shirts out there so he could be with them all the time by scent proxy.

Although we hadn't thought of it, a stick or two of furniture from their old home might have been a nice, homey, comforting touch.

Nice to Smell You

There should be no whisker-to-whisker meetings in the beginning for the first week or so. Keep the new guys in their room or on their own floor, separated from the resident cats. Let them smell each other and play through the crack under the door. You'll have to play Shuffling Cats, swapping them between territories. If you can install a screen door on the new cats' room, this is a good time to open the main door and let them get a look at each other. Feed the resident cats in the new cats' sanctuary. Following the rules you read in the earlier section, once the new cats feel comfortable with their territory, open the door and let them meet under close supervision. In the event of an altercation, a water pistol helps cool overheated tempers. Don't leave them unsupervised until you haven't seen any hissing or growling for a few days.

You can visit the newcomers, but don't openly pay attention to them in the resident cats' presence. Go out of your way to pamper the residents. They're usually the ones to get their noses out of joint because it's their territory that's being invaded.

When you finally let them all out together, give each cat his old food and water dishes. Mingle the scents on a kitty brush to create a new improved communal smell.

You may try another method in which each owner sits across the room from each other holding their own respective cats. After a while, put the kitties in their own room for a few minutes, then trade cats and repeat the process. (You smell like my owner and I smell like yours.)

TAILS FROM THE TRENCHES

Sondra York has fostered thousands of cats for north Texas humane organizations. She managed one of the first cageless (no-kill) cat shelters in the country. When a new cat arrived she puts him in a cage for a few days and then cages the resident cats and lets the new guy run free for several more days. (OK, so they had a couple of cages.) This allows them to adjust to each other's sight and smell. In her method, the cats hiss and spit but can't get to each other. After a week, she opens the cages. The resident cats already know the new cat by sight and smell. Opening the door is just a formality. She says make sure the cage is backed against a wall (a corner is even better) because the cat is protected on that side. On release day, there's some posturing and rearranging of the hierarchy. She always watches to make certain the resident cats aren't ganging up on the new kitty. Sondra says this method should never be used on timid cats.

Keep the first meeting between cats short, no more than a few minutes, and then gradually let them spend more time together. Food is a powerful incentive. Feed the different groups in their own personal bowls at opposite ends of the room so that all the cats associate food with the strange cats. While this is great for training purposes, remember, you should have feeding stations in different parts of the house so the dominant cats don't guard the bowls.

Getting Their Whiskers in a Twist

In the beginning there's going to be posturing. But rest assured that most disagreements between cats are settled through quick skirmishes and intimidation. Cats rarely make full contact. (For more on cat-to-cat aggression, see the chapter "Family Feud.")

Don't permit continued aggressive behavior. Many behaviorists find **Bach Flower Remedies**, natural remedies similar to homeopathy, to be helpful in aggression situations. You'll find a complete list of flower remedies to help cats deal with aggression, fear, and new situations and physical and emotional trauma in the Shopping Guide section.

Location Logistics

It may be easier to feed everyone and clean litter boxes if they're all right together, but it's better for the kitties if you break up your home into lots of mini territories. Place cat trees, cubbyholes, cat beds, litter boxes, and food bowls throughout the house.

Just as we humans feel uneasy about sharing the bathroom with strangers, cats dislike sharing their litter boxes with an intruder.

If any of the cats start peeing outside the box, take them to the vet; there could be some health issues or aggression problems. (Learn all about your cats' litter box preferences in the chapter "Everything You Wanted to Know about the Litter Box But Were Afraid to Ask.")

If you take the time to slowly introduce your new cat, you won't have to spend all your time being a referee. As with humans, proper introductions go a long way toward building a lifelong friendship, or at the least, cats that can tolerate each other.

CHAPTER SIX

The Pissing Contest

Do not meddle in the affairs of cats, for they are subtle
and will piss on your computer.
—**Bruce Graham**

DURING WORLD WAR II, A cartoon face captioned with the words, "Kilroy was here," appeared all over Europe. James Kilroy was a shipyard construction inspector who scribbled the long-nosed image on the bulkheads of new ships with a yellow crayon to certify the rivets. Troops being transported to the war in Europe saw the cartoon and believed it to be left behind by another GI. When the Americans landed, as a joke they began leaving the graffiti all over creation. The first American troops to enter territory captured from the enemy claimed to find the

Everyone marks territory in some way. Cats use pee because they don't have opposable thumbs to operate a spray paint can.

Once again, Howard from down the street made off with the personals before Kilroy had a chance to check them out.

phrase already posted. "Kilroy was here," a human form of territorial marking, irritated the German and Japanese who came across the drawings.

"Kilroy was here" has been found at the summit of Mount Everest, on the torch of the Statue of Liberty, the underside of the Arc de Triomphe in France. It's even drawn in the dust on the moon.

Like those soldiers who spread the word "Kilroy was here" from there to eternity, cats have the innate need to leave their own graffiti behind. Instead of using yellow crayon, cats use a yellow spray paint of sorts. Call it peepee graffiti. When cats spray, they are leaving behind a message similar to Kilroy's: "I was here."

In the wild, a male cat marks his territory with pee, and an interested female will pee back a similar message that says something like, "My place or yours?" The cat will curl his lips into a *flehmen*, sucking scent into his *Jacobson's organ*. This way a cat can check out another cat's message, gleaning information a plain old sniff couldn't detect.

Cats use their sense of smell the same way humans use a community bulletin board to tell when a new cat has arrived and whether he's going to horn in on the female action. Of course, while he's smelling the neighborhood gossip, he's peeing messages of his own.

Making Sense of Scents

Generally, in the wild it's not a problem when a cat sprays peepee graffiti all over the neighborhood. But it's a huge problem when he sprays his thoughts and feelings around your house. When you find someone has hosed the house, the cat is trying to get a message across to you or another cat. He may be marking or he might be going to the bathroom. He uses pee to empty his bladder *and* to leave his mark. There are subtle differences.

FELINE FACT OR FICTION

Spraying Inside the House Is "Bad" Behavior

Well, it's actually normal for cats to spray and it's an important part of their survival instinct. It certainly clashes when cats follow their instincts inside our homes. Scent is a crucial form of communication. A cat will spray the outskirts of his territory to warn other cats to stay out or he might issue a challenge to another cat when he's considering a real estate expansion program.

IS IT PEE OR GRAFFITI?

HE'S PEEING IF:	HE'S MARKING IF:
he *never* uses the litter box properly, and usually squats *near the box*.	*he continues to pee in the litter box*, but you *also* find spots on the furniture, your bed, or in your dirty clothes.
there's a large volume of pee when he empties his bladder.	he sprays small quantity of pee when he marks.
he scratches to cover his pee.	he doesn't attempt to cover his pee.
he squats near the litter box.	he backs up to a vertical object, wiggles his tail, sprays urine, and wears a euphoric expression on his face.
he makes a round pattern with his pee. This is *usually* peeing (but not always).	he stands in the middle of a flat surface like a bed and produces a long stream or pee.
he never pees in the litter box.	he continues to pee in the litter box several times a day *and* sprays other places.
he usually pees in a discreet place.	he pees on unusual places, such as stoves and countertops, and on personal items, such as beds, worn clothing, purses, and used towels.
he pees in large amounts while squatting in the middle of the room.	he marks the middle of the room with only a small amount of pee.

I go into a lot of detail about the difference between inappropriate elimination and spraying in other chapters, but here's the redux. If a cat is squatting right *beside* a box he's probably either sick or he's not happy about the condition of his bathroom. You can *usually* tell the difference between a pee spot and peepee graffiti by the artistic design. Cats *normally* spray from the standing position so they can concentrate the stream at nose height to another cat. After all, if you're trying to get a message across, it makes sense to put it where he can most easily read it, or rather, sniff it. He's marking if he's backed up to a vertical object wiggling his tail spraying urine. There's a faux spraying behavior that looks like he's spraying, but he's shooting blanks—no pee passes—which happens when the cat is excited about something. If he's standing in the middle of a flat surface like a bed, producing a long stream, he's marking. A round pattern from a squatting position *usually* means he's peeing. *But not always.* While it seems like a contradiction, cats may also mark on flat surfaces while squatting. The clue is where he's doing it and whether he's peeing inside the box at other times, and if he only sprays a little pee rather than the flood that lets loose when he empties his bladder. If your cat is neutered and he's happily peeing in the litter box, that means squatting in the middle of your bed or in your dirty clothes is a marking action rather than emptying his bladder. If he *never* pees in the box, he's going to the bathroom. (See a vet and read the chapter "Back in the Box.")

Dr. Dodman says urine marking always involves interesting and varied locations such as countertops, windowsills, walls, drapes, new furniture (especially desktops), electrical equipment (computers, stereos), stovetops, refrigerators, shopping bags, personal belongings, peoples' clothes, or beds of the owner, and sometimes even the people themselves. This list seems to cover just about everything in the house, doesn't it? If a few of these targets have been hosed you can be fairly sure that he is marking rather than peeing.

You may notice a pattern, such as pee stains near a window or door. Vertical surfaces are often the target.

Regardless of whether it's spraying or peeing, it's always wise to have your vet check for illness.

Alter Your Cats' Outlook on Life

Although unneutered males are the most likely suspects for anointing the interior of the home, any stressed cat can mark regardless of whether they're male or female or even if they're altered. If you have a urine-marking problem, and your cat is neither pedigreed nor show quality, get him or her fixed. Altering your cats should decrease the occurrences significantly. Cats who want to reproduce aren't concerned about the condition of your carpets. They'll continue to post those wet personal ads on the floor as long as they're in the mood for love. In a multicat home, one spraying cat will usually result in the other cats spraying as well.

Intact males spray urine to claim their territory as early as six months. A girl in heat can mark when she's looking for a boyfriend, which can happen as early as four months. You can avoid this situation by having your cat or kitten altered as soon as possible.

FELINE FACT OR FICTION

Kittens As Young As Two Months Can Be Fixed

True. Vets can fix kittens as small as two pounds. Several studies, including one conducted by the Winn Feline Foundation, show that kittens who are altered before the onset of puberty stay friendlier than kittens altered at six months. They don't get breast cancer and other gender-associated diseases that still occur in older alters. You never have to suffer through a heat cycle or have unwanted kittens. And best of all, they don't generally spray. If your mature, intact cat is marking, there's a good chance that a little operation will nip his problem. However, with a rough and rowdy two-year-old, it's not an instant fix. It can take a month or even longer for the hormones to dissipate. It depends mainly on the age of the cat; mature male cats, whose veins flow heavily with testosterone, will take longer than a five-month-old kitten. Adjust your expectations accordingly.

After all, according to Dr. Dodman, "Inappropriate elimination is the number one cat behavior problem and is tough for owners to tolerate, making it the leading cause of surrender of cats to shelters and pounds (which usually results in euthanasia). Urine-marking is probably the most common form of inappropriate elimination and used to be the most difficult to treat."

But it's far from hopeless.

A frustrated family once asked me to take their four-year-old, blue-eyed tabby girl. The unspayed kitty was peeing all over the house. They said if I didn't take the friendly lap cat, they were going to euthanize her. Once I had her fixed she never soiled the house again. She soon went to a more deserving home. Moral to the story? Even with an established tagger, sometimes all it takes is a trip to the vet's office.

Marking the Sprayer

If you have an anonymous Kilroy in your home, a magic potion might help you pinpoint your culprit. Pick up an ultraviolet light at the pet store and ask your vet for a solution of fluorescein (fluorescent stain used to diagnose eye injuries) and water, which can be given orally to leave an indicator in the cat's pee. Fluorescein-enhanced pee glows bright apple green in ultraviolet light, whereas untreated pee will appear glowing yellow in florescent light. Check the walls, baseboards, and furniture. Color test your carpet with the mixture in an out-of-the-way corner before you administer it to your cats (see the chapter "Cleanup on Aisle Two").

This Land Is Your Land, This Land Is My Land

Think of your home as a real-estate community. On a big chunk of land the developer builds to satisfy all sorts of tastes, desires, and budgets. Some pieces of property are more valuable than others. You've got your high-dollar property, such as restaurants and fitness centers, and lots of individual homes. And then you have your low-income housing, those tiny little houses at the end of the airport runway or near the floodplain.

As a rule, when you want to see the dominant cat, look up. He (or she) likes to be elevated so he can survey his domain. Think of it as the high cat on the totem pole or maybe the fat cat in the penthouse. As you might expect, the dominant cats are going to seize control of the prime real estate like the food bowls and litter boxes, window perches, and high points on the cat trees. Don't be surprised if your sprayer feels protective about who approaches the high-rent district. He'll spray to warn other cats that those assets belong to him. The other cats will spray in return, reacting to the stress of a controlled world. In your home, a cat sprays to post a warning to other housemates or to signal a turf takeover.

Both inside and outside cats having overlapping territories and they time-share prime real estate. Pam Johnson-Bennett says, "Cats 'time-share' territories, so the urine marks enable the cats to space themselves out so that they don't often meet."

In addition to stress, cats spray urine to show dominance. In a herd of cats, you'll find cats of many different ranks—from the alpha cats to the pariah. The rankings in the clowder is thoroughly discussed in the chapters "Family Feud" and "Cat Psychology 101." The key to shutting down the spraying valves lies in creating a less-stressful, less-threatening, and more fulfilling environment for your cats. Let's begin by making sure everyone has enough space from the lowest cat to the most dominant cat.

Break up your home into a lot of different territories. The more territories available, the less the cats are stressed. Territory doesn't need to be wide-open spaces the way a multidog home might need a large yard. Instead create separate areas where they can hang out alone, so they can eat and go to the bathroom without another cat bothering them.

Don't just add litter pans, food bowls, and scratching posts; decentralize them by placing them in two or three different areas of the house. After all, unless your alpha cat has a clone, he can't guard them all. Create clever hiding places and hangouts in every room where the cats are allowed to go. Think in three dimensions. Cats want to be high up. You can add space with tall cat trees, lofts, shelves, and modified bookcases (see the chapter "Happy Habitats" for more ideas). Cats also like hidey-holes like baskets, boxes, and even new covered litter boxes with a bed inside instead of litter. Open up space at different elevations.

Despite the increase in living area, some cats may never get along. You might have to completely separate some kitties, breaking up your home into different countries that require passports to travel between. Watch out for those bully border guards!

To increase territory, think outside the house—no, I don't mean opening the front door and letting the cats run amok. I mean cat fences, enclosed porches, window enclosures, and window perches. Being able to run, play, and climb is a great stress reliever for cats. It uses up excess energy that would otherwise be spent tormenting less-dominant cats or destroying your home. Going outside in safety permits your kitties to get in touch with their inner feline. (You can read about safely enlarging your cats' territory in the chapter "Happy Habitats.")

Cats mark for a number of different reasons. When it's not for love or a medical reason, it's possibly because of stress. What stresses a cat? Seriously, everything. Well, almost everything: changes around the house, a change in your cats' schedule, a change in your schedule, a conflict with a human family member, a conflict with one of your other cats, even something as minor as changing the bedcovers from winter to summer.

When you discover the identity of your little offender (there may be several sprayers), you have to figure out what his motives are. After you've ruled out medical and litter box problems that lead to marking, look around the environment to find out what's upsetting your cats. You can find out about the medical conditions that can cause your cats to go astray in the chapters "Back in the Box" and "Health First." If you have cats who are spraying right in front of you, it's obvious they are trying to communicate with you.

Back in the days when I let my cats roam the neighborhood, I had a little black-and-white spayed girl named Chani. She loved to sit in the trees in the front yard watching traffic. When I first learned about the dangers to cats around Halloween, I brought everyone inside for a few weeks before the holiday. Chani cried repeatedly for me to let her out. Eventually, she made direct eye contact with me, backed up to the wall, and sprayed for all her six pounds' worth. While it didn't open the doors for her, her actions certainly got the point across that she was one stressed little kitty who wanted to go outside. Being new at this cat thing, I just cleaned up the mess and ignored her.

When you catch your cat in the act of spraying, don't scream or rub his nose in it. The time to react is *before,* as he's positioning himself to spray, not during or after. As you watch him backing up to his target (before he opens the floodgates), toss a magazine or drop a can with pennies, but make sure not to hit him! Don't let him see you do it. It's more effective if he thinks it comes from out of nowhere. If he realizes you're causing the ruckus, he'll just wait until you're not there.

Havoc in the Herd

When your cat feels stressed or picked on, he may seek out his favorite person's clothes or bath towel and mark them because he finds that scent comforting and he's blending his scent with yours. Or he may spray a possession of someone who scares him. Take Houston, my very first cat, who actually belonged to my ex-husband. Every time my ex would yell at him, Houston would poop in his dirty underwear that hadn't made it to the hamper. After my ex learned to pick up his clothes, Houston adjusted and went on the bath mat while my ex was showering. Houston's the reason I fell in love with cats. He expressed his stress in a very tangible way. I admired that.

Unlike the gentle face marking when they deposit scent by rubbing their cheeks or forehead against someone or something, marking with pee and poop is like TYPING A MESSAGE IN ALL CAPS!

Just as humans can be stressed by our relationships with family members, work associates, and even occasionally our good friends, cats—being territorial creatures—become stressed when the home becomes overcrowded. There's a strong correlation between marking behavior and the number of cats in the home.

I'm going to tell you the unfortunate and stinky truth. In any cat environment, pee happens. In a best-case scenario, in a home with only one cat, there's a 25 percent chance that he will spray. Yup. You read right. Even one-cat homes have problems. But wait, there's more—in homes with ten or more cats, there is almost a 100 percent probability that someone is marking somewhere. Bummer. The more crowded the conditions, the more likely they are to spray. This is another excellent reason to keep only as many cats as can live comfortably in your home and to set up different territories throughout the house.

Desensitizing Cats to Things They Fear

In a high-density home with ten or more cats, or as I call them a "megacat home," you'll most often be dealing with dominance aggression or territorial aggression. Territorial aggression happens when a home or territory has more than one intact male. Other common causes are when a new cat enters the household or when a kitty returns from the vet's office. The stress that follows the confusion results in the more dominant cats going on the warpath. When the house is filled with turmoil, it's not surprising that subordinate cats figuratively sleep with one eye open lest the bully kick their tails.

To quickly reduce stress, plug in some **Comfort Zone Diffuser with Feliway**. (For more about Comfort Zone see the Shopping Guide section.) Then, why not try reconciliation? Remember, cats want to know what's in it for them. You might convince the bully and the cat he tends to pick on it's in their best interest to get along. Counterconditioning and desensitization are the basis for treating anxiety that often causes territorial and dominance aggression. Make the bully want to be around the target, and vice versa. I cover all those strategies in the chapters "Family Feud" and "New Kit in Town."

Confuse a Cat

When you have a cat spraying because he's dominant and a paper tiger marking because he's stressed or afraid, you have to change the way they look at each other, or rather sniff each other.

Monty Python fans may remember a skit called "Confuse-a-Cat." A woman with a depressed cat hired behaviorists to perform bizarre antics to bring the cat out of his depression. It worked. Everyone lived happily ever after.

Now, I'm not recommending that you hire "Confuse a Cat," but you might borrow a trick from their repertoire. If you have a dominant cat continuously bullying a timid kitty, try confusing his nose. Cats are so dependent on scent for recognition, if you change the subordinate cat's scent, you may be able to change his perception of the lower-ranking guy.

Rub the bully's fur with a clean, dry cloth. Then rub the other kitty with a second clean cloth. Now comes the confusing part. Switch the cloths. Rub the bully with the lower-ranking kitty's scent and vice versa. Attitudes change when scents mingle because nobody can smell who's who any longer. There are many more of these strategies in the chapters "Family Feud" and "New Kit in Town."

Other Causes of Stress

Besides bullies, legions of different things can cause stress in a multicat home. You've got to try to comb through the clues and put the pieces together to figure out this puzzle. Dr. Dodman says that urine marking may indicate some other hard-to-handle stresses in the cat's life, such as:

- significant change in the house (new furniture, new pet, remodeling, new carpeting, death of a person or another pet)

- a move

- bullying by a kid, or another cat or dog

- illness

- stress or fighting among people

- abuse

- fear

Cats are creatures of habit. They don't respond well to even subtle changes like moving a piece of furniture from one part of the house to another. I've learned after a few mishaps when I've packed my suitcase in preparation for a trip to lock it up in an empty bathroom. Imagine my surprise one day when I open my suitcase to change for my high school reunion and found to my horror that Nixie had sprayed my clothes. These days I travel with an odor neutralizer, just in case. Nixie knows, as do the other cats, that when the suitcase comes out there will be a major disruption in her life. She's either going to be loaded in a carrier and taken on a long trip or I am leaving. Both are terrible possibilities when all you want in your day is the status quo.

Cats sometimes mark grocery bags. The question here is, do they just like the plastic or is it the new smell in the house? Who knows? Often when new objects come into the house, highly territorial cats may find the need to anoint them to make them smell right. (Kilroy was here!) Someone might feel the need to spray the guest bed after company has left or to christen the new sofa.

When I started dating my husband, Weems, most of my cats adored him— all except for wall-spraying Basil. Weems began a campaign to win him over. Every time my new sweetie came to the house, he brought treats. Basil would hiss at him, eat, and leave. It didn't take long for them to become best friends. Every night for the next fifteen years they slept all curled up together. (New spouses and significant others can win huge points by volunteering to operate the can opener.)

Cats of all levels of importance will get their knickers in a wad when threatened by outsiders, human and animal.

The Intruder from Without

While you might not be around to witness a pissing match, the location of the marking gives you a clue to the source of the cats' stress. You're sure to get a meltdown reaction out of any self-respecting feline when a neighborhood cat stakes out Kilroy's yard. If you find vertical pee marks near a window, windowsill, or on the curtains, blinds or by the door, the real cause is probably a wild animal, stray, or neighbor bugging the pee out of your cat. If you don't think your sweet little kitty is itching to defend his yard (territory), think again.

Eyeing a threat through the front window often results in frustration. It's enough to set off a series of "Mine, mine, mine" graffiti.

If wildlife or neighborhood cats stir up your gang and open up a sequence of indoor sprinklers, you'll either want to eliminate their view to the great outdoors or keep the critters away. Try covering the bottom half of the window with the dark opaque film used in limousines. If that doesn't work, completely

TAILS FROM THE TRENCHES

In 2006 a true David and Goliath tale occurred in West Milford, New Jersey. A ten-year-old cat named Jack treed a bear who had wandered into his neighbor's yard. Jack chased the bear up a tree not once, but twice. The fifteen-pound declawed orange-and-white cat spends his day standing sentinel over his yard and the yard next door. Prior to his bear hunt, he had been known to chase off all sorts of animals from his home range. That afternoon, Jack confronted the adolescent black bear and ran it up a tree where it stayed aloft for fifteen minutes before venturing down. But before Yogi could make his escape, Jack chased it up a second tree where the bear cowered for another fifteen minutes. Jack stood his ground at the base of the tree spouting feline obscenities in the form of hisses and growls. A neighbor concerned about the bear phoned Donna Dickey, Jack's owner. Donna called Jack to come inside, which he did.

"He doesn't like anything in his yard," Ms. Dickey explained.

He's not the only one. Chances are, some of your cats may feel almost as strongly about interlopers in their yard. While your cat may never have an opportunity to tree a bear, he may be straining at the window yowling, "Let me at 'em. Let me at 'em."

block all access to that window or keep the cats out of that room whenever animals are likely to be foraging or prowling for females.

If the presence of other animals in your yard causes your cats anxiety, you can use some devices that will keep intruders from stirring up a hornet's nest. ⊛ **CatStop Ultrasonic Cat Deterrent** is an ultrasonic repellent and the ⊛ **Scarecrow Motion Activated Sprinkler** sprays the intruder with water.

Getting Pee-ce and Quiet

None of the steps you've taken will make any difference unless you completely remove the odor of cat pee from your home. Remember, pee and poop contains pheromones that draw your kitties back to the same location time after time. With your cats' superhuman sense of smell, if the odors aren't completely removed you'll never be able to break the cycle of marking. As far as your cats are concerned, until the pheromone has disappeared, the stain may as well be a sign that says: Bathroom. There's a guide to odor neutralizing products in the chapter "Cleanup on Aisle Two."

Working It Out

You feel better when you get a good workout at the gym and get your blood flowing and your heart pumping. Cats do too. Give everyone an outlet for their stress and aggression and you might just solve your spraying problem. Interactive toys that simulate prey will make your cats jump, run, and leap, using up calories and wearing them out—the perfect solution for venting pent-up stress. When he gets enough exercise, the bully may not have the energy to go after a lesser rival. Twenty minutes of active play with a toy like 😺 **Da Bird** (ten min-

TAILS FROM THE TRENCHES

After the carpet has been cleaned in a high-spray area, Beth Adelman, a certified cat behaviorist from Brooklyn, likes to hold catnip parties. She says cats mark the periphery of their territory, not the interior. She sits on the floor with the cats, sharing all forms catnip: fresh or dried or a potent catnip toy. The catnip needs to be fresh with a strong, minty fragrance. After all, catnip with no scent is like a basketball with no air. To avoid duds, use what the Rainbolt Test Kitties showed a preference for: 😺 **Bell Rock Catnip Bouquet** and 😺 **Bell Rock Live Catnip**. If you can't smell the mint, throw it away.

Scatter loose catnip on the floor. Catnip parties change a spray spot into the party room, and cats don't pee in the party room. Food and water bowls, beds, and of course their favorite toys will make the area a less-inviting target.

utes, twice a day) will help vent some of that energy that the dominant cat would have spent harassing the subordinate cats. (I talk about neat games you can play with your kitties in "Happy Habitats.")

Encourage play inside the area that the cat(s) like to spray. Cats who spray or mark in a specific area may stop if the context of the area changes. They don't usually spray where they eat, sleep, or scratch. So, do whatever you can to turn the area into part of the cat's main territory. (Look for an additional list of strategies for stopping the marking in the chapter "Family Feud.")

Take the Fun Out of Spraying

Just as with true inappropriate elimination, you either have to make their marking area unattractive or bring it into their main territory.

Your cat has the occasional need to freshen up those marks he's been depositing on the wall and furniture. So while you're working to break your cats' habit of spraying specific areas, you'll have to deny the graffiti artists access to their favorite palette.

If you can't keep them out of the room, then take the fun out of it. Now let me remind you: cats can be determined little creatures. Some of these strategies may work like a charm on one or more of your cats. Others may be miserable failures. Only your cats will know for sure.

Try placing one of the following over the area where he would stand to spray his favorite target:

- 🐾 **Sticky Paws XL**
- plastic carpet protectors with the pointy side up
- aluminum foil
- contact paper
- bubble wrap

Or put the following down on or right next to the spot:

- 🐾 **Ssscat**
- 🐾 **Comfort Zone**

- solid orange air freshener

- your cologne on a cotton ball

- food and water bowls directly over the freshly cleaned spot

- a play area

If you've tried all of these tricks, including creating multiple core territories, using Comfort Zone, interactive play, and other planned activities, you may need to resort to drug therapy, for yourself or your cats! I cover all the drug options in the chapter "Family Feud."

Unfortunately, sometimes the only way to reduce stress that causes marking is to reduce the number of cats in your home. If the strategies above can't help you gain control, you might want to consider finding other homes for your most adoptable cats.

CHAPTER SEVEN

Everything You Wanted to Know about the Litter Box But Were Afraid to Ask

*A cat is the only domestic animal I know who toilet trains itself
and does a damned impressive job of it.*
— Joseph Epstein

CATS HAVE CERTAIN EXPECTATIONS ABOUT their bathroom similar to your own. You want your toilet to be clean and not smell like a sewer. You'd like it to be big enough so you can disrobe without banging into the walls. Nobody wants to go into those filthy portable restrooms found on fairgrounds and construction sites. They're disgusting, nasty, and there's not enough room. With what you see and smell in the typical portable potty, you're probably going to want to find a private little bush someplace nearby.

Then, there's your Aunt Audrey's bathroom that's so clean you could eat off the floor, but the strong pine cleaners she uses, combined with the flowery plug-in air freshener, turn your stomach. Because you've gotta go, you use it begrudgingly. But you sure don't linger. If *she* had a shrub available, you might just be tempted to seek it out.

Even at home you have specific expectations about your toilet. Unless you live in an area where you have water restrictions, you and your family probably flush every time you go. After all, it's pretty disgusting to go in and find someone else's waste, even if they're your beloved family members.

Your cats want exactly the same things. Their bathroom should be clean, have enough room to move around, and it shouldn't stink.

Most people want to avoid the vile subject of cats' bodily waste. Often they put a single, covered cat box in a disused corner of the house down in the basement or in the laundry room so they don't have to smell it and their delicate sensibilities aren't offended by having to watch the cats go to the bathroom. They expect every cat in the house to happily traipse downstairs, climb into a covered litter box, and hold his breath because of the combination of poop and floral scented litter. He has to try to avoid stepping in all the poop and pee obstacles left there by all the cats that beat him to the clean box. As soon as he's finished, he runs from the box as if escaping a vet brandishing a rectal thermometer. This cat's a trooper.

You need at least one litter box per cat plus one extra.

His actions are very clear. He's a few poops short of jumping the good ship *Litter Box* and swimming out to Exile Island to find a good, clean sandbar.

If you observe these reluctant behaviors, you have problems brewing. You may not have experienced potty problems, but the crystal cat ball sees them in your future.

Litter Box Rules

Kitties have rules regarding the litter box. Unless you want to constantly swab the floor, you'd be wise to go along with them. The rules become more complicated in a multicat home and even more so in a megacat home. You do your job, understand their simple needs, and they'll do their job where they're supposed to.

Rule No. 1. Fill the Box with Sand Imported from the Egyptian Desert

Your pets are descended from desert cats. In the old days, their bathroom felt and smelled like sand. Your cats are looking for similar qualities in their toilet. If Egyptian sand isn't readily available, maybe you can compromise. Use unscented litter with a sandy texture.

In the early 1990s, Peter Borchelt, a Forensic and Applied Animal Behaviorist in Brooklyn with vast experience in feline litter habits, conducted a series of cat litter studies to discover what qualities in their litter cats really prefer. According to Borchelt's studies cats prefer an unscented, sandy-textured litter because it feels softer against their sensitive paws. Litter box happiness, it seems, is sand shaped and unscented. Later, the Rainbolt Test Kitties and I conducted informal preference tests for different magazines and litter companies. They confirmed Borchelt's studies.

Scratch and Sniff

With all the hundreds of litter options, cats' preferences boil down simply to scratch and sniff. Period. In order to keep your tabbies happy and using the litter boxes Peter Borchelt suggested scooping frequently and choosing a litter the cat likes and enjoys digging in.

"I hate to think of a cat that's started eliminating inappropriately ending up in a shelter—unadoptable—because someone just used the wrong litter," Borchelt said. "It's very unfair to the cat."

Litter That Doesn't Make Scents

Cat box fillers sport all sorts of additives from sickly sweet perfumes to herbal attractants. Are you looking for an effective cat repellent?

You may think scents make your house smell better, but your cats think those little extras stink, literally. Borchelt's cat litter preference studies showed that while no single litter appeals to all cats, one blanket statement can be made: kitties hate scented litters. Period. The bolder the fragrance, the more they avoid using the box.

Dr. Nicholas Dodman says peeing outside the litter box is the number one behavior problem in cats and ultimately the number one cause of cats' death in the United States. Scented litters are the main reason they avoid the box. They're made to appeal to nasally challenged humans, not the cats who find them very pungent. After all, people, not the cats, control the purse.

Besides their supremely sensitive sense of scents, cats may have another good reason they don't like scented litter. In a 1991 Danish study of occupational asthma caused by industrial perfumes, researcher I. Petersen determined that perfume in scented cat litter caused asthma in workers at the litter manufacturing facility.

Cats avoid scents of all kinds. Imagine that to a cat even the faintest scent is magnified at least one hundred times your ability to smell it. Worse still, your cat's nose is only an inch or two from that stench. Stick your nose that close and see how pleasant it smells. And it doesn't end when he leaves that stinky box. Both the litter scent and the ammonia cling to his fur. Until he cleans himself up (and how nasty is that?) the odors are going to follow him wherever he goes. From your cats' perspective you're simply mingling one intolerable odor (ammonia) with another (perfume). If you need the added scent because the box stinks, it needs to be cleaned not masked.

Borchelt says that new parents know a human baby needs to be changed by the odor. "When we smell that smell, we change the baby; we don't just buy deodorized diapers."

And if after scooping the litter pan, the house still stinks, the smell is probably coming from the plastic in the pan itself, the floor, walls, or furniture. (I'll tell you how to get the smell of cat pee out of everything in the chapter "Cleanup on Aisle Two.")

It Seemed Like A Good Idea at the Time

Even with no added perfume, pine and citrus litter receives a paws-down from a great many cats. On the surface, using waste from the citrus industry sounds like a good idea. And orange and lemon *do* make wonderful bathtub cleansers, but citrus is also the active ingredient in many natural cat repellents. That would be like putting a skunk-scented plug-in in your bathroom and expecting guests to happily use it. It's enough to inspire a litter box mutiny.

When the Test Kitties checked out citrus litter, only one brave soul used the citrus litter, but he never repeated his performance. Not only did they avoid the citrus litter, they avoided their favorite box next to it. I've often wondered how many ecologically aware cat owners have taken their cats to shelters when the real culprit is orange and lemon rinds in the box.

Scratching Out the Truth about Textures

Litter texture can be as much of a deterrent as scent. In Borchelt's preference study, cats gave the nod to finer-grained scoopable litters. Cats don't like pellets because of the uncomfortable size and texture. They're too big compared to a cat's paw, Borchelt said.

Before making your cats use any litter, test the way it feels. Press your hand down (even better, your inner arm) against some clean litter. It should feel soft and soothing. If it doesn't, don't use it.

The Scoop on Clay Litters

There's a dark side to both clumping and nonclumping clay litters. Some preliminary research has associated the use of nonclumping clay litter, which contains dust, with feline asthma. All clay litters, but especially cheap nonclumping litter, contain crystalline silica dust that may present hazards to both the one who pees in the litter box and to the one who cleans it. Repeatedly breathing silicate dust has been associated with lung cancer in humans. Clay automotive absorbents, which are basically very dusty clay cat litter, are required to carry a label warning the consumer that exposure to silicates can cause cancer.

Borchelt says that clay (crystalline silica) cat litter exacerbates if not contributes to the development of feline asthma. While there are no definitive studies linking clay litter to asthma in cats, Borchelt headed a lung wash study published in the October 2001 issue of the *Journal of the American Holistic Veterinary Medical Association* that he says "raised some tantalizing questions." The study concluded that "silica may act as an airway irritant in those cats with airway disease."

Clay clumping litter *may* pose another problem. It forms hard balls, and if a cat somehow swallows enough clay, so the story goes, it can cause an intestinal blockage. There have been no studies to my knowledge and no verified cases of clump blockage have wound up in the hands of academics. Anecdotal cases usually, but not always, involve kittens. But that doesn't mean it doesn't happen. Litter manufacturers warn cat owners not to allow kittens under six months to use clay-clumping litter.

Silica Gel and Silica Grain Litter

The Mercedes of the cat litter world are the silica gel and silica grain litters (not to be confused with crystalline silica). Like a Mercedes, it's going to cost more. It acts as a desiccant that absorbs moisture. Until the grains start to become saturated with pee, it completely neutralizes the odor. The used litter acquires a stale and musty odor, but doesn't have the usual ammonia smell. A four-pound bag takes care of a single cat for a month. You do the math. *The fine-grained silica sand litter was very popular with the Test Kitties.*

Grain-Based Cat Litter

Crumbled-corn, corncob, and flaked-wheat litters make up this group of natural grain-based clumping litter. Few of the manufacturers of grain litter, to their credit, have added perfumes to their products. If you want to use a clumping litter but have a family member (human or feline) who is asthmatic, this is the way to go. They're safe to use with even tiny kittens. Unlike clay litters, if a cat ingests some, it will break down in the digestive system and end up in the box a second time.

✿ **World's Best Cat Litter,** the crumbled corn litter, was the top alternative for its ability to control odors. It had all the advantages of the clay clumping litter: good, solid clumps; low tracking and feline approval, combined with the healthy benefits of alternative litters; minimal organic dust; no added scent; no clumping danger for kittens; it's flushable and light to carry. It never sticks to the box. *This was the Test Kitties all-time favorite alternative litter.*

Wood

None of the test kitties seemed to like the wood pellets. *The cats showed a decided preference for the unscented hardwoods over cedar, which they still preferred over pine products (and the strong natural pine smell).* Another problem with the wood pellet litters, at first they don't absorb all the pee. It tends to pool at the bottom of the litter box. Consequently, the litter box itself can begin to smell of old pee. Only flush the pellets that cling to the poop. Once they turned into sawdust, the cats used it more readily. At that point, they also tracked it significantly.

Paper By-Products

Paper litter comes in fine grains, soft fluff, and compressed pellets. The Test Cats weren't impressed with paper pellet litters. Paper litter doesn't control odors well. Think about how wonderful pee-soaked newspaper smells. The litter should be scooped daily and the box washed and changed twice a week. *The Test Kitties preferred the softer texture, usually used as bedding for pocket pets.*

Poopsy Challenge

In order to keep your kitties happily using their litter boxes Borchelt suggests scooping frequently and choosing a litter the cat enjoys digging in. Keep in mind that different cats may like different textures, or as the pros call it, substrata. To find out your cat's litter preference, set up a cafeteria-style line of two or three boxes. It's not hard to tell which are preferred and which litters are avoided like, well, lemon cat litter.

I make different litters available to accommodate my cats' different preferences in litter.

You can tell your cat has a problem with his litter if your cat uses his box, but scratches at the sides of the box, on the floor, or on other objects nearby instead of in the litter pan itself. He's telling you he doesn't like the litter if he won't dig in it or he shakes off his paws when he's finished as if he's trying to sling something icky from his feet. He may do a circus contortionist act, putting his feet up on the edge of the box to avoid touching the litter. He may bolt out of the box as soon as he's finished because he just wants to get the heck out of Dodge.

If some of your cats are dissatisfied with the contents of their boxes consider switching to one of the 😺 **Precious Cat** cat box fillers. They are designed to make cats want to use it. Although they're not perfumed, they're spiked with a proprietary herbal attractant that most cats find irresistible. 😺 **Senior Attract**, a fine-grained silica gel litter (not crystalline silica), is the Test Cats' all-time favorite cat litter. It was very effective in a cat who had suffered from a lower urinary tract infection. The attractant tempted him back to the box after quite a long hiatus. Because of the soft, sandy texture, it's also a great choice for declawed kitties or any cat with paw sensitivity. *Senior Attract litter received more use than any litter in the house.*

Rule No. 2: Scoop Early and Scoop Often

Let's be honest. Sometimes the boxes don't get scooped or cleaned as frequently as they should. There are wet spots or clumps and poop all over the box. Every cat has a point where he holds up his paws and say, "No way." Eventually he'll pass that dirty box, as if to say, "I'd have used it if someone had just flushed."

In a multicat home, it doesn't take long for the conditions of the boxes to reel way out of control. In only one day the box may look like it hasn't been cleaned since the turn of the millennium. The cats shouldn't have to navigate a poop-mined obstacle course to go to the bathroom.

To keep your herd heading for their proper facilities, scoop at least once a day. Scoop the poop *and* wet spots and change the traditional litter no less than two or three times a week. Regardless of your regular changing schedule, change traditional litter when the litter looks wet and soggy; it should look and feel clean and dry. With a houseful of cats, it's hard to say specifically how often you should change the clumping litter and wash out the box. Every time you finish scooping the box, stick your nose down at kitty nose level and take a sniff. If it smells, it's time to throw out the old litter and wash the box.

People who use scoopable litter need to avoid certain features like sharp corners or indentations in the floor of the litter box. Channels along the edge make it almost impossible to remove the clump without breaking it up. These small broken pieces that remain behind will eventually begin to smell. Rounded corners and flat bottoms help cut down on the dreaded Smelly Box Syndrome and makes scooping easier. Spraying the box with Pam Cooking Spray helps prevent broken clumps.

Getting the Poop on How to Scoop

Just because you scoop daily doesn't guarantee you're cleaning up all the mess.

"Some people don't know how to use clumping litter," Borchelt said. He warned against using light plastic litter scoops. You can't feel the ball, and it breaks up. When that happens, you're defeating the purpose of clumping litter.

I use 🐾 **Litter Lifter** and 🐾 **DuraScoop**. They're rigid, comfortable, and makes fast work of multiple litter boxes. Also both are dishwasher safe so they can be sterilized.

Borchelt added, "Keep the litter deep enough so the clumps lift right out."

Properly set up, clumping litter should allow you to pull out all the pee clumps and the poop intact. Sticking to the bottom ensures a breakup. And breaking up is hard to do because it leads to Smelly Box Syndrome and wasted litter. The litter should be one and one-half to two inches deep—deep enough that the clumps can float around on top rather than sticking to the box floor as happens with too little litter. As often happens, pee clumps cling to the side of the box. A gentle bump on the outside of the box will loosen clumps so you can scoop them from beneath. Wipe that area down (and any brown goop you see) with a damp towel. Don't forget to swab down the inside of the hood with a damp paper towel for the benefit of your box sprayers.

Rule No. 3: Gimme Those Wide Open Spaces

According to Borchelt's study, most cats—especially the big boys—preferred large, open litter boxes to covered boxes. Open pans are perfect for multicat households where the one-box-per-cat law (plus one) must be obeyed. No-frills open litter boxes have become so inexpensive that they are disposable. One lady told me she used to clean the boxes with bleach and scrub them down. Now she just buys new ones once a month.

Remember your special needs cats. Seniors, kittens, and cats who have a disability or sickness may need a box with lower sides.

TAILS FROM THE TRENCHES

Even as a kitten, Karen Wormald's Yul never squatted to pee. Instead, he stood tall, spraying pee over the side of the box. She was at her wit's end to keep him from hosing whenever he went to the bathroom. She tried covered litter boxes, but Yul is so large, when he stood up he took the hood right off the box. Desperate for a supersized box, she bought a fifty-eight-quart storage container from a discount store to use as an open litter box. Problem solved. Yule had plenty of room to go to the bathroom, and the sides were high enough to keep the walls pee-free.

You can also buy a plastic sweater box or large plastic storage container. Cut one side down low enough so the cat can get in and out easily. Make sure you leave at least four inches beneath the opening so the litter doesn't come out when you scoop. With the lid on, the storage box doubles as a bed, by placing the lid on it and throwing a towel or blanket on top.

When the Test Kitties investigated bathroom facilities, they preferred open boxes over hooded boxes, and the bigger the box, the more use it received.

The ✿ **Petmate Giant Litter Pan** may not be a work of visual art, but then, beauty is in the eye of the beholder. The Test Kitties didn't care what it looked like. It had everything a cat wants in a bathroom facility. It's open and roomy, with high walls, and holds a hefty thirty pounds of litter. It has two storage compartments for scoops and other litter accessories. This box was used more than all of the other boxes combined.

Like scented litter, covered boxes have been invented for the benefit of the owner, and they're a common causes of litter box indiscretions, especially for large cats. Hoods hold in odor; it's harder for you to see and smell when it needs to be cleaned. Your cats won't appreciate having to hold their breath when using the box, and you might miss important symptoms like the cat's straining to go, bloody poop, or the presence of tapeworms. And the timid cats in your herd may be afraid to use one because they can't watch for the bully cat while going to the bathroom. However, occasionally covered pans provide some kitties with a sense of potty protection if he suffers from the prying eyes of children. It helps keep litter in the box while he's digging to China. If your kitty likes to spray inside the box, a covered box will help keep the walls of your home clean. Don't forget your older kitties. They night have difficulty getting in and out of the box because of arthritis.

🐾 **Marchioro Deluxe Enclosed Litter Pan with Door (Bill2-F)** is one of the few commercially available covered litter boxes designed for Colossal Kilroy. The extra-large Marchioro is roomy and inviting, but comes with a cat flap-style door that none of the test cats would use. Once the door was removed, they happily entered and used the box. *This was the Test Kitties favorite covered box.*

A Royal Flush

Automatic self-scooping and self-flushing boxes are the Rolls Royces of the cat toilet world. Like a Rolls, they are often larger (in overall size) than traditional boxes with a substantial price tag. They also get mixed reviews from behaviorists, cat owners, and cats.

Let's start with the drawbacks. The self-scooping feature usually comes at the expense of the working room for the cat. When looking at mechanized boxes, make sure there's enough room for your cat to stand up in the box, easily circle, and cover. Another disadvantage, you don't get to see the condition of the poo. But the reality is, in a multicat home, you might have difficulty doing this anyway.

Now comes the fear factor. Some cats are fearful of new things and don't like the noise of the motor, while others don't mind it at all. When I tested my first LitterMaid, as the motor ran its cycle, cats converged from all over the house to watch it—spellbound. Granted, not all cats have the same sense of adventure.

The major brand of electronic boxes have motion sensors that prevent the unit from operating until the cat has been out of the box for a certain number of minutes. However, in some multicat homes with cats who startle easily, this could be a problem, as a second cat may be heading to the box as it starts its cleaning cycle. Watch your cats to make sure you're not creating a bigger problem than having a dirty litter box.

Most self-cleaning boxes require a high-quality, fast-clumping litter. The only alternative litter I've found that works in them is World's Best Cat Litter.

Now, the plus features. If you have cats who simply will not use the box after another cat, the self-scooping box is always clean. Overall, the box cuts down on the amount of contact that a person has with the cat's waste so it's good for people who don't want to or can't handle cat poo.

My favorite (as well as the cats' favorite) automatic litter box is the new **LitterMaid Elite Mega-Advanced Automatic Self-Cleaning Litter Box** made for multicat homes and larger cats with more inside box space than most other auto boxes.

Rule No. 4: A Box for Every Cat Plus One Extra and One on Every Floor of the House

Many cats won't use a litter box if another cat has already used it, and some cats only pee in one box and only poop in another. Of course, there's the occasional dominant cat who feels the need to guard the boxes, or the aging cat who struggles to get from place to place. Regardless of the reason one cat strays, it opens Pandora's litter box and a game of Follow the Pee-er. Prevention is much easier. So let's prevent. You can try different styles of boxes and various types of litter to appeal to the diversified tastes of your cat population.

Rule No. 5: Location, Location, Location

Ask any real estate agent and she will tell you the location of a piece of property makes it either a coveted commodity or a discount listing. So make sure to place the litter boxes in prime spots—that is, prime for your cats.

Behaviorist Alice Moon-Fanelli says never put a box in a high traffic area. Cats need privacy. You don't want to use the bathroom where there's a lot of activity. Your cats don't either. Is there any nearby noise that might bother them—a furnace coming on, a noisy clothes dryer, or another loud machine operating? That tennis shoe bouncing around in the dryer could scare the pee right out of him. Air blowing from a vent is a huge bathroom turnoff to most cats. Before you set up a box anyplace make sure the breeze from the vent isn't aimed at the box.

Like human housemates, cats don't want to eat in their bathroom. So keep their food and water bowls well away from the box. Nothing kills your cat's appetite like the smell of cat poop at mealtime, even if it's his own poop.

Position the boxes in quiet corners so your timid cats have several possible escape routes. This comes in handy when they're stalked by the bully cat, the hound from hell, or the neighbor kid voted by his kindergarten classmates as most likely to be a parolee. Don't put all your pans in just one cluster so the bully can guard all boxes with little or no effort. Scatter them throughout the house in different core regions.

If the location is too inconvenient, some cats may have difficulty just getting to the box. Your elderly cats may not be *able* to make it up or down the stairs to the litter box. But before you start throwing around words like "incontinent" and "euthanasia" or "get rid of the cat," let's think about all the things that can cause an older cat to miss the box. Aging cats can suffer from a myriad of health problems that make it difficult to get to where they need to go.

Remember how miserable it was to wait in line to use the bathroom when we were kids? Cats are no different. In a multicat home, like any multihuman situation, you're going to have personalities who tolerate a lack of facilities better than others. Some will use whatever you put out there, wherever you put it—no matter what—even if they have to wait.

If you have your own ambush predator (a cat who attacks other kitties while they use the litter box, or a cat who guards the boxes), additional boxes are vital. After all, unless the bully has a clone, he can't guard all the boxes at the same time.

Rule No. 6: It's Too Clean

Can you believe it? After all this talk about how cats hate dirty litter boxes, the litter pan can actually be too clean. When you scrub out his box, don't use pine cleaner, citrus cleaner, bleach, or anything with a strong scent. Your kitty may revolt all the way to the carpet. (Pine cleaners, including Lysol, aren't just obnoxious, they're toxic to cats.)

Although we don't understand this type of feline reasoning, a cat likes the way his pee smells. The familiar scent assures him he's using the right place. The *faint* hint of pee is very appealing to cats. But they avoid the overwhelming stench of a dirty cat box. That's why when the odor of the pee isn't thoroughly removed from the carpet, the cats will return again and again.

As long as you rinse the box thoroughly with hot water, you shouldn't be able to smell anything. Unlike Captain Kirk of the starship *Enterprise*, your kitties don't want to go where no cat has gone before. If you totally remove their smell, which they have worked very hard to put there—thank you very much—then they won't recognize it as their box.

"You can use anything you want to clean a cat box as long as it's warm running water," Dr. Dodman said. "Clean anything off the sides and make it visibly clean. But you don't want it to be too clean. Cats are attracted to the site where they have already eliminated and to spots where other cats have gone."

Rule No. 7: Don't Move the Box

You may not like the location of one of the litter boxes, but the cats will take it very personally if you arbitrarily move it. If the cats uses the floor at the original place—put the box back. If you must move the litter box, move it gradually or add a new one to the new spot. He may be avoiding the plastic floor runner or litter mat. Many cats don't like walking on plastic. Others love to pee on it.

Rule No. 8: Don't Suddenly Change Litter

If you want to switch brands or kinds of litter, scoop out the poop and clumps and refill the amount you've removed with fresh litter in the new brand. Pretty soon the box will contain only the litter you want.

Rule No. 9: Cats Don't Like Litter Box Liners and Some Litter Mats

Borchelt's studies showed that cats don't like box liners. It makes the litter feel wrong. Even with traditional litter, cat claws catch and rip the liner. Pee collects between the box and the liner. That really smells good after a few days. It makes far more work for you in the end (no pun intended).

REALITY BITES

Now you know what the experts say, and how you should keep your litter boxes clean—the kind of clean that both you and your cats deserve. But you have a life. And when the schedule becomes too complicated, the cats' care is often the first thing to slide. In my work as an animal behavior consultant, I had a client who had multiple cats, but she scooped only once a week and changed even less frequently. Because the boxes were overflowing, the cats peed everywhere. It was like an avalanche. It seemed impossible to reverse.

How does a cat eat a whale? One three-ounce can at a time. How do you climb out of an abyss of cat poop? One scoop at a time. If you are in that overwhelming situation, you probably have fantasies of a clean house. For you, let's scoop all the boxes today. While you're at it, totally empty, wash, and change one box. Just one. Tomorrow scoop them all and clean one more—just one. In just a short time all the boxes will be clean. My client did this and was delighted. Once the boxes were clean, the cats started holding up their part of the bargain. Little by little she got a grip on the disaster. She's happier. So are her cats. Don't procrastinate. Put the book down and go scoop those boxes.

FELINE FACT OR FICTION

Simply Having a Cat in the House Will Injure Unborn Baby

False. The much-feared toxoplasmosis is caused by a single-celled parasite. According to the Centers for Disease Control (CDC) Web site (www.cdc.gov/ncidod/dpd/parasites/toxoplasmosis/factsht_toxoplasmosis.htm) "more than 60 million" Americans may be infected with it, but most don't even know it because "a healthy person's immune system usually keeps the parasite from causing illness. However, pregnant women and individuals who have compromised immune systems should be cautious." You can get toxoplasmosis when you "accidentally swallow cat feces from a Toxoplasma-infected cat that is shedding the organism."

This happens if you've been gardening, cleaning the cat box, or when you brush hair out of your mouth with a dirty hand. Although the cat is the most maligned suspect, he certainly isn't the only culprit. You can get toxoplasmosis by eating or handling raw or undercooked meat, or even cutting raw meat, then chopping veggies with the same knife.

If you want to get pregnant, then get yourself tested. According to the CDC, the good news is, if you've already had toxoplasmosis for a while everyone should be fine.

The CDC reports, "There usually is little need to worry about passing the infection to your baby." The truth is, cats only spread toxoplasmosis in their poop for a few weeks after they first get it. After that, you no longer have to worry about them shedding it.

If the test is negative, take the necessary precautions, like wearing gloves when you tend your flowerbeds. Wash your hands well with soap and water after gardening, handling raw meat, or cleaning the litter box.

Don't give up your cats even if you are at risk. Keep them indoors and try to prevent their access to prey. (There goes their entertainment center.) Take special care handling your cats' food if you feed a raw meat diet.

Houston cat vet Cynthia Rigoni breaks it down into one simple sentence: "Don't eat cat poop."

This is a great time to make someone else responsible to keep the boxes clean. The CDC says, "If this is not possible, wear gloves and clean the litter box every day, because the parasite found in cat feces needs one or more days after being passed to become infectious. Wash your hands well with soap and water afterwards."

The best defense is to wash your hands frequently, don't bite your nails, and keep the boxes clean. Contact your doctor if you think that you may have a parasitic infection.

CHAPTER EIGHT

Back in the Box

I have an Egyptian cat. He leaves a pyramid in every room.
—**Rodney Dangerfield**

REMEMBER WHEN YOU INVITED YOUR friend from work over to your house for the first and last time? As soon as she walked through the door, the smell of ammonia blasted her in the face. She placed her hand over her nose. "What is that smell?" If you'd had one, you would have handed her a gas mask. You smile sheepishly and explain, "Sorry. I'm having a little trouble with my cats."

The truth is, there's nothing funny about a soiled, ammonia-soaked house. People don't want to come to your home; you don't want them to visit you either. If you stop to think about it, there are probably days when you don't want to go home either. In "Everything You Wanted to Know about the Litter Box" you learned about cats' bathroom preferences. Now let's add to that and herd those strays back to the litter box where they belong.

Is It Peeing or Spraying?
If it looks like a duck and quacks like a duck, it must be a duck. That may apply to feathered waterfowl, but it doesn't apply here. Even if it looks like cat pee and smells like cat pee, it could still be marking. Granted, cats use pee to mark with, but the action of urinating and marking with urine are two cats of a different color, figuratively speaking.

There are three types of inappropriate elimination. None of them have any association with "bad cat." The most common is peeing in an inappropriate place because a cat is unhappy with some aspect of his litter box. He may be marking territory or suffering from an illness. It's critically important to discriminate between medical and nonmedical causes or a behavior problem.

Watching how he acts in and around the litter box should clue you in on the reason he's missing his bathroom. There's a thorough comparison between peeing and marking in the chapter "The Pissing Contest." In most cases, a cat who spends a lot of time squatting as if he needs to go but only pees a little or not at all is feeling under the weather. If he gets into the box, then leaves immediately with no digging or scratching, then he has a problem with the box or the litter. If he's peeing in the box and elsewhere, it's most likely marking.

Don't put off cleaning up and putting him back on the road to litter box reconciliation. The longer you wait, the more ingrained the habit becomes in the little pee-petrator's mind. Over time, more cats will join him in his litter box mutiny. All it takes is one sick or upset cat to start problems that could reverberate for years.

So when a normally well-mannered cat strays from proper litter box etiquette, it's his way of sending a medical SOS. Guess what would happen if a wild cat threw a fit and carried on, "Oh, it hurts. Won't someone help me?" Every coyote, fox, and stray dog within five miles will be offering him an invitation to dinner—as the main course.

When you notice that someone is peeing outside the box, the first step to correcting the problem is getting the culprit to the vet. The little offender could actually have a number of ailments, most of which are serious but treatable.

Feline lower urinary tract disease (FLUTD) is a catchall phrase to describe many different problems in your cat's urinary tract, including cystitis and bladder crystals. When bladder crystals combine with mucus, they turn into a plug, and a life-threatening blockage that prevents him from being able to pee. Male cats are especially susceptible to urinary tract blockages because of their long, narrow urethras. While blockages are uncommon in females, they do happen. In either gender, a blockage constitutes a bona fide lights-and-siren trip to the emergency clinic as it can kill a healthy cat in twenty-four to thirty-six hours. A cat with kidney disease would last only half that time.

Besides peeing outside the litter pan, look for other symptoms of FLUTD, such as:

no evidence of having peed at all (no clumps or wet spots in the box)

repeatedly squatting in the box with little or no results

bloody pee

crying out when he's using the box

frequently licking his private parts

OK, your kitty's sick; but that doesn't explain why he's missing his litter box. Any of the conditions associated with FLUTD burn like crazy whenever he tries to go to the bathroom. So when he goes to the litter pan, he thinks the box itself is hurting him. He thinks if he goes somewhere else, it won't hurt. Or a cat with cystitis or diarrhea may not be able to make it to his litter box in time. For FLUTDs your vet will likely prescribe antibiotics and may recommend switching to a diet that will change the pH of your cat's urine to prevent or reduce any future episodes.

FLUTD is just one of many medical reasons a cat has litter box problems. Or your cat may have developed diabetes, hyperthyroidism, kidney disease, or irritable bowel disease. Cognitive dysfunction (kitty Alzheimer's) and incontinence are two other senior health conditions that may cause inappropriate elimination. Your older cats may have difficulty actually getting into the litter box because of arthritis.(🐾 **Tobin Farms Antler Velvet** supplements are a natural way to help those with those achy joints.) A ramp to the box may be a godsend for a frustrated senior. Your vet can help provide your cat with some relief for these conditions. Also, cats who are given hard litter too soon after declaw surgery frequently develop an aversion to litter that hurts their feet, preferring a nice, soft carpet.

Even after treatment, he may avoid the evil litter box, fully convinced it will hurt him again if he goes near it. Sometimes during the illness the cats may shift their potty preference from cat litter to the carpet, your clean clothes, or the linoleum, or whatever else he's been using.

Here's What You Need to Do to Stop the Spiral

Figure out the source of the indiscretions. You may be surprised how many different culprits you have.

Don't punish them.

Have your vet check them out for medical issues.

Find and clean up accidents as soon as possible.

Make several types of litter available.

Scoop at least daily. In a multicat home scoop two or three times a day. (That's the price of having cats.)

Don't wash the litter box with strong-smelling cleaners like pine.

Make sure there are enough litter boxes for your herd in places they like.

Offer an assortment of litter boxes, both open and covered. Buy the largest ones you can find.

Deep-six litter additives except for charcoal and baking soda and Cat Attract. Avoid litter box liners.

Watch out for the bullies.

Give each of the little offenders lots of extra attention every day with some strenuous interactive play.

Get all your cats fixed.

Make inappropriate areas unpleasant or restrict their access.

Retrain the perps.

Create multiple core areas with food and litter boxes where the cats can hang out. Don't put the food too close to the boxes.

Nab Your Culprit

I love to watch the old detective movies with all the usual suspects—the good guy, the bad guy, and all the red herrings. Sometimes it's not just one guy; it's a conspiracy of several guys. Figuring out the Yellow Carpet Stain Caper isn't unlike those old movies, except your heist is in vivid Smellavision. Like the detective, you're going to have to look for clues to pin your suspect.

If you only have two cats, it's easy to figure out who's peeing or pooping outside the box. As you add kitties to the mix, it becomes more difficult to determine the culprits.

You may have to resort to marking your cats' pee the way a bank marks bills. By the process of inappropriate elimination, your vet can help you pin or exonerate your most likely suspects by supplying a concoction of fluorescein (fluorescent eye stain) and water. This is all outlined in "The Pissing Contest." When you find an inappropriate eliminator, take him to the vet. There are also specialized cat litters and litter additives that can help you monitor cats with a history of FLUTD. You can read about them in the chapter "Health First."

You may even have to go high tech to catch everyone. Set up a video camera but don't stop when you nab your first suspect. There might be other offenders.

Don't Punish Them

Now that you've pegged him, take a breath. He's not peeing on the carpet to spite you. He's peeing on the carpet because it's the only way he knows to deal with his situation. Because we humans can and do retaliate, we assume our cats do, but they don't. As aggravating as it is, don't discipline him or scream at him, and especially don't punish him after the fact. Hitting (even a light swat), yelling, clapping your hands, throwing a can full of pennies, squirting water at him, rubbing his nose in it will intensify his stress and he'll associate punishment with the actual act of going to the bathroom. Now he's scared of the box *and* you.

What's Bugging the Pee Out of Him?

You've already addressed the medical issues. If the vet determines your cat is healthy, you need to figure out other motives. Other than marking or feeling sick, Kilroy might have any number of reasons why he can't or won't use the box. Some of these might surprise you. The following are some of the most common causes for misses:

- He doesn't like the smell or feel of his litter or it's not deep enough.
- He has to dodge pee and poop landmines to use the box.
- You cleaned boxes with harsh chemicals.
- There aren't enough boxes or they're set up on one area.
- He has to choose between small boxes, covered boxes, or worse still, small covered boxes.
- He doesn't like litter box liners.
- Food and water bowls, or beds are too close to the box.
- He's declawed and his feet are sensitive.
- He's just stressed, darn it.
- He's been frightened or intimidated while he was using the litter box by other cats, dogs, or even kids—again.

To try to figure out what's bothering your gang, sketch the floor plan of your home. Draw in the location of the bowls, litter boxes, appliances (washer, dryer, furnace, even air vents, speakers), windows. Mark (in pencil!) each cats' favorite places to hang out. When you see the whole picture, you might find some missing clues on the motives behind the litter pan mutiny.

If all your work and retraining continues to bear nothing but soggy carpets, it might be time to call in the big guns—a cat behaviorist who can treat your cats' problem holistically, looking at the entire family (people too), not just the single cat.

Answering these questions might help you trace the causes:

Where do they pee?

Is it right next to the litter box?

What do they pee on—paper, towels, dirty clothes, carpet, counter?

When did it start?

What happened around that time?

Is it in the same spot every time or all over the place?

Are there other signs of anxiety? Excessive licking? Hiding? Biting?

Are other cats aggressive toward the cat?

Is the pee on vertical or horizontal surfaces?

Is there conflict between the cats?

Bully, Bully

You'd be surprised how often an accident isn't the fault of the cat making the puddle but is caused by an alpha cat giving him the evil eye. Go back to the chapter "Family Feud" to review the signs of subtle aggression.

The key to outsmarting the bully isn't just adding more litter boxes to the same location, but spreading the boxes throughout the house. After all, the bully can't block them all. Another method of taming the beast includes regular individual exercise with a tease toy.

If that doesn't work, you may need to break up the house into more literal turfs. Give one cat the front of the house or the upstairs and the other can have the downstairs. As Rudyard Kipling said, "Oh, East is East, and West is West, and never the twain shall meet." In some feline conflicts, this philosophy can ease tensions. As an added bonus, your house will smell better too.

While we're talking about ambushing, don't become the bully yourself. Don't wait until your cat is using the box to medicate him. That's as much an ambush as Butch the Bully jumping into the middle of his vulnerable moment.

You need to be a detective and a therapist to figure out what your cat is telling you before the problem becomes insurmountable.

Another way to reduce kitties' stress level is Comfort Zone with Feliway in a diffuser or pump spray. (The Shopping Guide gives you the full story on

TAILS FROM THE TRENCHES

Cat author Anne Leighton from the Bronx owns twenty-one cats. She started noticing that one of her cats had pooped near a windowsill and on paper that had fallen to the floor from her desk, and there were pee spots on a counter. Lassie, a shy gray-and-white Norwegian Forest Cat wannabe liked to hang around Anne's office. Occasionally he'd leave his office domain and get into fights with other cats. If cats came into her room, Lassie would hide and growl. Anne tried to get Lassie to use the boxes in other rooms, but the messes kept materializing. Finally, she realized that Lassie was afraid of some of the other cats. Anne set up a litter box in the office and supercleaned all the soiled areas. Neither Anne nor Lassie had any more problems.

Comfort Zone.) Once the stress level is lowered, cats may not feel the need to guard resources or litter boxes with quite the same voracity. Try giving him the Bach Flower Remedy Agrimony or Willow or Anaflora Spraying Cat Formula to help with stress.

Rekindling Their Love Affair with the Litter Box

Finally, to get him back on a friendlier basis with his litter box, make his facility more fun and the carpet less pleasant. Anytime there's a litter box issue immediately try switching to 🐾 **Cat Attract** or 🐾 **Senior Attract** cat litter, which contains a proprietary herbal attractant that entices kitties to use the litter box again. They act like kittens playing in a litter box, digging, rolling, and scratching. In addition to the attractant, the litter has a nice, soft, sandy texture. The herb blend is also sold separately, so you can add this to your own brand of cat litter.

If he shows he's not happy with his freshly cleaned box, he's telling you he prefers a different substrate (that's the stuff you put in the box). Consider your own preferences. If you live in a cold climate, you may object to a tiled floor

Cats and people have different expectations when it comes to litter boxes.

because it feels cold against your bare feet. You probably don't like walking barefooted on rocks. Although cats usually prefer a softer substrate (sheets, underwear, bath mats, plastic trash bags), some cats prefer open, reflective areas such as linoleum, wood floors, tile, sinks, and bathtubs. If he's peeing on newspaper, put sheets of newspaper in his box. Going on a hard shiny floor? Try him out in an empty litter box. You might need to fill his box with carpet squares, printer paper, clean clothes, dirty clothes, plastic bags, or towels. Once he's using the litter box with the newspaper or your dirty underwear, you can slowly add an attracting litter like Cat Attract.

Substrate preferences other than cat litter are extremely common, especially among longhaired cats. Sometimes a bit of poop clings to his breeches or fine-grained clumping litter may stick to the tufts of fur on his paws. Trimming the fur from the paws pads sometimes helps or try 🐾 **Precious Cat Longhaired Cat Litter**.

Another special substrate situation to consider is the problem of an outdoor cat converting to living a strictly indoor life. If he doesn't catch on to cat litter, he might benefit from a pan filled with organic potting soil (no fertilizers or chemicals) or play sand from a garden supply store. Change the dirt or sand a couple of times a day. Then slowly add your preferred unscented filler.

Making Inappropriate Elimination Unpleasant

It's the nature of any animal, ourselves included, to do what is pleasant and avoid what is objectionable. So, in addition to making the litter box a fun place to go, after cleaning up their accidents, you need to make the formerly soiled spots objectionable. Since kitties are creatures of habit, continue to make the area icky for three to six weeks after your guys are using the boxes to fully break the habit. There are a lot of ideas about how to keep him away from his spots in the chapter "The Pissing Contest."

Kitty Rehab

Like so many of today's celebrities, your kitty has had some indiscretions, so he's going into rehab. You need to sequester him to a cage, small bathroom, or other confined area with his litter box on one side of the area and his bowls and bed on the opposite side. In these cramped spaces he should feel compelled to go *in* the box. You're not punishing him. You're confining him to a small area because cats instinctively won't use the bathroom where they eat or sleep.

Go into his room and play with him, talk to him, read to him. You can let him out for supervised excursions, but when you are unable to keep an eye on him, he's back in his room. While he's out on leave, if you notice him sniffing the floor or other inappropriate venue, gently and with no ado, pick him up and put him in the box. Praise him and give him a reward if you have one readily available. Check the area later with a black light and I'll bet you find an old pee spot that needs cleaning.

When you see him using a litter box, you can let him out for longer periods. Continue to keep deterrents up until you are confident he's been rehabilitated. You can then let him out on parole, but keep your eye and nose on him. He might be a repeat offender. Don't expect results overnight. It took a while to establish this bad habit. It will take at least three weeks of the same routine to develop his new habit.

CHAPTER NINE

Cleanup on Aisle Two

Never hold a Dustbuster and a cat at the same time.
—Unknown

YOU'VE HEARD IT BEFORE. AS you stroll down the aisles of your favorite pet supply warehouse, a voice booms across the public address system, "Wet cleanup on aisle two." You know exactly what they're talking about. With a house full of cats, messes are inevitable. When we think of cleaning up after cats, most of us immediately think of mopping up pee. But there's more to it than that. There are two other *P*s that form the triad: poop and puke. There are also hairballs and loose fur thrown into the mix.

The key to maintaining sanitary sanity with multiple cats is finding the right cleaning products for the job, knowing how to clean up the messes, and when the time comes, replacing your present home trappings with other surfaces that are easier to keep clean.

Although cats live up to their reputation as self-cleaning pets, they certainly don't contribute to the concept of a self-cleaning house. After all, we know that Kilroy may occasionally sneak up onto the kitchen counter to inspect what's for dinner. Sometimes Fluffy's litter box aim lacks Olympic accuracy. Do we even need to mention the hairballs on the linoleum? As a consequence, we cat lovers find ourselves mopping, blotting, vacuuming, and scrubbing more often than our friends with a solo cat.

This brings us to the real question: How do we clean up after our furry friends without endangering them? While cats reputedly have nine lives, the official issue is really just one life. Let's not take unnecessary chances with it.

Read the label warnings and take them to heart. But remember, the warnings are for people. Because the feline body is so sensitive, these products pose far more danger to a cat than to a child or even to a similarly sized dog. The injuries cleaning products can do run the gamut from irritation to the digestive tract to causing serious chemically burns to the mouth, esophagus, and stomach, and even fatal liver failure.

When cleaning your house, never allow your cat access to the area where cleaners are used or stored. Wipe up the spill of a concentrated product immediately so the cats don't track through it and ingest it while licking their paws.

Hoping to keep their cats safe, you might turn to natural products because we often equate "natural" with safe. The two aren't necessarily synonymous. Tobacco, strychnine, and arsenic are all natural, but deadly. The dilemma is further complicated by the fact that manufacturers are not required to disclose the ingredients contained in their products unless they are dangerous to people. Cationic detergents are in many cleaning products deemed "natural" or "safe" around people, and therefore not mentioned on the label. They use strong acids, such as hydrochloric acid, as the neutralizing agent, which can burn a cat's skin and cause mouth ulcers. Cats are so sensitive that cleaning chemicals can be absorbed systemically through their pads or even when they walk through an area filled with fumes. Cats will be doubly affected by licking the compound from their paws or coats. When using cleaners, make certain the surface has been well rinsed and then thoroughly dried before giving your cats access to it. The same logic should be used when cleaning carpets or mopping the floor. Before having your carpets cleaned, find out what kind of chemicals the company plans to use.

Avoid using phenol-based cleaners with ingredients that contain "sol" or "nol" in their names. Phenols are toxic to cats; they slowly kill the liver. You can usually tell if cleaners have phenols because they turn white in water. Check with your veterinarian or the ASPCA/Animal Poison Control Center (APCC) to see if your cleaning products are safe to use around your cats.

Looking at the cautions printed on the label will give you a hint of the danger involved. If a product warns you to wear gloves, keep out of reach of children, wear eye protection, or dilute, you need to be concerned about the affect it would have should the cat accidentally come in contact with it.

Three factors determine the dosage of what is toxic to cats:

- Concentration. Is the concentration of the potentially toxic substance 1 percent or 95 percent?

- Quantity. Is the amount that the cat ingested one or two licks or ten teaspoons?

- Size of the cat. Does the cat weigh one or fifteen pounds? Those fourteen pounds make a big difference.

Stronger isn't necessarily better. A chemical that is safe at a weaker strength may burn your cats at a higher concentration. Most products are safe around cats when used according to directions. Cat owners get their cats into trouble when the label says to dilute one tablespoon per gallon, and instead you dilute it in a quart of water—even with a cleaner as "safe" as citrus oil.

FELINE FACT OR FICTION

Citrus Is an Odor Eliminator

False. In reality, the strong scent simply blocks the olfactory senses causing you to lose your sense of smell temporarily. That's why citrus acts as a cat repellent. In the wild, cats depend on their olfactory sense to detect larger predators and a potential mouse meal. Citrus temporarily compromises that ability to smell, putting the cat's life in peril. It's believed that's why cats avoid citrus rather than risk compromising their ability to smell. Instead of going into a citrus polluted area, he leaves.

> ## REALITY BITES
>
> ### In Case of Emergency
>
> Take the ASPCA/APCC number below and tape it to the inside of your medicine cabinet, your fridge, or next to the phone along with your human poison control center phone number. Also, jot down your veterinarian's phone number and emergency animal clinic's address and number.
>
> If you suspect that your cat has ingested a toxic plant, cleaning supply, or medication, immediately call the APCC at 1-888-426-4435. The vet on the other end of the line will charge a $55 flat consultation fee to a major credit card (VISA, Master Charge, American Express, or Discover). Or, if you don't have a credit card, you can call 1-900-443-0000. A charge of $55 is directly applied to your phone bill. Follow-up calls by either you or your vet are at no additional charge. The hotline operates twenty-four hours a day, seven days a week, even on holidays.
>
> If you're concerned about the safety of a product, call your local poison control number or the ASPCA/APCC or the American Association of Poison Control Center (1-800-222-1222). Tell them it's not an emergency. Every product label should have the company's phone number. Call the company and ask how to use the product safely around cats.

Shedding a Little Ultraviolet Light on the Subject

Before you can clean up his messes, you've got to find them—all of them. That's not as easy as it sounds. Especially when there are multiple spots, the nose no longer knows. You can smell the ammonia, but it can't give you good directions to its exact location. Just as a ventriloquist can throw her voice, cat pee can throw its smell. Fortunately, those invisible stains become visible under the right conditions. Enter the number one (pardon the pun) weapon in the pee problem arsenal: the black light. It's also called an ultraviolet (UV) light, or a Woods lamp. Buy a light from a pet supply or a janitorial supply house. Don't waste your money on cheap novelty boutique black lights; they are fine for

> ### REALITY BITES
>
> ## Carpet Cleanup Necessities
>
> Since time is of the essence when cleaning up the three Ps, have a Pee Kit ready to go. It should include:
>
> - Ultraviolet light
> - Odor neutralizer
> - Old sponges
> - White towels or white paper towels
> - Spatula pooper scraper
> - Silica gel litter
> - Mop

psychedelic posters, but they don't work well on cat pee. (A UV light is more effective if you let it warm up for fifteen minutes before you start your search.)

Under the cover of darkness, your cats' indiscretions will be crystal clear (or rather florescent yellow). It's the salt in urine that fluoresces, so UV light pinpoints the exact location of the odor regardless of how old the stain is. Mark each glowing spot with a piece of masking tape, turn on the lights, and reclaim your home.

Not only will the UV light show you where the spots are, it will help you figure out whether your cats are peeing or spraying. If the spots appear as round stains on the floor and nowhere else, your cat is probably peeing. If the walls, baseboards, and carpet glow, or the stain is located in the middle of the floor in a long shape, your kitty is marking or spraying. You can learn more about this in the chapters "Back in the Box" and "The Pissing Contest."

Minding Their Pees and Qs on Carpet

Once you've pinpointed all the locations, it's time to do some toxic waste cleanup.

Left untreated, cat pee is the gift that keeps on giving—a little reminder of a cat who may have died years ago. Through the ammonia rising from your floor, your late pet could live on in your carpets, mattresses, furniture, or any porous surface for years. Even though the smell may have disappeared to your satisfaction, an olfactory phantom could return the smell to life on rainy days. Humidity seems to give new life to old cat pee and entices your current generation of cats to stray from their box. The fading smell of cat pee is a signal for your cats to freshen up their scent.

The other reason you need to clean up the mess as soon as you find it, is because cat pee can bleach or fade the carpet.

When you find a brand new pee spot (meaning still wet), put a white cloth or paper towel over the spot and blot it up by pressing down or stepping on the towel. Use white because colored cloth may bleed dye, further staining the carpet. Do this until you can't pull any more moisture from the carpet. Don't rub the spot; that will just force the pee deeper into the pad.

Professional carpet cleaners say, "The solution to pollution is dilution." After you blot as much of the excess liquid as possible or use a shop vacuum that can safely extract water, pour water on that area and blot it up again. Repeat the process three or four times. Now the area is ready to saturate with a product that removes the odor. Just to be safe, before you apply odor removers color-test the carpet and upholstery.

A pee stain is like an iceberg in that you're only seeing the tip. A visible stain the size of an Eisenhower silver dollar expands up to a ten-inch area in the pad. If you don't treat the entire area, you're wasting your time.

Even when the carpet surface is clean, the carpet pads can hold the stink forever. Treat the pad by injecting an odor neutralizer into it with a medical syringe—sans the needle. Saturate the entire area. Even the best odor control product won't work if the entire affected area hasn't been thoroughly soaked. You may have to re-treat the site several times in order to pass feline muster. Be sure to completely neutralize the odor before you steam clean the rug. Any lingering smell of pee will be locked into the carpet fibers by the steam. Don't forget to scrub the walls and baseboards.

When the ammonia odor persists or your cats return to the spot, pull the carpet up and treat the wood or concrete subflooring. When the subfloor has dried, seal it, then saturate the carpet with odor removers. Failing that, you may have to replace badly saturated floorboards, as well as the carpet and padding.

Another thing to keep in mind: products described as "stain removers" won't work if the carpet has already been discolored. After a while, cat pee permanently bleaches out carpet. If the fibers have faded, then an effective treatment will remove the offensive odor but can't replace the lost color. This is one of the main reasons to clean up a soiled spot as soon as you discover it.

Avoid cleaning products that contain ammonia. Cat pee also contains ammonia and the lingering smell from some cleaners will encourage your cats to refresh the spot with some ammonia of their own.

Kinds of Odor Control Products

Don Aslett, who has been cleaning up after other people's pets for forty-five years, is the author of the best-selling book *Pet Cleanup Made Easy*. In an interview he said odors are made up, chemically speaking, of a chain of molecules. When you break one part out of the chain the rest of the odor falls apart. He added that in chemistry you can change a molecule by cutting one part of the chain. A single cut may change a molecule into a plastic. Cut another part and the same molecule becomes liquid. Cut another and it becomes gas. A true odor neutralizer actually changes the chemical shape of odor molecules. Once you neutralize an odor, it won't revert to its original shape or smell.

Until twenty years ago there weren't any effective odor control products on the market. The older chemicals simply masked the smell. Fortunately, now a broad range of effective products are on the market that handle pet odors. They eliminate, change, absorb, or mask odors, often in several combinations. Below are the most effective neutralizers, how they work, and the advantages, disadvantages, and limitations of each:

- Molecular odor eliminators. This odor neutralizer eliminates odor at the molecular level creating a permanent bond with the odor molecules. By forming an irreversible bond, it permanently converts an odor molecule into a nonodor molecule. They work immediately and permanently, but they are rather expensive.

- Oxidizers. These cause a chemical reaction that adds oxygen to the molecule, changing its composition. They break down odors into carbon dioxide and water. The process is frequently used in wastewater treatment plants and in the purification of drinking water. Unlike the bacteria neutralizers, oxidizers aren't affected by cleaners previously applied to the carpet. Oxidizers work very quickly. These products are more expensive than enzymes and bacteria products.

- Bacteria only. These are solutions containing bacteria produce enzymes that break down the odor and consume it. Are bacterial products hazardous to your health? Not at all. Manufacturers have strict regulatory standards of operation. All the "friendly" bacteria contained in these cleaners have been laboratory tested for safety. And when their job is finished, they're gone. Unfortunately, bacteria have a short life span and can die before the job is finished so you may have to keep treating the spot. It takes about twenty-four hours for the bacteria to work. They only work when the carpet is moist. You may run the risk of developing mold or mildew. Bacteria products have a limited shelf life and are sensitive to temperature extremes. Chemicals or detergents previously used on the carpet will kill them.

- Enzymes. These are made of proteins that break down the odor molecules. Enzyme digesters break down odor-causing residue but will not digest it. They're not living organisms like the bacteria products, so they're not vulnerable to chemicals and extreme heat and cold as are live bacteria. Some other products like detergent and pesticides won't affect the enzymes. Unlike bacteria, the enzymes will dissolve detergent residue from earlier carpet cleanings. Enzymes don't work under every circumstance. Enzymes are pH sensitive, and pH fluctuates as the odor breaks down, working best under a neutral pH between six and eight. They only work when they are moist, and like bacteria they take about twenty-four hours to work and mold may grow.

- Bacteria and enzyme teams. In some products, bacteria and enzymes work in tandem. After the enzymes break down the odor molecule, the beneficial bacteria consumes the organic material, and the fluids turn into CO_2 and water, which then evaporate. With the food source eaten and the carpet dry, the bacteria die. Unfortunately, the bacteria can die before the odor has been completely removed so you have to keep it moist and add fresh solution for twenty-four hours. Be forewarned that you could run into mildew problems if you live in a hot, humid climate. A large, older stain may require thirty-two ounces of the bacterial/enzyme solution to do the job. If after twenty-four hours you still smell pee, you didn't use enough of the product.

- Encapsulators. In encapsulation a molecule attaches to and surrounds the odor molecule like the outer coating on an M&M. They do not contain enzymes or bacteria. Because of this, the product is not affected by the heat or cold of a warehouse. Since it doesn't contain a living organism, it has a shelf life of seven years. It removes the odor immediately. The effects are often temporary. The encapsulating molecule may eventually release its hold on the odor molecule, and the odor returns to its original shape and smell.

Absorption

Absorbents remove odor with a positive-negative ion reaction—like a magnet that straps the odor molecule. But enough chemistry mumbo jumbo. Baking soda and the volcanic ash Zeolite are two of the most popular absorption products. Sprinkle the powders on the carpet, leave for an hour or so, and vacuum.

REALITY BITES

Odor Removers that Work

⊛ **Zero Odor** is a molecular odor eliminator and my very favorite product for removing pet odors.

⊛ **Urine Erase** was the most effective bacteria/enzyme neutralizer with a peroxide component.

⊛ **EnzymD** got the best results when I tested enzyme/bacteria odor removers.

⊛ **Urine-Off Odor & Stain Remover** is a bioenzymatic cleaner containing enzymes, bacteria, and minty surfactants.

This is probably the most helpful way to freshen up when surprise company is on their way over.

Since odors are picked up rather than removed, you will need to continue to treat the affected areas.

The Poop on Poo

There are two kinds of poop to clean up: easy and hard. Easy is nice and firm. Pick it up with a paper towel or a plastic bag. Unlike pee, this is a surface mess. You just spot clean the carpet with any cat-safe carpet spotter or cleaner or even detergent.

Diarrhea is another story. Don't rub it in. Cover it with silica gel litter to pull out the moisture. After a few minutes, run something thin and flat (like a spatula or cookie sheet underneath the mess and lift it up. Saturate the area in **Tuff Oxi** solution, let sit, and blot (don't rub). When you don't get any more moisture, saturate the area again. It's only clean when you aren't picking up colored liquid.

REALITY BITES

Finally a Use for Stinky Carpet

Your kitty may have developed a preference for a carpeted bathroom. If you have to replace a section of carpet, hang on to some scraps of that soiled carpet. You can put it in a litter box to speed up retraining. When he begins to use the carpet inside the box, start adding **Cat Attract Cat Litter** or **Senior Attract Cat Litter** to the corners. Gradually add more litter. When he's using the litter, you can pull out the saturated, ugh, carpet leaving behind only cat litter. At the same time, block his access to the place he used to soil by placing a carpet runner (points up) over the spot. Read all about retraining your cats in the chapter "Back in the Box."

Barfing Up the Blues (or Reds)

Kitty loses his lunch for a number of reasons: food allergies, hairballs, or illness. Don't assume vomiting is just because of hairballs. Read the chapter "Health First" to find out why he's tossing his cookies. And just look at the puke—either it's hair or it's not!

Cleaning up gastric eruptions is one job that stinks. Cat puke contains stomach acids that can bleach out carpet, upholstery, and break down wood flooring finishes. So, clean it up right away, otherwise you could find your carpet has taken on a leopard-spot appearance.

If you have some silica gel cat litter on hand, pour it on the mess to soak up the liquid. Otherwise, use a hand towel or a plain white paper towel, no printed designs or borders because the color could bleed into your light-colored carpet. Scoop up the solid, or should I say semisolid, matter. Then blot, don't rub, the liquid just as you do with pee. When you've swept or vacuumed the silica litter, dilute those discoloring stomach juices with water. Continue to blot until you don't pick up any more liquid.

Treat the remaining stain with an oxygenating product like 🐾 **Tuff Oxi** or club soda, which will help remove any of the red dye in some cat foods that could permanently stain your carpet. Always color test your carpet before you use peroxide cleaners.

The best way to avoided red puke polka dots on your carpet is to feed your kitties a higher-quality food that doesn't contain food dye. Cheap food isn't nearly as cheap if you have to buy new carpeting.

Wood and Laminate Flooring

Wood flooring is popular in many multicat homes, but it can be as big a pain in the tail as carpeting. A couple of well-placed piddles and your wood floor is ruined. When you find it, wipe the pee up immediately. Follow with a clean wet paper towel. Then spray your favorite odor remover on the floor. I prefer the molecular odor eliminator and oxidation products because they are fast acting and cause less damage than keeping the floor wet.

With a wood floor, it's potentially a no-win situation. Your flooring manufacturer says don't use water-based products. The odor removal manufacturers say the same thing. They tell you to clean with recommended cleaners. But the recommended cleaners don't contain anything that can neutralize the smell of the pee. They're both covering their tails legally. The products that *do* remove odors can potentially damage your beautiful wood floor. But if you don't use odor removers, you have a bigger problem. There are tiny cracks between the planks where liquid collects, inviting your kitties to come back and pee. This has a greater risk of damage. I use 🐾 **Zero Odor** because it works so quickly and you can wipe it right off. This is an off-label use and you risk damaging your finish. Tough choice, but you have to make it.

TAILS FROM THE TRENCHES

Marion Lane, special projects editor for the national office of the ASPCA, has had experience with hardwood floors and multiple cats and dogs over many years. Her flooring company recommended two coats of 🐾 **Fabulon**, a finish similar to that on bowling alley floors. If the finish can stand up to spilled beer, ground-in nachos, and dropped bowling balls, it can stand up to cat pee. Marion said the Fabulon worked fabulously. Everything beads up and wipes away clean. She has also replaced her laminate kitchen floor with ceramic tiles because the laminate had water damage.

One Hairy Little Problem

Vast quantities of cat hair is an ongoing problem for those of us with multiple kitties. Many years ago, pet hair wasn't a problem for me. I had a black cat and two black-and-tan dogs. You never caught me wearing anything but navy blue or black. My furniture was dark brown. My clothes never betrayed my pets, but I did look like I worked in a mortuary. These days, I have a cat to contrast every outfit. My sofa has stripes—the dark blue stripes show off the white Turkish Van fur; the white stripes brilliantly emphasize Midnight Louie's lustrous black fur.

Coordinating your wardrobe and decor to blend with your cats' colors may work for a while, but it certainly limits what you wear or sit on. Now, unless your cats are all the same color, there's no practical way to hide the hair. Your only choice is hair removal.

One of the best ways to cut down on that Contemporary Persian look is to brush your cats frequently, especially during those times of seasonal shed-

In our house, cat hair is a condiment.

ding—when they change from their heavy longjohns into their lighter summer wear. For all but the longest-haired cats, a soft slicker brush, a brush with soft wire bristles that removes loose fur, should catch a great deal of the loose hair that would eventually find its way to your furniture. To protect your furniture, use slipcovers or throw a stylish sheet over the sofa or chair. After all, you can machine wash it as often as necessary.

TAILS FROM THE TRENCHES

Mary Anne Miller, who rescues cats in Oregon, throws the cat bedding in the dryer with two wet dryer sheets for twenty minutes before putting them in the wash. The fur becomes trapped on the soggy sheets and in the lint filter. She removes cat hair from her sofa with a metal currycomb.

Next time you buy furniture, consider this: some fabrics trap cat hair worse than others. Slick fabrics with tighter weaves such as cotton/polyester blends, polyesters, acrylics, and rayons are easier to clean and cat hair doesn't become woven into the fibers the way it does in looser fabrics that have a lot of texture or nubby surfaces.

Since cats have favorite lounging spots, you can cover just the places where they hang out with a throw or a towel. If company comes over unexpectedly, you can quickly whip off the cover and stash it. Also you can buy really nice machine-washable couch and chair covers.

Pet hair sponges remove the fur from most furniture. A new, barely dampened kitchen sponge can work just as well as some of these sponges. Unfortunately, this leaves the fabric damp. Some fabrics can't handle applications of water and it's not much fun to sit on afterward.

Adhesive lint rollers are a more-expensive option. For that matter, a huge roll of masking tape from a hardware store does just about as well for a fraction of the price. The masking tape can be more of a pain to use, but if you're watching your pennies, you might consider this option. Tapeless lint rollers work fine in a one- or two-cat home, but they're not practical in multicat situations. These products use a sticky rubber to remove the fur and lint. On a superficial level it does lift the fur off clothing and upholstery, but you have to rinse the hair off with *warm* water and then wait until the roller dries to use it again. With more than one cat or with a longhaired cat, it's too much trouble.

Here are some of the most effective hair removal products I've found:

- 🐾 **Handi-Brush**
- 🐾 **Pet Hair Eliminator**
- 🐾 **Petmate Pet Hair Magnet**
- 🐾 **Sticky Sheets**
- 🐾 **Magnet Broom**

If you have problems with cat hair collecting in your computer keyboard, order a 🐾 **Micro Vacuum Attachment Kit**. It pulls dust and cat hair out of computer keyboards.

X Marks the Spot, and X Is Everywhere

Right now your house is as it is. However, a fortune teller may see remodeling in your future. If that's the case, some changes in your home's surface may help keep your sanity and home value at a reasonable level. With cats, home decor needs to be accomplished on a variation of the KISS principle: Keep It Simple, Sweetie.

Feline-Friendly Flooring

Cats and carpets don't mix. When it comes time to replace the carpet—don't. Carpeting is difficult to care for under the best of circumstances. Add the three Ps and it becomes an olfactory nightmare.

Even laminate flooring is less than ideal because it can't be sealed. If pee isn't cleaned up right away it will seep between the planks causing them to swell. The planks are then ruined.

TAILS FROM THE TRENCHES

Megacat owners unanimously recommend ceramic tile. A long-time cat foster mom and president of the north Texas feral cat rescue organization Barn Cats, Inc., Peggy Atkerson designed her home around her feline companions. Her number one rule: anywhere you find cats, there's tile. According to Peggy, tile makes everything 100 percent easier.

"If they pee on it you clean it up," she says. "With the tile you know you're getting it up."

She has no feline administrative assistants, however. Her home office is one of the few designated cat-free zones. Every place else has slick, scrubbable surfaces like Corian counters, shutters in place of curtains, and a flat cooking top in the kitchen. To keep cats out of restricted areas, she has glass doors. BG (before glass) her cats would wait outside the closed door and caterwaul.

Her tile sunroom, built specifically for the cats' amusement, has shelves, cat trees, and plastic furniture. Everything can be wiped, or if necessary, hosed off or thrown in the washer.

Before installing new flooring, treat the subfloor with an odor remover like ⊛ **Tuff Oxi**. (After all, if it affected the pad, it affected the subfloor.) Use very hot (steaming) water and then pour the solution on the stinky spot. Be forewarned, these products don't have fragrance. The ammonia is going to be strong enough to lift weights. When it's dry, seal it. Treat the walls and baseboard too.

Tracking the Litter

There's no feeling like it. You get up in the middle of the night. On the way back to bed, you pass by the cat's litter box. Then you climb into bed, all cozy and snug, only now you feel cat litter between the sheets. Neither you nor the bed will feel clean until you do something about it. Next to odors, tracking is one of the cat owner's biggest housekeeping problems. As a cat uses the box, litter becomes trapped between his paw pads. After he exits the box, the litter works its way out with each step he takes. You step in it or it clutters the look of a clean room.

Tracking can be controlled in two ways. You can use litters that reduce tracking, but you sacrifice a comfortable texture and risk litter box avoidance. The second option is to use a litter mat to limit the amount of tracking. When a cat steps out of the litter box, paw pads separate and release trapped litter. Some mats actually help open the paws, others catch the litter as it drops naturally.

Sorry to use an often-loathed and overused cliché, but as with so many aspects of cat care, mat size does matter. Litter mats won't remove all the litter from the cat's paws before the cat returns to the floor, but larger mats catch more than smaller mats. If you have hard floors look for some kind of backing, otherwise they'll slide across a hardwood floor like a pair of inline skates. Avoid artificial grass mats because a lot of cats don't like the texture against their paws. In some multicat homes cats have a tendency to either mark or pee just outside the box, so look for a mat that has a waterproof backing.

My favorite litter mats are the 🐾 **Drymate Miracle Litter Box Mat** and the 🐾 **Welcome Mat**.

In your battle with odors and cat messes it's easy to become overwhelmed by a Siamese stampede or bushwhacked by a Burmese. Sure it's more work to clean up after multiple cats, but you can keep a step or two behind the herd and keep an ample supply of white paper towels and odor eliminators. Read the chapter "Back in the Box" to learn why your cats may be straying from the litter box. Pretty soon you'll be able to say you're "in the pink" not "in the pee."

CHAPTER TEN

Dinner Is Served

The best way to call a cat is to turn the handle of a can opener.
—Unknown

DINNERTIME PRESENTS A STRATEGIC NIGHTMARE in the multicat home. Any given feline family may have a twenty-year-old cat with kidney disease, an energetic four-month-old, a bowl-guarding alpha who wears a Wide Load sign, and an older cat who resembles a supermodel because she isn't permitted to eat when the alpha is around. How do you get a house full of cats to peacefully break bread, or rather mice, together?

Feeding Time Logistics

In the wild, cats don't need a lunch monitor. A cat's busy work schedule revolves around putting food on his personal dinner table. Unless a queen has kittens to feed, she's not interested in chatting with other cats over supper. Unlike lions, there's not a lot of coopera-

Winky no longer needs to use intimidation to block the food bowl. Now he blocks it with his butt.

tive hunting going on. It's hard to divvy up a single mouse. So in the cat world, it's each cat for himself.

Since they eat alone in the wild, few cats like the idea of someone else's nose (or butt) in their food dish. Because they need their space, every cat in the house should have his own food bowl. Spread them out so there's plenty of elbow room and dominant cats can't push the timid cats away from their food.

Just as I recommended with litter boxes, strategically scatter food and water bowls in different rooms around the house. Do this even if you free feed. Unfortunately, if you feed in a cluster, old or shy cats get pushed out of the way. If they're spread out, cats won't have to trespass into each other's territory in order to eat.

Since your herd may represent a variety of nutritional needs and several personalities who need to be catered to, you have to decide if your home would operate more smoothly with managed feeding times or by allowing your cats to graze whenever they want. Not every cat food and not every feeding strategy works in all situations. If you want to free feed, you have to feed dry. Unfortunately canned and fresh food do not lend themselves well to an open food bar because they will begin to spoil thirty minutes after you set them out. For wet food, managed or at least scheduled meals are the only way to go. Homes with cats who want to eat everything that's not still moving or with cats who must have medical diets have to go with managed meals.

Kibble gives you more flexibility. If you feed dry, you can either give them full-time access to their food or set out their rations on a schedule just like you would with canned food. You can always free feed and give them a taste of canned once or twice a day. That way they look forward to seeing you. It's a great time of day and it's a bonding experience for you and your kitties.

The Lunchroom Monitor

One advantage to feeding at specific times is being able to monitor who is eating what and how much or how little. When you have multiple cats, managed feeding is the only way for you to fully control portions. Your kidney cat can keep to his renal diet. Your fat cats begrudgingly chow down their lite foods, while the kittens scarf up their growth formula. Simple, right? This is where wrangling comes in.

If you can't manage different rooms, stagger dinner seatings as they do on a cruise ship or in schools. Separate your fat cats from the skinny minnies and the shy guys. If isolated dining facilities aren't an option, sit on the floor and monitor the activity. This way, you can see eating patterns, catch problems, or halt troublemakers from hogging the food.

REALITY BITES

Between-Meal Snacks

Give your kitties something to do while you're away. Keep them busy with a treasure hunt. Hide treats throughout your house. You can hide frozen bits of fish around the home for your cats to sniff out. The cats' job is to go seek out the munchies. Like their wild counterparts, they get to hunt. It gives your furry couch potatoes something to do.

Take the treasure hunt a step further by hiding not just single treats but treat balls. These are small, hollow, goody-filled balls. When your cat pushes it around with his paw or nose, it dispenses treats or food a bit or two at a time. You're mimicking the opportunities he'd have in the wild. Treat balls and food puzzles will help keep your cats' attention focused on foraging and less on beating up their roommates.

They say we humans should eat slowly because it takes a few minutes for our brains to tell us our stomachs are full. It's the same way with cats. By eating a little bit at a time throughout the day, Kilroy is keeping his metabolic furnace fired up all day long. It takes more energy to digest throughout the day than it does to process one or two big feedings.

When it comes to free feeding, Dr. Cynthia Rigoni, a Cornish Rex breeder and owner of All Cats Veterinarian Clinic in Houston, said her rule is to feed the entire group based on the cat with the most crucial nutritional needs. The nutritional needs of the twenty-year-old trumps all the other cats in the clowder, so she would give the group a senior diet.

While a kitten does need a diet higher in fat and protein to stay healthy, he would have fewer problems following a senior diet than a senior cat with kidney disease on a high-protein kitten diet. (If you free feed a low-fat, low-protein food, make sure the kitten has three or four special meals of a growth formula during the day.)

Sometimes the special kitty's nutritional needs are so specific it would be detrimental for him to sneak a bite or two out of the communal bowl. In these cases you have no choice; you have to set up a separate little apartment, but you don't have to imprison him. After everyone has eaten their dinner pick up the food dishes and let them all hang out together. When dinnertime rolls around, the special cat goes to his own room.

TAILS FROM THE TRENCHES

Free feeding eight cats a prescribed kidney diet could bankrupt you. Lulu from south Texas was experiencing this firsthand. She had twelve cats, one of them with kidney disease. The other cats loved the kidney diet and frequently squeezed the patient out of the food lineup. Lulu started feeding her kidney kitty in private at mealtime whenever she went to the restroom. Like Pavlov's dog, whenever Ruger saw her walk into the bathroom, he knew it was mealtime.

Switching to Managed Dining

Cats who are used to munching at will won't appreciate having to eat on a schedule. But once they get used to their new scheduled feedings, I guarantee your cats will develop time-keeping skills that rival the Swiss.

The night before the big switchover, right before you go to bed, pick up all the food bowls. When your herd checks out the empty place mats they will be less than amused. In the morning put out their food for thirty minutes. You'll need to supervise, otherwise the gluttons will help the more casual diners lick their plates clean. If one cat wolfs his food down and then helps himself to the neighboring bowls, you'll have to feed him in a separate room. That night, feed them again. After thirty minutes, toss the leftovers. A cat who can no longer snack throughout the day should be ravenous by the next meal. He'll eat most of his food, but may leave some leftovers thinking his full bowl will mysteriously return later. In a few days, everyone will adjust to managed feeding and eat when they have an opportunity.

Regimented feedings don't apply to kittens, pregnant or nursing queens, or ill cats. They get two or three more meals than the common rabble. You might even give them a special territory of their own.

Wet or Dry? It's Not Just the Weather Report

Go to the pet store and you'll see aisles and aisles of cat food. Dry food, wet food, bags, cans, jugs, pouches, cheap stuff, expensive stuff, even freeze-dried and frozen products. All those choices can cause a brain freeze.

Meat Me for Dinner

Remember your mom saying, "If you do that you'll go blind"? Some things she wasn't kidding about. For cats, it's eating a vegetarian diet. Kitties are obligate carnivores. That means they have to eat meat or they will die. Their bodies need an amino acid called taurine, which only comes from a meat source like a mouse or a lizard (not grains, not broccoli or soy). They also need fatty acids, other amino acids, and vitamins. Unlike many other animals, their bodies can't manufacture these essential nutrients. If they don't get enough of them, they will go blind or develop a deadly heart disease called cardiomyopathy. Feeding them dog food will do the same thing because dogs don't need as much protein as cats.

The Why of Dry

The least expensive and most convenient cat food option is dry food. Kitty kibble comes in easy-to-pour jugs and hulking, economical bags. It typically contains 10 to 15 percent moisture. It's not as tasty as canned food, but it has little odor obvious to our insensitive human noses. Kibble doesn't require refrigeration or attract bugs the way other foods do.

Dry food gives you the option of either free feeding or scheduling a prompt dinner. Remember, cats are designed to eat many times a day. Under normal circumstances cats can free feed dry food throughout the day without any problems. Most cats will eat their fill, returning when they are hungry again—eating little by little as their hunting skills would naturally permit. If your schedule is erratic, this method allows your cats to eat to their heart's content, and you don't have to worry about them going hungry. However, it's not such a great idea for your eight-year-old with a waistline approximately the circumference of Denver.

One reason many people feed dry food is to keep Kilroy's pearly whites pearly and white. J. R. "Bert" Dodd, who teaches dentistry at the Veterinary Medical Teaching Hospital's Department of Small Animal Clinical Sciences at Texas A&M, says that one easy step to reduce tartar is to feed dry food rather than wet food. "Dry food will keep the teeth cleaner a little bit longer than canned." However, many holistic vets believe that a raw meat diet contains enzymes that are more effective at reducing plaque.

Because of its low moisture content, cats who eat dry food are more prone to kidney disease. Besides that, crunchies aren't as tasty as canned food. Plus they contain more grains, fillers, and preservatives than other types of cat food.

Canned or Wet Food

Wet or canned food is more appetizing than dry. It contains fewer fillers and preservatives than its dry counterpart. Since individual cats have preferences in the texture of their food, you have a choice between buying pâté, ground, slices, or chunks of meat. For containers, you have a choice of rip-open pouches or cans. Wet food is better for the kidneys than dry food; because it contains 80 percent moisture it keeps the cat's kidneys more hydrated.

Left out, uneaten wet food grows a healthy population of bacteria and attracts insects. Pick it up and throw it away after thirty minutes. After that long, most cats don't like the smell either. You have to refrigerate unused food. Since cats prefer food that's the same temperature as the body temp of a mouse, you'll either have to warm the leftovers in the microwave set to thaw, or risk them turning tail and walking away when you plop down their ice-cold dinner.

Unfortunately, wet food doesn't give you the option of allowing your cats to graze. Finally, it's much more expensive than dry.

Raw or Homemade Diet

These are controversial cat food options. Raw and homemade aren't necessarily the same thing. Raw diets don't have to be homemade, and home cooked diets aren't necessarily raw. These are usually fresh meals that you prepare in your own kitchen. Although some raw diets can be purchased in almost ready-to-serve form like freeze-dried or frozen.

Holistic vet Jean Hofve said cats eating a raw diet chew their food more than they would eating canned or even dried food. Also, enzymes in the food help contribute to breaking down the food properly. "Done correctly, a raw meat diet can be beneficial to some cats, but you must work with a qualified holistic vet to assure the cat is getting a balanced diet," she says.

Since I seldom cook my own dinner, I certainly don't have the personal discipline to prepare meals for my cats. However, I know a few breeders and cats lovers who have dedicated their time to preparing their cats' diets. They swear by their cats' increased energy and improved coat quality.

When you prepare the food, you know the meat is fresh and not diseased and it contains no mystery ingredients. The supplements came from your neighborhood health food store, not the Dung Quak plant in Beijing.

Raw or homemade cat food has a very dark side, however. Preparing meals incorrectly or inconsistently could potentially cost your cats their eyesight or even their lives. You must be fully committed to the food preparation for the long term.

Dr. Hofve stresses that the diet takes dedication and perseverance. You and your vet must agree on a recipe or prepared food that contains all the nutrients your cat's body requires. Make sure you have all the ingredients and they are top quality. Don't get them at a discount store; buy them at a health food store.

Do your research. Make sure you understand the importance of each ingredient. If you know the reason it's in the recipe, you're less likely to cut corners and leave it out. When you run out of bonemeal, you have to go buy bonemeal (or whatever the missing ingredient is). You can't wait until next week to buy it.

FELINE FACT OR FICTION

Cats Give Pregnant Women Toxoplasmosis

The truth is people commonly get this parasite from mishandling uncooked or undercooked meat. You could do this while preparing your cat's next meal or even your own dinner. Always wash your hands after touching uncooked meat. Don't use the same knife to cut meat and vegetables without scrubbing it in hot water. (I go into a great deal of detail about this in chapter "Everything You Wanted to Know about the Litter Box, But Were Afraid to Ask.")

"If your heart isn't in it, you can't do it," Hofve says. She quotes Yoda from *The Empire Strikes Back*: "Do or do not. There is no try." If you want to feed your cats a raw or homemade diet you have to be totally committed. Steer clear of Internet recipes from self-proclaimed natural nutritionists. They could have your kitties securing the services of a guide dog.

REALITY BITES

Since preparing raw diet recipes can be time intensive and subject to variable results, consider feeding a prepared frozen or freeze-dried raw diet. 🐾 **Animal Food Services** has a line of frozen and freeze-dried cat food complete with a guaranteed nutritional analysis.

If you want the advantages of a raw diet without the hassle, Dr. Hofve suggests adding a small scoop of raw meat to your cats' current food. But only feed them small amounts. If you give them more than 10 percent of their diet as raw meat, Dr. Hofve says you have to go the whole way.

You will have to convert your herd to a raw diet slowly. If they're on dry food, switch them to canned first to make the switch more gradual. Once you have them eating canned begin adding raw meat to the diet.

Food for Thought (But Not for Eating)

If all those things I've already talked about weren't enough to ruin your cats' day, there's a whole list of foods your cat can't safely eat, either. The ASPCA/APCC warns against feeding kitties fatty foods, which put your cats at risk of developing pancreatitis. Cooked chicken and turkey bones can splinter and become lodged in their throat or puncture his esophagus, stomach, or intestine.

There's no end to the possible cuisine disasters facing felines. On the do-not-feed list is anything containing garlic, onions, or chives as they can cause anemia. Grapes and raisins have the potential to cause kidney failure. Also avoid avocado, coffee, macadamia nuts, walnuts, moldy or spoiled foods, salt, even uncooked yeast dough.

When it comes to sweets, most cats couldn't give a tail flip about them. Recent studies show that cats lack the ability to taste sweets. But chocolate is still a no-no. Cat owners should never let their kitties eat anything containing the artificial sweetener xylitol. If a cat swallows enough of it, it can cause a sudden drop in blood sugar resulting in depression and even seizures. Your kitty needs to stick to plain old unadulterated water. Even small amounts of alcohol can cause fatal respiratory failure.

Water

And speaking of water, let's not forget the most important ingredient in your cats' diet. Your cats' bodies contain 70 percent water. They might be able to survive for weeks without food, but they can only live for a few days without water. It regulates body temperature and helps them digest food. Without it they can't eliminate toxins through their poop and pee.

"We do know that cats that eat a dry food diet consume less water than cats that eat canned food diets," says Linda A. Ross in an interview, associate professor of small animal medicine at the Cummings School of Veterinary Medicine at Tufts University. "Remember that water comes not just from drinking, but from the food as well—and canned food is about eighty percent water, dry only about fifteen percent. Cats that eat only dry food are at increased risk for developing lower urinary tract disease (blood in urine, straining to urinate, urinating in abnormal places)."

Each healthy cat should take in about two cups per day including moisture from canned food. Cats with kidney disease, diabetes, or thyroid disease will drink more than that. Increase your cats' water intake by switching from dry to canned food. Your cats should always have fresh water available. Empty and wash water bowls every day.

Multicat homes should set up several water bowls around the house. Don't put food and water bowls right next to each other because cats have a tendency to drop their food into the water, mucking it up.

The Skinny on Cat Food Labels

Buying cat food seems like it should be fairly easy. After all, you simply go to the grocery or pet supply store and grab a can of cat food or a bag of dry food. Tada! Dinner is served. The truth is, I can't tell you which cat food is the best for your cats, but I can help you weed through some of the criteria that will help you make an informed decision.

If you free feed and you have a variety of ages, look for a cat food formulated for kitties of "all life stages." This diet is likely to be a safer bet in multicat homes where ages and your cats' nutritional needs may vary.

Look at the list of ingredients. Manufacturers can make it sound like there's lots of meat in it, when it may be only an illusion. Call this one the Disappearing Nutrition Trick. If the "Mirthy Moggy" label lists chicken meal first, but it's followed by ground corn, rice meal, corn gluten, ground wheat, corn bran, and wheat flour, you may have to get your reading glasses not only to read the label, but also to find the meat. That means it's only fit to be fed to an animal with more than one stomach.

You'll also need your glasses when you check out the ultrafine print on the label. The ingredients must be listed on the label in descending order by weight. But some pet food companies are tricky. Moist ingredients like turkey or fish may contain 70 percent moisture or water. Because it weighs more, a moist ingredient will be listed ahead of the dry grain or filler ingredients like wheat flour, soybean meal, and rice, which contain very little moisture. Individually, the dry contents may appear second or third on the ingredients list, but combined with all the other fillers the grains may exceed the amount of meat.

But wait, there's more. Fillers can also contribute to food allergies, creating a situation at the other end of your cat. There's nothing like finding a pile of kitty puke between your toes on a midnight jaunt to the bathroom. What's worse is cheap cat foods contain food dyes to make it look like there's more than a thimble full of meat in them. When your cat's graciously returns the icky food to your carpet, that red dye stain is a nightmare to remove! (The chapter "Cleanup on Aisle Two" has suggestions that will help dealing with red food dye.) While it may not seem to make sense, premium foods are cheaper in the long run. They contain more meat so the cats have to eat less to feel satisfied.

FELINE FACT OR FICTION

Premium Cat Foods Save You Money

True. And if that's not enough to make you upgrade your cat food, the litter boxes of cats who eat cheap "Mirthy Moggy"-quality food could gag a maggot. You know what computer geeks say: "Garbage in— garbage out." It's the same thing with cats. Feed them cheap, stinky food and that stinky filler winds up in the cat litter. Multiply that stench times the number of cats in your home, and I can only hope that when you scoop, you use a mask and have an oxygen tank nearby. Trust me, corn and other fillers smell worse when they've been recycled through a cat. Premium cat foods cut down on vet bills, make your cats healthier, and you won't have to put up toxic waste signs every time your kitties go to the bathroom. Remember, "the more the goop, the worse the poop."

Think about what a cat living in the woods would eat. Five to ten times a day, he'd snag himself a perfectly balanced single-serving food unit—you know, a mouse. The mouse contains everything a kitty needs—little mouse bones provide enough calcium for strong bones and good teeth. But a mousey is more than muscles and bones; he's got a little bitty liver and other vital organs that balance out a kitty diet nicely. Old Mickey Meal may even have a few grains and some plant matter in his tummy. The rest of the mouse is unadulterated flesh, bone, and fat in just the right proportions. News flash—if you ground that mouse up and listed the ingredients in order of weight (like a cat food label does), the grain in his belly, like corn and rice, would be listed way down in the list—not up at the top like it is in the "Mirthy Moggy" variety of foods.

Unfortunately pet food manufacturers don't sell processed mouse. Because kitties are obligate carnivores they aren't designed to metabolize large quantities of carbohydrates. All those grains in the dry foods are just empty calories. And do they spread the waistline! Unfortunately, it's hard to make dry cat food without these fillers.

Doing the Dishes

Cats have definite bowl preferences. Some like stainless steel. Others like ceramic or glass. If you notice your cat is not eating from a food bowl, put his food on a small plate instead. Their whiskers are very sensitive. Kitties don't like to soil them or bump them when they eat. Steer clean of soft plastic bowls. They scratch easily and hide bacteria that can cause feline acne.

You may have to experiment to see what type of bowls or water source your kitty prefers.

Although they look like a good idea at the pet store, pitch the food and water combo bowls. You waste a lot of cat food because it gets wet and the cats always drop food in the water.

Dinner is the highpoint of your cats' day, whether you decide to set up a specific feeding schedule or you allow your cats to free feed. The few simple steps contained in this chapter can make the difference between a dinnertime melee and a satisfying meal. Choose the right food and give everyone plenty of room to spread out, and you and your kitties will have a more manageable and pleasant dining experience.

CHAPTER ELEVEN

A Disaster Waiting to Happen

PREPARING FOR MULTICAT EMERGENCIES

Many of the survivors of Katrina have lost their homes, their jobs
and, in many cases, their loved ones. It's time for us to step in to ensure that
those who have lost everything are not forced, in their darkest and
most desperate moments, to abandon their pets as well.
—**Newt Gingrich**

DISASTERS COME IN ALL SHAPES and sizes, from the train derailment that requires the entire town to evacuate to hurricanes or earthquakes of biblical proportions. Then there are the more personal disasters like a gas leak that sends a family fleeing from their home in the middle of the night. And finally, the most personal disaster: your own death.

Now that we have arrived at such an unhappy note, let me remind you that, unfortunately, disasters don't just happen to the other guy. Sometimes that fickle finger of fate points right at you. If you don't have a plan when you get the finger, your cats will get caught in the crossfire.

Natural and Unnatural Disasters

We all saw those horrific videos from the areas leveled by Hurricane Katrina. We bit our nails for days, even weeks, waiting for rescuers to get the all clear to go in and start saving pets who had been left behind. Before Hurricane Katrina hit the Gulf Coast in 2005, the ASPCA national office estimated that 230,000 cats and 205,000 dogs lived in the area of impact. There's no way to know how many people took pets with them, how many animals died in the storm, or how many perished awaiting help. But one fact is certain: many animals who initially survived the storm died waiting for someone to rescue them.

As of early December 2005, about fifteen thousand pets had been rescued after Katrina. Of those, only three hundred sixty had family reunions to celebrate. So in the event of another similar disaster, if your cats get left behind, a happy reunion is probably not in the tea, uh . . . catnip leaves.

Hurricane Katrina provided a hard-learned lesson for the government and pet owners alike. Prior to Katrina, pets had no place in emergency evacuation plans. As a result, many committed pet owners in the Gulf region died because they wouldn't abandon their cats and dogs. One visually impaired man was even forced to abandon his Seeing Eye dog. In 2006, President George W. Bush signed the Pets Evacuation Transportation Standards (PETS) Act requiring local and state emergency preparedness authorities to include pets and service animals in their disaster plans in order to qualify for grants from the Federal Emergency Management Administration (FEMA). The act also granted FEMA the authority to help states and local communities develop disaster plans to accommodate pets and service animals, and to authorize federal funds to help create pet-friendly emergency shelters.

When it comes to disasters, I have good news and bad news. The good news is you don't have to worry about hurricanes if you don't live near a coast. And you may not have to worry about tsunamis if you live in Minnesota. But the bad news is that no matter where you live, there's something to worry about, whether it be earthquakes, wildfires, floods, power outages, chemical spills, and who knows what terrorists might cook up someday in your area. That makes it all the more important that you plan ahead for the safety of your cats.

Even though the PETS Act has been written into law, don't expect the government to help out much in a disaster. You know the old joke: "I'm from the government and I'm here to help." During a disaster, government agencies are often overwhelmed. As in Katrina, they couldn't address the basic needs of people, much less of the animals. In times of trouble, the only one you can count on is you. *You* need to form a plan to assure your cats are safe and cared for long before a crisis begins brewing. Some disasters, like hurricanes, can be predicted well ahead of time. But often you have little or no warning. The trick is making the process easy. Humans, being the procrastinating creatures we are, won't do anything at all if it gets too complicated.

Be the (Wo)Man with the Plan

You never know when some guy wearing a badge will bang at your door telling you to get out because something nearby might explode. If this happens, take your cats with you, even if authorities promise you'll only be out of the house for a few hours. A situation too dangerous for you is too dangerous for your cats. When you evacuate, *never* leave your kitties behind—no matter what

TAILS FROM THE TRENCHES

In 1996, a train carrying liquefied petroleum gas, propane, and sodium hydroxide derailed in Weyauwega, Wisconsin. More than twenty-three hundred people were evacuated from a radius of a mile and a half. Over half the people who owned pets left them behind because they thought they would be back in just a few hours. But when exploding train cars sent fireballs up three hundred feet, it quickly became obvious that it could be weeks before folks would be allowed back in their homes. After two days, some pet owners revolted. Under cover of darkness, they formed an illegal scouting party and retrieved their pets. Two days later the governor called in the National Guard to assist the remaining pet owners.

Once the smoke cleared, a study showed that more than 20 percent of the households with pets didn't evacuate, a higher percentage than families without pets. The likelihood a family would refuse to evacuate increased about 30 percent for each dog or cat they owned. Clearly, families with pets are more likely to stay behind and face danger together, and possibly die together.

officials on the scene say. If your home is damaged, the cats could be killed out-right or escape and fall prey to hungry coyotes and other predators. Even if the house isn't touched, your cats could starve to death before you can get back to them, as so many Katrina pets did. Police and the National Guard may later forbid your return for weeks.

Even if you're not at risk for natural disasters like earthquakes, hurricanes, floods or tornadoes, you could be at risk for the unforeseen catastrophes like the Weyauwega train wreck, a fire or chemical spill, or even a terrorist attack.

TAILS FROM THE TRENCHES

Alice Moon-Fanelli, assistant professor and a certified-applied animal behaviorist with Cummings School of Veterinary Medicine at Tufts University, can attest firsthand that a crisis can happen when you least expect it. Recently, a fire broke out in her chimney.

Her husband discovered it. As he leashed the dog, he yelled at his wife to get the cats. Easier said than done. The crates were in the cellar.

"Who plans on having a nightmare?" says Moon-Fanelli.

As soon as the carriers came out, the cats performed a feat of magic and vanished. The excitement and commotion, along with the appearance of the vet transportation vehicles, aka carriers, sent the two cats to points unknown.

In order to avoid the same problem, Moon-Fanelli recommends that you leave the carriers out in the open all the time. You must have a carrier for every cat. If you have ten cats, that's ten carriers. Place a towel inside so it's comfy and inviting. From time to time toss some treats inside so the cats keep checking them out. This transforms it from the evil vet box to a place where good stuff happens sometimes. In times of crisis try to behave normally (yeah, right!) and entice the cats into their carriers. If you're afraid they'll still go into the carrier kicking and screaming, have a cotton pillowcase handy for every cat. Since they aren't afraid of the pillowcase, they won't run. Simply slip it over the cat's head, then give him a little shove. Leave the end open so he can come out whenever he wants to. Because it's dark inside the pillowcase, your cats will find it comforting. Once the cat is safely contained in the pillowcase, slide him into a carrier and prepare another pillowcase for your next evacuee. I know from experience pillowcases work like a charm.

Step One: The Nose Count

Cats often become frightened and hide when dangerous weather approaches. Even normally outgoing cats often hide or run away before a hurricane, tornado, or even earthquakes. Since the predictable concerns are usually weather

TAILS FROM THE TRENCHES

Susan Hamil knows firsthand about disaster planning. She has been the director of the Blue Bell Foundation for Cats in Laguna Beach, California, for the past ten years. She and the cats in her shelter have been through three different disaster evacuations, including two wildfires and a mudslide. Susan says at the first hint of trouble, do a nose count. Like Santa Claus, you're making a list and checking it twice. You already know who's naughty and nice. What is important to know is exactly where your cats are. Keep a list of all your cats' names on the refrigerator, or in a place where you won't have to look for it. No, I'm not kidding. In a panic, you might forget somebody. Remember the movie *Home Alone*?

related, when you hear there may be a dangerous system in your area, turn to the National Oceanic and Atmospheric Administration (NOAA) weather radio station. Monitor the advancement of dangerous weather or turn on the local news to keep track of other types of disasters.

If it looks like you might have to evacuate or if dangerous weather is brewing, confine your cats to specific rooms so you don't have to waste precious minutes or hours looking under beds and inside cabinets. That's time you could spend driving to somewhere safe or taking shelter.

Step Two: Assemble the Carriers

With the cats safely confined to a room, Susan says it's time to get the carriers out. Fully assembled crates take up so much room, and nobody has a spare wing to store five or ten, or more, carriers. So it may be impractical to keep ready-to-go carriers for every cat. But let's face it, assembling carriers under the best of circumstances is a pain in the tail. In a crisis, screwing together bolts and washers or snapping stubborn latches eats up valuable time. Susan says rather than wasting time fumbling with bolts, keep a big package of cable ties (available from any home improvement warehouse or hardware store) with the carriers. Use them in place of the bolts. Cable ties don't rust. It only takes a second to thread them through the holes. Replace the cable ties every couple of years because they can grow brittle.

If a disaster warning has been issued for a wildfire or hurricane, the staff at Blue Bell loads the cats in carriers and leaves them together in a cluster in a room. They usually monitor the news and start catching cats when the fire reaches within two miles of the shelter. They don't put them in the van until it's time to evacuate.

Families with more than ten or twelve cats need to consider whether they have enough room in their vehicle and enough drivers to escape with everyone.

Instead of placing a litter box in each carrier, Hamil says they have a large dog cage or crate that acts as the community bathroom once they're on the move. Cats take turns using the privy. This way they can use smaller carriers for the cats.

Before the crisis, write your name and contact information directly on the carriers with a permanent marker. Try to have containers that are comfortable for the cats because they may have to stay in that carrier for days. For housing purposes, a carrier should be large enough to hold a shoebox litter pan and two dishes and still permit your cat to stand up and turn around.

Poop happens. If the port-a-privy isn't an option, you can still provide your cat with toilet arrangements even without a mini litter box. Line the bottom of the carrier with a thick carpet of crumpled paper towels. They are absorbent and the cats can use them to cover up accidents. It traps waste in one area of the carrier. After kitty goes, just pull out the dirty wads and replace them with clean ones. Or simply line the floor of the carrier with puppy pads. I like 🐾 **Hartz LIVING Puppy Training Pads for Dogs and Puppies**. They don't take as much time to use as crumpling paper towels, but your kitties will be forced to sit in their own poop until you can clean it up.

It might be tempting to toss two or three cats in a single large carrier, but don't. Evacuating is stressful enough, but cram those poor territorial creatures three to a box and watch the sparks and the fur fly. Not to mention how much fun they'll have sitting in each other's poop. Large carriers holding multiple cats present another problem. Three cats and a carrier could easily weigh thirty-five to forty pounds. You don't want to add a truss to your postdisaster wardrobe. I've pulled a muscle in my back picking up a litter of two-month-old kittens in a single carrier.

Finally, resist the temptation to cut corners by using cheap cardboard carriers. They are notorious for the bottom dropping out, literally, especially if the cat pees in it. You don't want to be looking at a bottomless, catless carrier saying, "It seemed like a good idea at the time." If you have no choice but to use them, or if you're uncertain about the reliability of any carrier, bring along a roll of duct tape to provide added support.

Make sure you have a harness (not a collar) and a leash for each cat. Eventually you'll have to take your kitties out of the carrier to clean the litter boxes. A harness gives you (or a disaster volunteer) more control in case one of your terrified tabbies thrashes around or tries to make a break for it.

For long trips or stays in the carrier, I like the 🐾 **Petmate Double Door Deluxe** carrier and the 🐾 **Sturdiproducts CarGo**, a roomy car cage that doubles as a hotel cage.

Step Three: Make Your Reservations

Getting outta Dodge is just half the battle. You have to find someplace to stay.
Have a list of pet-friendly hotels. At the first sign that you need to bail, call outside the danger zone and make reservations for yourself and your cats. If you
wait too long there may be no room at the pet-friendly inn. Here's a list of some
of the national hotel chains that take pets:

- Accor Hotels (Motel 6, Studio 6, Red Roof Inns), www.accorhotels.com

- Baymont Inns and Suites (1-866-999-1111), www.lq.com

- Best Western (1-800-780-7234), www.bestwestern.com/

- Comfort Inn, Quality Inn (1-877-424-6423), www.choicehotels.com

- Days Inn (1-800-329-7466), www.daysinn.com

- Four Seasons Hotels and Resorts (1-800-819-5053), www.fourseasons.com

- Some Holiday Inns, call first (1-800-315-2621), www.holiday-inn.com

- Hotel Monaco (1-800-546-7866), www.kimptonhotels.com

- Howard Johnson (1-800-446-4656), www.hojo.com

- La Quinta Inns and Suites (1-866-725-1661), www.lq.com

- Loews Hotels (1-800-23-LOEWS), www.loews.com

- Ramada Inn (1-800-2Ramada), www.ramada.com

- Super 8 (1-800-800-8000), www.super8.com

- Travelodge (1-800-578-7878), www.travelodge.com

- Westin Hotels, W Hotel, Sheraton, Starwood (1-800-937-8461),
  www.starwoodhotels.com

Step Four: Retrieve Your Emergency Kitty Kit

Anyone smart enough to own cats should be savvy enough to put together a cat
evacuation kit. Every pet in the house should have his or her own personalized
emergency kit ready, or one large kit for all the pets. Store your emergency gear,
which includes copies of the all-important proof of vaccinations, in an out-of-
the-way place but one that's easy to get to. Not in the basement under three-

hundred pounds of wine-making equipment that your dad used once in the 1960s. If you think about it ahead of time and create a plan, you'll be much calmer if or when that disaster strikes.

The ASPCA recommends storing emergency items in a sturdy, preferably waterproof, container that can be carried easily (plastic tub, duffel bag, backpack, ice chest on wheels, new covered trash can, etc.). Date each food package, bottled water, and medication container. Swap them out every twelve months. Whenever you move your clocks forward or back, take a look at the kit and make sure none of the food or meds has expired. Don't forget 🐾 **Bach Flower Remedies** and 🐾 **Rescue Remedy** to help keep the cats calm during evacuations. Photocopy the list in the following sidebar and tape it to the container holding your pets' provisions.

If you have the benefit of an early warning, get a head start in evacuating out of the affected area. You don't need to take as many supplies with you because wherever you go, there should be an infrastructure, says Lauren Bond, disaster response program coordinator with the HSUS. In those cases a three-day supply of food, water, and litter is reasonable. If you're going to evacuate locally and stay in the potentially affected area, prepare for two weeks.

When putting together your personalized evacuation kit, the items need to be as close as possible to what your cats use at home. Cats are creatures of habit. They feel more comfortable in an uncomfortable situation if they can eat from the same kind of dinnerware food bowls they use at home. The safest bowls for travel are stainless steel and plastic that won't break.

When using nonclumping litter, aluminum baking pans make great waterproof, disposable litter boxes. You can put together single-use cat litter pans in zippered freezer storage bags. Once you've used the litter box, hang on to the bag; it can double for poop disposal. For evacuations, a flushable litter like 🐾 **World's Best Cat Litter** is lighter to carry and easier. Most hotels welcome litter that is easily disposed of. If you use corn or paper litter, carry enough for a few weeks. Most animal shelters can provide clay litters.

Wet food in Mylar pouches work better than cans because they're lighter, they're easier to open, and less trouble to dispose of. Store dry food in airtight containers or keep it in zippered freezer bags. Bring along bottled water since

Disaster Necessities

These are the items you will need:

- List of your cats by name so you can do a nose count
- Pillowcase for every cat
- Carrier for each pet
- Food and bottled water
- Food and water bowls
- Litter, litter box, litter scoop
- Plastic grocery bags and zipper plastic bags for trash, poop, and used litter
- Puppy pads, newspaper, or paper towels
- Paper towels and/or baby wipes
- Your cats' medicine
- Tranquilizers or calming remedies (Bach Flower Remedies, Rescue Remedy, Comfort Zone)
- Current individual photographs of your cats
- Copies of ownership papers and medical records
- Harness, leash, ID, and rabies tags
- List of phone numbers including your veterinarian, pet-friendly motels, emergency clinic, APCC, area animal shelters
- Cat first-aid kit
- Comfort items—favorite toys, treats, bed
- Brush/comb (for longhaired cats)
- Odor neutralizer
- Duct tape
- Cable ties
- Neighbor's key

strange tap water may cause diarrhea (and trust me, you don't want to be trapped in a car filled with cats with the runs).

People who live in disaster-prone areas also need to keep a two-week supply of their cats' maintenance medication. Ask your vet for pills, unreconstituted powder, or keep an unfilled drug prescription with your cat's evacuation kit. Protect the label with clear packing tape so it remains readable.

This is where the individual kits come in. Buy stock in the company that makes the zippered freezer bags and the giant zippered storage bags because you're going to be using a lot of them. They help keep things organized. Have a freezer bag labeled with each cat's name in permanent marker. Inside, store the harness and leash, medication, and anything special that your cat will need (lactated ringers, syringes, etc.).

While you're getting emergency meds or prescriptions from your vet, ask for photocopies of your cats' records. They will be priceless if the clinic is damaged or records become lost. Every time you have blood work or lab work done ask your vet for copies. (And in single-cat emergencies, those records could be a lifesaver when you take a sick cat to an after-hours emergency clinic.) For transport across state lines it's important to have rabies vaccination records. You never know when your pets could be forced to stay at a shelter of some kind.

Predisaster Precautions

In an interview with the ASPCA Companion Animal Programs advisor Jacque Schultz, she indicated that as a preventive measure it's important to swap house keys with a trusted neighbor. "In the event of an unexpected evacuation, if either of you are away from home, the other person can get the pets out of the line of trouble. Even if you just go to the grocery store, you may not able to get back home."

Then designate a meeting place, like a church or a Home Depot, to meet family members and neighbors with your pets if the damage is limited to a small area. Depending on your disaster de jour, you need an alternate site. After all, your original location may not be accessible. The meeting place may be critical since cell phone communications, as well as landlines, are frequently disabled during a disaster.

Doing Your Paperwork

You should gather all the following paperwork in one giant storage bag:

- Medical and current rabies and other vaccination records plus your pets' city licensing registration. Include a written prescription for maintenance medicine your cats are taking. (Swap the prescription out annually, since they are only valid for one year.)

- Photocopies of ownership papers (registration information, adoption papers, proof of purchase, and microchip information.)

- A list with each of your pets names, their breed, age, sex, color, and markings.

- Your pet insurance policy number, and the address and phone number where you or a contact person can be reached if you are not at home.

- Individual photos of each cat (in case you and one of your cats become separated and you need to post lost cat signs). Hopefully the plastic bag will keep all the photos and records readable if they get wet.

Practice Makes Perfect

One time, just for grins, why don't you try loading up all the cats and emergency gear and swing around the block once or twice? That way, should you ever need to leave with the cats, you'll have a better idea how much time it takes to load up and how conveniently (or inconveniently) carriers and kits are stored. My husband and I have held rehearsals twice. It was an eye-opening experience. Should evacuation ever be necessary, things may not roll perfectly, but we'll have a better grip on things.

Up-to-Date ID Is a Must

Keep identification tags on cats. If they don't normally wear collars, then fasten them to the emergency harnesses. Put your cell phone number on the tag so authorities can reach you. Even if your cats wear tags, consider getting a little body piercing. Instead of a nose or the earring, how about a stylish microchip right between the shoulder blades? A microchip, a device the size of a rice grain, is encoded with a unique number. Microchips provide added insurance. Using a handheld scanner, animal control officers can scan your cat for the chip. For that happily-ever-after ending so many Katrina victims didn't experience, it's vital that cat owners have their animals microchipped because it's the only permanent, positive means of identification. After all, to most people all tabby cats look alike, so do black cats.

Getting the chips implanted by a rescue group or a vet runs between $25 and $50 depending on which chip you get and who implants it. Most of the time there's an additional payment to the database provider. Some are a one-time enrollment fee and others charge an annual data maintenance fee. Zoos microchip everything from aardvarks to zebras, so you know it's safe. After all, one of your guys could lose his breakaway release collar, leaving him with no ID and no way home.

Each chip identification number is traceable through a central national database like American Kennel Club Companion Animal Recovery or United All Breed Registry where either your vet's or your contact information is kept on file. Alternate contacts should include an out-of-state friend or relative who's not likely to be affected by your disaster. After all, your next-door neighbor, who is at the top of the list if your cat gets lost on an average day, probably won't have phone service either.

REALITY BITES

Paying for chips for every cat in the house will cost you a paw and a tail if you do it all at once. You can get one cat done every couple of months until everyone is wearing a microchip under their skin. Also don't forget, if you should move or change phone numbers, update the records with the database registry. All the microchips in the world won't return your pets if the contact data is incorrect.

Disasters of a More Personal Nature

Then there's a disaster of a much more personal nature: your becoming disabled or your death. Especially if you live alone, make sure to designate someone to take care of your cats in case you're in a car wreck or involved in any other accident. We have no guarantee we will actually arrive home on any given night. Keep a pet alert card in your wallet to tip off officials if you are injured in an accident or if you are hospitalized for a few days. On the card write your name, the name of your significant other, address, phone number, and e-mail address. List each of your pets. Include name, species, description, age, and sex. Most important, provide the names of your pets' foster family or families, their phone numbers, and e-mail addresses. Give one of these people a key to your house. In a car crash your significant other might be injured as well. So ask someone outside your immediate family.

Because cats usually live fifteen or twenty years to our eighty or ninety, we assume we will outlive them. In most cases, that's true. But if you keep cats for your whole life, eventually the Grim Reaper will catch up with you. Then what will happen to your kitties?

Don't assume that because your kids or siblings love you, they'll be happy to take in your pets. Ask them if they are willing to handle the responsibility. You may have friends and loved ones who would volunteer to take a cat or two if something happened to you, but remember, cats sometimes bite and so does reality. Your pet's new caretaker may run into financial problems. A kid could become allergic, or the new boyfriend might not like cats. Off go your cats to the shelter.

In just the last year I have been asked to take in two sets of older foster cats. The first pair were a seventeen-year-old tabby named Slim and a seven-year-old gray companion cat, Silver, who had belonged to an elderly couple. When the parents went into the nursing home, their daughter planned to take the cats to the vet to be euthanized. A neighbor intervened begging Animal Allies of Texas to save the cats. We did. The gray kitty was adopted into a nice home. I kept Slim.

If you think this is an isolated case and your kids or family would never do that to your cats, think again. Just a few weeks ago I got a call from an area animal control officer. An elderly woman was dying. Her adult son dropped off her pets at the shelter. The three-year-old declawed tabbies were brothers, Tank and Patton. Rather than making any effort to find a home for these sweet boys, the son left them at a shelter that euthanizes cats every week. Shelter workers took pity on them and asked me to take them.

It's doubtful these people ever imagined that their precious cats would be killed when they became incapacitated. Tank, Patton, Slim, and Silver are not unusual cases.

The point is, once you are out of the picture, you have no control over what happens to your beloved pets unless you take action. Make arrangements *now*. If you don't, you have no assurances that your children or heirs will honor your wishes and care for your cats and other pets. It is especially critical when you have more than one cat. A single cat may be easily integrated into a friend or family member's home even if she already has a cat or two. But most people are ill equipped, physically and emotionally, to take on the burden of more than one kitty.

Kathryn M. Kollmeyer, a Texas attorney with two Russian Blues and an interest in pet law, said there are several ways to protect your pets when you become incapacitated. The easiest is to create a *power of attorney for pet care* and a *statutory durable power of attorney.*

The power of attorney for pet care takes effect whenever you specify, or if you become mentally or physically incapacitated and can't manage your pets' care. Through this document, you can thoughtfully select and designate a person as your *pet care agent* whom you trust to care for your pet during your disability or permanently. You should also list an alternate, in case the first person can't undertake the duties. You may authorize the pet care agent to spend money for your pets' care, including food, litter, and veterinary expenses.

Under a *statutory durable power of attorney*, you appoint someone as your *attorney-in-fact,* that is, a person authorized to act in your place. These documents grant the attorney-in-fact general powers to conduct your day-to-day business (pay your bills, dispose of property, etc.), except for those actions you specifically exclude. You can specify that the document take affect only in the event you become incapacitated. In this document, you should specifically authorize your attorney-in-fact to pay any expenses, fees, and costs that the pet care agent incurs while caring for your pets. You can direct that the expenses be paid to the service provider, reimbursed to the pet care agent, or both.

The two documents can be combined into one if your attorney-in-fact is also your pet care agent. Note, however, that whether executed as two documents or combined into one, these powers of attorney end after your death, leaving your pets unprotected.

To protect your cats when you die, you can create an *inter vivos* trust. This trust is created while you are still alive and becomes effective at the time of its creation, as opposed to a trust that becomes effective when you die. You can fund the trust with just a little money to start with and add to it at any time, like a savings account deposit. Also, you can make a provision in your will (called a pour-over provision) to add money from your estate into the trust during probate.

Probate usually takes a while, however. You can provide the trust with immediate funds upon your death by listing the trustee (in trust) as the beneficiary of nonprobate assets, including any insurance policy, government bond, annuity, retirement plan, IRA, or bank account as the pay on death payee. These moneys would pass to the trust you set up for your pets without having to go through probate.

Be aware that not every state has passed pet trust legislation. Even some states that have such laws treat these trusts as honorary. This means the trust can't be enforced in a court. In other states, like Texas, pet trusts are enforceable.

You can first create a pet care power of attorney, then bequeath your pets to the pet agent in your will. Then, so that the pet care agent will have funds immediately upon your death, name your pet care agent as beneficiary in nonprobate assets (life insurance, bank account, etc., as with the inter vivos trust) in whatever amount you wish to go to the care of your pets. Let your pet care agent know about your will's terms and who the executor is. Make the executor of your will aware of the pet care agent and your wishes regarding your pet.

Your executor needs to be someone you trust and who agrees not to contest the bequest. Also insert a no-contest clause in the will (if the named heirs contest any bequests, including the ones regarding your pet, they forfeit the bequests you left to them). If you can trust no one to obey the will's directives and your wishes, then use a professional fiduciary as the executor of your will (banks are set up to do this). Of course, all of this has its price.

Remember, I'm not an attorney. You should consult your own lawyer to formalize these arrangements.

The HSUS offers a free estate planning kit called "Providing for Your Pet's Future without You." It includes a six-page fact sheet, wallet alert cards, emergency decals for windows and doors, and caregiver information forms. Get the kit by writing to petsinwills@hsus.org or HSUS, Humane Legacy, 2100 L Street NW, Washington, DC, 20037, or call 1-202-452-1100.

Retirement Homes for Cats

If you're concerned you can't count on anyone or no one is willing to take your cats, look into finding a retirement center for them. Your cats will be allowed to live out their lives in a comfortable, safe setting. These kitty retirement communities are especially a blessing for elderly cats and any cat over five years old, because it's so difficult to find adoptive homes. You can name the retirement home as your pet care agent rather than a friend or relative, making the organization the beneficiary of insurance policies and government benefits, as well. Because wills can be tied up in court for years in some cases, kitty retirement communities usually require upfront enrollment fees.

Although these foundations are a labor of love for the people who run them, they are not free. To prearrange a space in a kitty retirement home can require an upfront financial commitment, ranging from $3,000 to $25,000 per cat. Consider it an investment in your cats' futures.

If you find a facility that appeals to you, visit it to make sure your cats will get the kind of care you expect. This way you'll know the living conditions are as good as you are led to believe. Do your own investigation to be sure the group is on the level. You can check out the foundations' finances, nonprofit status, and its plans for perpetuity at GuideStar, the nonprofit watchdog organization (www.guidestar.org). Also check out complaints with the Better Business Bureau. Sadly some of these homes turn out to be too good to be true.

If the organization checks out and you like the way they treat animals, have your attorney look over the contract and make suggestions on how to fund the enrollment fee. When you've enrolled your cats in a program, tell your family, friends, pet sitter, vet, and of course your attorney about your arrangements. Putting it in your will may make you feel better, but your wishes won't be revealed until your death. That could be many years off. When you die, it could be weeks or months before the will is read. By that time, your pets could already have been taken to the pound or otherwise disposed of. Keep copies of the enrollment papers with your power of attorney.

While this is neither a complete list nor an endorsement of these facilities, the following organizations listed alphabetically by state may be able to help you. It's your responsibility to check them out before you commit to their programs.

California

The Bluebell Foundation for Cats
Bertha's House
20982 Laguna Canyon Road
Laguna Beach, CA 92651
1-949-494-1586
www.dovecanyon.org/bluebell/

California Feline Foundation
Fresno, CA 93728
1-559-233-8554
www.valleyanimal.org

Sylvester House
P.O. Box 896
Lompoc, CA 93438
1-805-735-6741
www.viva-animal-shelter.org

Living Free Animal Sanctuary
Mountain Center, CA 92561
1-951-659-4687
1-951-659-4684
www.living-free.org

National Cat Protection Society
Retirement Centers
Newport Beach, CA 92660
1-949-650-1232
Spring Valley, CA 91977
1-619-469-8871
www.natcat.org

Callie's Home for Cats
Riverside, CA
kritrkamp2@msn.com

Colorado

Cat Care Society
Lakewood, CO 80214
1-303-239-9680
www.catcaresociety.org

Connecticut

Vivisection Investigation League
The Last Post
Falls Village, CT 06031
1-860-824-0831

Florida

Rainbow Ranch
Candler, FL 32111
1-352-680-1707
www.rainbowranch.org

Palm Meow, Inc.
Hallandale, FL 33009
1-954-929-8230
www.palm-meow.com

Illinois

Assisi Animal Foundation
Continuing Pet Care Program
Crystal Lake, IL 60039
1-815-455-9411
www.assisi.org

Minnesota

Home For Life
The Animal Sanctuary of St. Croix Valley
Stillwater, MN 55082
1-800-252-5918
www.homeforlife.org/angelcar.htm

New Jersey

Kitty City
Newark, NJ 07114
1-609-693-1900
www.ahscares.org

New York

Kent Animal Shelter
Calverton, NY 11933
1-631-727-5731
www.kentanimalshelter.com

The Sunshine Home
Honeoye, NY 14471
1-585-919-6557
www.thesunshinehome.com

Bide-A-Wee Home Association
Golden Years Retirement Home
New York, NY 10016
1-212-532-6395
www.bideawee.org

North Shore Animal League America Surviving Pet Care Program
Port Washington, NY 11050
1-516-883-7900, ext. 389
www.nsalamerica.org

Texas

Texas A&M University
Stevenson Companion Animal Life-Care Center
College Station TX 77843-4461
1-979-845-1188
www.cvm.tamu.edu/petcare

CHAPTER TWELVE

Health First

The best trick a cat does is a disappearing act when a medication is due.
—Bob Lovka

PICK UP ANY NEWSPAPER AND you'll probably read the latest study about kids in day care swapping germs and diseases. Unfortunately, healthy multicat and megacat homes bear a striking similarity to a mom's day care dilemma. A multicat home is a Pandora's box full of trouble and a hotbed of potential viruses, infections, and parasite problems.

How much germ swapping you have, and your expenses in vet bills, depends greatly on you and whether your cats stay inside or outside, whether they get vaccinations, if you bring in other unvaccinated cats, the quality of their diet, the level of cleanliness, and how quickly you isolate a sick kitty. The more crowded your conditions, the more likely you are to have health problems.

Preventive Care

Cat and cars have something in common. A little proper maintenance rewards the car owner with a long-lived and smooth-running driving machine; tune-ups and checkups do the same thing for our little Jaguars.

Mechanics tell us that, depending on the model, cars should be tuned up regularly every twenty-five thousand to fifty thousand miles. But let's face it, an old Lynx is going to take much more frequent care than a new Cougar. A twenty-year-old Kilroy is probably going to require more attention than two-year-old Fluffy. Oil change, a lube job, and checking the fluids should be performed every three thousand miles as good preventive car care. Likewise, vaccinations, regular vet care, and careful monitoring will help prevent your cats from passing diseases back and forth.

Since many viral shots only require boosters every three years, you still must make a point of having your kitties seen by a vet annually. Even a yearly tune-up is the equivalent of your seeing a physician every seven years.

I'm sure you know, the more cats you have, the more difficult it is to monitor the health of each individual cat. You may not know exactly who ate when or who's not pooping. Just as you would periodically check the dipstick for oil levels, you need to give everyone a quick once-over every month just to make sure those motors keeps purring. And, silly as this sounds, every day conduct a nose count. Have a checklist and eyeball every cat. In megacat and even multi-cat homes, it can be hard to keep track of when you last saw everyone. A daily roll call, and subsequent search for anyone who's missing in action, will help you locate sick or injured kitties long before you might ordinary realize they're missing. It will also help you find kitties who may have become trapped in a closet or alert you that a kitty may have snuck out the door.

If you can't pinpoint the sick kitty, you may have to round all of them up for a trip to the vet.

Preventing Disease

Vaccinations are important in a single-cat home, but they're vital in a multicat or megacat environment. Before the availability of routine vaccinations, cats died by the scores of common diseases. Today the cheapest kitty health insurance you can buy for your herd is to make sure they stay current on their shots. Since most viral shots are very effective and inexpensive, it doesn't make sense to not to get them.

Vaccines protect because they contain either parts of dead viruses, live virus particles that have been modified, or a part of a live virus. Fooled by the fake disease, the body's immune system mounts a full-fledged defense by unleashing antibodies to kill the (mostly) harmless invaders. When kitty comes in contact with the real disease, the antibodies are ready to protect him. Without these antibodies, invading virus, bacteria, or organisms can come in and take over, sometimes killing your cats. There's a hitch here. The shots only protect the cats when they're received them *before* they've been infected. There are two kinds of vaccinations: core and noncore. Core vaccines protect against common and serious diseases. Every cat should receive core vaccinations. These include feline panleukopenia (FPV, which is also called distemper), feline herpesvirus (FHV-1, formerly known as rhinotracheitis), and felines calicivirus (FCV). Distemper, herpes, and calici are usually packaged in one shot—FVRCP, sometimes called, *a three-way vaccine*. The other core shot is rabies, which is required by law in most states. Noncore vaccines should only be given to cats who are at risk of coming in contact with the diseases. These include chlamydiosis (chlamydia), feline leukemia (FeLV), feline immunodeficiency virus (FIV), feline infectious peritonitis (FIP), and ringworm. Annual booster shots were the standard until recently. It's now known that the immunity lasts longer than originally believed. In the FVRCP shot the FPV vaccine is certified for three years, but homes with more than three cats, breeders, foster homes, and cats who go to boarding or grooming facilities or cat shows may benefit from booster vaccinations prior to being around other cats, and then receiving yearly boosters.

Early on, kittens get their resistance to disease from their mom. Mother's first milk passes on antibodies that protects the kitten until he's about seven or eight weeks, then gradually dissipates. To maintain continuous immunity, kittens should receive three sets of shots starting at eight weeks. Hand-raised kittens should start their shots at six weeks. To provide the most uninterrupted protection, they should receive additional shots three to four weeks apart until they reach sixteen weeks—with a total of thee shots.

Shots aren't like starship force fields. Unfortunately, they don't make your cats impervious to disease. The amount of protection they provide varies from cat to cat. You can give your cats added protection by reducing their exposure to infected cats or contaminated areas. Inside cats are much safer than outdoor cats.

Shots That Hurt

Despite all their benefits, some of these serums hold rare but potential dangers. Vets have found an association between some shots and cancers located at the vaccination sites called vaccine associated sarcomas (VAS). These rare but deadly cancers start out as a routine swelling at the injection point at the time of the injection. Most of the time the swelling goes down within a few days. However, the sarcoma swelling persists for months and continues to grow. Researchers believe some forms of the rabies and the FeLV vaccines have more incidents of VAS than others. It's believed that the serums containing killed virus and an adjuvant to help boost the immune response may be at the heart of the problem. You can ask your vet to give your cats the modified live rabies and FeLV shots rather than the killed virus containing the adjuvant. If you notice swelling at the shot site a few weeks later, see your vet.

Multicat Diseases and Their Vaccinations

More so than solo kitties, cats in multicat situations face numerous diseases that can devastate your cat population. Most of these diseases can be completely prevented by either vaccinating your cats, keeping them indoors, or both.

Rabies

This always fatal virus most often invades the body through bites or saliva entering a scratch. It attacks the brain of mammals, including cats. Skunks, raccoons, coyotes, bats, and other wildlife most commonly spread it. Presently, feline rabies cases reported in the United States far exceeds cases reported in all other domestic animals. Although rabies can be prevented with vaccinations, it can't be treated once a cat is bitten. These shots are vital especially if your cats go outdoors. It's not just a good idea, it's the law. Most states require all cats and kittens over three months to be vaccinated for rabies by a licensed vet. If your kitten was vaccinated earlier than four months, he'll need a booster within six months.

FELINE FACT OR FICTION

Indoor Cats Don't Need Rabies Shots

That's not necessarily true. According to Dr. Rigoni, in 2006 two people in Houston died after being bitten by bats that were inside the house. If a bat can bite a human, it can bite a cat.

Rabies inoculations contain either the killed virus with the adjuvant, which is certified for three years of protection, or a modified live serum needing annual booster shots. Since the adjuvant has been connected with vaccine-associated sarcomas, you must decide if you want the three-year shot along with a rare chance for the sarcoma or the safer annual shot.

FELINE FACT OR FICTION

Cats Can Get Rabies from Mice and Rats

False. Here's some good news for the mighty little hunters in our midst. The Centers for Disease Control says rats, mice, and other rodents rarely get rabies.

Feline Panleukopenia (FPV)

Panleukopenia, which is also known as feline distemper or FPV, is a very contagious and deadly virus spread from cat to cat by direct contact. It's caused by the feline parvovirus. It targets kittens, sick cats, and unvaccinated cats. Most often, it's spread by infected poop in the litter box. But it's also found in mucous, blood, and saliva lingering on food and water dishes or even on your hands, clothes, or in cat beds. Right out of a 1950s' horror film, the virus is almost indestructible once it enters your home. In survives extreme environmental temperatures and moisture in the home for months and even years. The virus is also resistant to most household disinfectants. You can kill it with a solution of one part bleach to thirty-two parts water. Because of the success of the vaccine, this once-feared disease cat killer has grown uncommon.

It attacks the immune system, bowels, nervous system, and destroys red blood cells. Ninety percent of kittens under six months who get distemper don't make it. Symptoms of FPV include depression, loss of appetite, fever, vomiting, lethargy, and dehydration. Infected cats are often seen hanging over the water dish. In advanced cases, the virus can cause death within hours. As the symptoms are varied, any sick cat should be brought to a veterinarian for diagnosis.

As soon as you suspect a cat may have distemper, isolate him in a clean, warm room free of drafts. According to the American Veterinary Medical Association Web site, a recovering cat needs "plenty of tender loving care" because these cats often "lose the will to live."

The heartbreak and expense connected to a homewide epidemic can be easily and inexpensively avoided by vaccinating your cats. Adult cats only need one shot for protection. After the series of three shots for kittens and a one-year booster, this vaccination can be given every three years. If you have a mega-cat home, you might want to talk to your vet about annual shots.

If there's an outbreak of distemper in your area, keep your cats inside. Wash your hands after handling other people's cats and even when you've been to the pet store to buy cat food.

Feline Infectious Peritonitis (FIP)

Of all the diseases cats and their owners must face, feline infectious peritonitis (FIP) is the most frustrating and frightening. It's a disease without any answers or resolution. For cats suffering from FIP there's no definitive test, no cure, no treatment, and worst of all, no hope. At this time, there's only one possible ending, and unfortunately it doesn't include the words "and they lived happily ever after."

FIP is a progressive disease in the coronavirus family. There are many strains of feline coronaviruses, and FIP starts out as the relatively harmless feline corona virus (FeCV). FeCV is widespread in the cat population, especially in multicat lifestyles. Catteries with dense populations of related cats and multicat homes with more than six unrelated cats have a 100 percent chance of experiencing the harmless FeCV. It's estimated that 80 to 90 percent of all the cats living in a multicat home become infected with FeCV. Cats with a new case of FeCV usually have mild symptoms, if any at all. They might experience sneezing, watery eyes, diarrhea. Usually in a short time, they get over the virus. Unfortunately, a few weeks after the initial infection the virus in a handful of cats will mutate into the lethal strain.

It's really a genetic craps shoot. The cat has to catch FeCV, which mutates into the deadly virus. The cat must also be genetically predisposed *and* stressed *and* a little under the weather. The stress could be going to a new home, getting fixed, an illness, or even a move. The timing has to be right, or wrong, depending on how you look at it: under a year and a half or very old. All the factors have to come together to roll the unlucky snake eyes.

Although the viruses seem like different diseases, FIP comes in two forms: wet and dry. Sometimes a cat may even develop a combination of wet and dry.

Wet FIP, or effusive FIP, is the most lethal form. Cats with this form usually die within a few days or weeks. To fight the invading virus, the body launches a futile defense. Tissue around the blood vessels become inflamed causing the blood vessels to leak. That fluid accumulates in the abdomen or chest. With all that fluid progressively pressing against his lungs and abdomen, each breath becomes a struggle as the cat drowns.

Dry FIP, or noneffusive FIP, has a slower progression and may temporarily respond to supportive care. Instead of accumulating fluid, a cat with this version suffers from weight loss, depression, anemia, ever-present fever, eye inflammation, or neurological problems such as paralysis, unsteady gait, and seizures. He might experience liver or kidney failure, pancreatic disease, or a host of other complications. Vets have a difficult time diagnosing FIP because the symptoms vary from cat to cat, especially in the dry form. Which symptoms he experiences depends on which organs are affected. Diagnosis is further complicated because the symptoms mimic so many diseases, from an upper respiratory infection to irritable bowel disease.

Susan Little, president of the Winn Feline Foundation, calls FIP the "Great Imitator" and the "Great Imposter." Not only do the vague and varied symptoms complicate diagnosing the virus, there are no definitive tests for it. The most common "FIP test" is actually a titre test that looks at the number of corona virus antibodies in the cat's blood. The test doesn't discriminate whether those antibodies are for the harmless FeCV or the deadly FIP. And it can't tell you whether the cat will later develop FIP. Because many vets don't fully understand the corona virus test, never put a cat to sleep based entirely on the corona titres. You can't just look at one aspect. You have to look at the whole picture, said Dr. James Richards, the late director of the Cornell Feline Health Center. Look at the cat's history, clinical signs, the environment, *and* the test. A vet should look at a four-month-old kitten from a cattery with a fever and a big belly full of fluid with a positive titre differently than an eight-year-old solo cat who's been with the same family his whole life.

Because there's no test, cure, or treatment the best you can do is make your cat more comfortable and treat the symptoms as they appear. The vet will drain excess fluid from around the chest and abdomen to ease breathing. Unfortunately, it doesn't stop the progression of the disease.

FELINE FACT OR FICTION

Cats Only Purr When They're Happy

False. Some breeders call FIP "the purring disease" because cats with the disease often purr. That doesn't mean that they're feeling content. Studies have revealed that vibrations between the frequencies of 20 to 140 hertz are therapeutic to help ease difficulty breathing and pain relief. It speeds up fracture healing and reduces swelling. A cat's purr falls within that vibrational range. Rather than being content, the FIP cat may purr to try to relieve pain.

There is a vaccine for FIP, but it's not without its controversy. Some studies show that the intranasal drops protect from 50 to 70 percent of vaccinated cats, but it's never effective in any cat that's already been exposed to FeCV. The manufacturer recommends that kittens receive their first vaccination at sixteen weeks, but most four-month-old kittens from breeders and shelters have already been exposed to the coronavirus. Since it's a waste of money and time to vaccinate the cat for FIP if the cat or kitten has already been exposed to FeCV, you should have your cat titre tested before getting the vaccination. Vets are also concerned because they don't know how long immunity lasts.

There's some good news, though. The current conventional wisdom among the veterinary community is that FIP isn't considered an infectious disease. If a cat dies of FIP, it doesn't necessarily increase the likelihood others will get the disease, especially if they aren't related. It's possible for all the rest of the cats to test positive for the titre but not develop FIP.

The best thing you can do for a cat diagnosed with FIP is provide a safe, stress-free environment, and plenty of love. Steroids can greatly reduce symptoms and discomfort that occur with FIP. Hard as it is to accept, a kitty with FIP won't be around for very long. Since your goal is to keep him comfortable, don't worry about the long-term effects of steroids.

FIP infects susceptible cats and kittens through contact with another infected cat or by indirect contact with the infected saliva, pee, and poop of an infected cat. But poop is the most common source. The best prevention is to keep the place clean, reduce stress around the house, and don't bring in new cats. So keep the litter boxed scooped. Food and water bowls need to be squeaky clean. Feed your kitties well away from the litter boxes.

Follow the one-litter-box-per-cat rule. The virus can survive for weeks caked on a litter box or on a scoop, but can be easily killed by most household detergents and disinfectants. If your cats have a genetic predisposition to FIP, wash your litter box and scoop in a diluted bleach solution. (Don't use stinky pine cleaners or anything with strong scents like Lysol because it may act as a repellent and they're toxic to cats.) The more frequently you remove poop from your cats' environment, the less the chance they will become infected.

Keep your kitties in small groups of fewer than five cats who get along. If you've had the same healthy cats for years and haven't added new kitties to your population, your cats aren't at risk of FIP. The danger comes from introducing a very young or very old cat to the group. Try to decrease your cat population; if that's not possible, try not to increase your numbers. Dr. Richards said the more cats you have, the higher the likelihood of FIP.

Feline Immunodeficiency Virus (FIV)

Feline immunodeficiency virus (FIV) infects victims through a cat bite. It's a retrovirus that belongs to the *Lentivirus* family of viruses known for their life-long infection and slow progression. Even though it's part of the same virus family as human immunodeficiency virus (HIV), FIV is species specific. Neither you nor the family dog can catch it.

The virus is found in all body fluids, but the saliva is teeming with it. Most cats get FIV from a bite wound during a cat fight when it can actually be injected into the cat's system. Unlike other killer cat diseases adults, not kittens, are at high risk.

Theoretically it's possible for mothers to pass it on to their kittens, and through casual contact like sharing food bowls and grooming other cats, this rarely happens. If your cat is diagnosed with FIV, that should put an end to his days as an unattended outdoor cat. Leaving him outside puts other neighborhood cats at risk of becoming infected with FIV. Also, in his weakened state, he could easily catch secondary infections, diseases, and parasites from other cats that can further wear down his immune system. With your protection he can live for many years with FIV.

FIV is known as the disease of angry cats, because it's passed from one cat to another by deep cat bites, usually in the passion of tomcat battles. That's why most of its victims are unneutered males from three to five years on the prowl for a good time. FIV is an entirely preventable disease. All you have to do is keep your cats inside and don't permit cat fights.

This retrovirus contains an enzyme that inserts its genetic material into the cat's DNA. It invades the disease-fighting white blood cells, which normally act as the body's first defense against disease. However, these altered cells hitch a ride via the lymphatic superhighway throughout the cat's body where they are either stored or replicated into white blood cells with FIV DNA. When the infected cells reproduce, they copy the corrupted cells.

The virus further challenges the immune system because it mutates. So the body must constantly produce new antibodies to fight each new version of the disease. Over time, the cat's population of healthy white blood cells decreases, leaving him vulnerable to bacteria, disease organisms, and other viruses. Infected cats often die from the secondary infections rather than from the virus itself.

When he's first infected, the cat may have swollen lymph nodes, but he might not show symptoms for many years. In the early stage, some cats get fever, anemia, or diarrhea. The virus slowly depresses the immune system, which leads to a wide variety of health problems. FIV kitties may show a wide range of reoccurring symptoms, but the most common are chronic gum inflammation, weight loss, upper respiratory infections, diarrhea, and recurring skin infections.

With the immune system weakened, other chronic problems may plague the infected cat, such as pneumonia, skin disease, sinus infections, urinary tract infections, eye inflammation, and cancers, especially lymphoma.

Some FIV cats may have long bouts of good health between setbacks from opportunistic illnesses. Healthy periods will decrease as the disease progresses and the cat's immune system is challenged by repeated illness. Eventually the cat will lose his fight, not to FIV directly, but to these secondary infections.

Outdoor cats with gingivitis or unexplained chronic symptoms are suspects of having FIV. Your vet can use an in-office test to detect FIV antibodies in the blood. If that shows positive, your vet can send a blood sample off to a lab for a confirmation test called Western blot. Vets consider the results of this test definitive. The American Association of Feline Practitioners (AAFP) recommends that owners test their outside and at risk cats for both FIV and FeLV annually.

There is a vaccine for FIV and even though it's shown to be effective, there is a problem with it. Since the vaccine stimulates antibodies, the cat will test positive for FIV antibodies for the rest of his life. Unfortunately, there are no tests that distinguish vaccine antibodies from the actual disease. Before you have a cat vaccinated, have him tested. After he's received the vaccination, there won't be any way to tell whether the cat is just testing positive for FIV antibodies or if he really has the disease.

The vaccine may prove helpful to protect high-risk groups of cats. One thing to consider: if your cat becomes lost and is rescued, he might be euthanized on the suspicion of having the virus. (Microchipping your cat and registering the information through a national database should protect him.)

You vet may stimulate your cat's immune system with a number of immune-stimulating medications, including interferon alpha.

FIV isn't the death sentence that FIP or even FeLV is. Properly cared for, positive cats may live for many months or even years. After being diagnosed with FIV, the average cat lives five years.

My husband rescued a seven-year-old stray tomcat. At ten years old, Goofus developed gingivitis and tested positive for FIV. Eventually we had to have all his teeth removed because of the chronic gum disease, but he lived to be nineteen—more than twelve years after he contracted the virus.

Dr. Little says that in a stable household it's not necessary to isolate an FIV cat unless he's likely to fight with the other cats in the house. It's almost impossible for an exclusively indoor cat to get FIV unless he lives with a biting housemate. The virus is so fragile it can't live outside the cat's body. However, if the cat is combative and has a tendency to bite your other cats, you may need to give him a suite of his own.

Feline Leukemia Virus (FeLV)

Feline leukemia virus (FeLV), another retrovirus, is a serious problem in multicat households. Like FIV, FeLV implants its own DNA into the host's cells. When the cells reproduce, the virus also reproduces. As the disease advances and the immune system slowly fails, the cat gradually loses the ability to fight off infections.

This virus is known as the "disease of friendly cats." Infection usually occurs after repeated exposure. Cats can transmit or *shed* the virus in bodily fluids. They pass it from one cat to another through communal grooming and bites, but also through food bowls and shared litter boxes. Moms can pass it to their kittens via milk and the umbilical cord. Researchers believe that it takes pro-longed or repeated exposure to pass the virus around, because the virus dies quickly outside the body.

About a third of cats exposed to FeLV actually get the virus and die. An infected cat showing symptoms can live from several weeks to several months, depending on how far the virus has advanced before diagnosis. Another one-third of exposed cats don't *seem* to be affected; the virus lies dormant in their bodies until months or even years later until stress to the immune system trig-gers an outbreak. And the final third of cats can actually fight off the disease.

The final third show no symptoms at all, but like Typhoid Mary, these cats can shed the virus, exposing companion cats to danger.

The initial symptoms are subtle and include an unkempt coat, fever, swollen lymph nodes, lack of energy, and anemia. More advanced symptoms of FeLV are varied and often confusing and can include upper respiratory infections, weight loss, decreased appetite, diarrhea or constipation, bloody poop, swollen lymph glands, jaundice, drinking a lot of water, peeing a lot, and no energy. Because of their compromised immune system, some cats develop cancer.

Kittens are most susceptible. The chance of a cat getting FeLV decreases with age. Older cats are more resistant and may have milder symptoms. But it's a losing battle. They often die of secondary infections and diseases.

If one of your cats is diagnosed with FeLV, you need to take precautions to protect your other kitties. FeLV vaccinations can give you a high degree of com-fort, but they haven't been proven to be 100 percent effective. So there's still a risk.

Dr. Richards said the only way to protect your cats 100 percent is to pre-vent them from being exposed. Keep them inside and don't bring potentially positive cats into the house.

Four tests show the evidence of the virus at different stages. Your vet can test for the disease in under twenty minutes using an in-office ELISA antigen blood test. It can show positive results just twenty-eight days after exposure. But since one-third of new exposures can be defeated, it's possible for the cat's immune system to fight off the infection and later retest negative. I've had this happen. If the ELISA test shows positive for FeLV antibodies, wait another sixty days and request an IFA test, which is sent off to a lab. This test shows positive only in the later stages of the infection. You can also also request a Western Blot antigen test. It's considered a more definitive test. At-home saliva tests aren't considered reliable.

To protect your kitties, have any new cats tested before you bring them home. If one of your cats recently died of FeLV, you'll want to have your whole herd tested and get FeLV shots. Fortunately, FeLV can't survive in the environment. The FeLV virus clinging to your carpet can only survive for thirty days. To protect other cats against FeLV, scrub everything down with a cup of bleach to a gallon of water. Wash beds with bleach, wash bowls in a dishwasher with hot water, and throw away all the old litter pans.

You and your dog have nothing to worry about. No human or dog has ever caught FeLV.

Chlamydia

This feline pneumonia is caused by chlamydia bacteria, which causes mild to serious nasal discharge, sneezing, and conjunctivitis. It moves through a home directly from cat to cat, usually affecting kittens between five weeks and nine months. This bug thrives in multicat homes. While chlamydia vaccinations don't protect a cat from getting the infection, the symptoms aren't as severe. It's more common for cats receiving the chlamydia shot to experience mild reactions, but they can be treated. This vaccination is recommended for multiple-cat homes where a case of chlamydia has been confirmed.

Feline Herpesvirus (FHV) and Feline Calicivirus (FCV)

Combined, feline herpesvirus (FHV, also called rhinotracheitis), and feline calicivirus (FCV) cause 80 to 90 percent of all upper respiratory tract diseases. Most cats will come in contact with either or both viruses at some point in their lives. These kitty colds aren't usually serious in adult cats, but may sometimes be fatal in kittens. Sneezing, runny eyes, runny nose, and fever show up with the virus. In addition to respiratory symptoms, sore joints (which may make walking painful) and mouth ulcers occur with calici. For many cats, once they get these viruses, they never completely get over it. While they can remain snotters for life, it's not the end of the world.

Contrary to popular belief, cats usually spread FHV through direct cat-to-cat contact rather than from sneezing, since sneezed droplets only travel about three feet. After being exposed to snot and saliva containing FHV, infected cats can shed it for several weeks, and possibly for the rest of their lives. Just as there is no cure for the human cold, there's no cure for feline herpes and calici.

Pesky secondary upper respiratory infections can last for days or for weeks. If you don't isolate the sick cat, every one of them will come down with it. Vets treat the secondary sinus and bronchial infections with broad-spectrum antibiotics. As needed, they also prescribe eye ointment and subcutaneous fluids. Since cats can't take decongestants, set up a vaporizer with Vick's VapoSteam to help loosen the mucous. If he's really stopped up, you can try to get some saline drops up his nose to loosen the crud blocking his nasal passages. Make sure it's saline only without any decongestant or antihistamine additives. Just put one drop in each nostril and then get out of the way. When he's mouth breathing, it's OK to use drops six times a day—that's *if* you can get them in. The trick is getting the cat to hold still long enough to get the drop up his nose. Also the amino acid l-lysine helps limit the duration of the virus. Occasional outbreaks can be reduced by giving herpes kitties with 250 to 500 mg a day. I put it in turkey baby food. Make sure the lysine does not contain the preservative propylene glycol.

A newcomer on the scene, *virulent systemic feline calicivirus* (VS-FCV), tells a different story. Dr. Richards said there are a gazillion strains of calicivirus. But a newly recognized disease caused by a mutated calicivirus has vets shaking their heads and washing their hands. Unlike the kinder, gentler old calici, this new virus has dire consequences. In reported cases, vets have lost a shocking 50 percent of their *healthy adult* patients with this form of the virus. The standard three-way vaccine doesn't protect cats against this new threat.

A vaccine is now available for the new virus, although it's not clear how much protection cats will get from it. Dr. Richards said the serum contains two caliciviruses. The vaccine is so new, vets don't really know the degree to which cats are going to be protected. It won't protect completely against infection, but vaccinated cats shouldn't get as sick as nonvaccinated cats. AAFP highly recommends this vaccine for all cats.

With the new strain, isolation and hygiene are vital. Vets say it's so contagious that it can be passed by an owner touching a contaminated doorknob or keyboard. You can help curb the spread of feline herpes and calici by keeping food dishes clean and changing the water frequently.

FLUTD

Feline lower urinary tract disease (FLUTD) used to be called feline urologic syndrome (FUS), a catchall phrase for several ailments of the lower urinary tract. Regardless of the cause, it hurts to go to the bathroom. Kilroy may start going outside the box, go repeatedly, attempt to go but passes no pee, pees blood, or cries out when he tries to go. He may repeatedly lick his private parts. It can be caused by bladder stones or crystals, infection, or obstruction.

Bladder stones are crystals that form in the bladder and cause inflammation of the bladder and the urethra. Overall, it's a serious and painful condition. These crystals can mingle with minerals, mucus, and other debris to form plugs that block the urethra. These obstructions keep pee from passing. Untreated, a healthy cat can die in just two days. A cat with kidney disease can only last half that time. Your vet has to anesthetize your cat to insert a catheter up the urethra and into the bladder. The tube will permit the pee to flow again. He'll also be given antibiotics and fluids. In some cases surgery is required to change Uncle Charlie into Aunt Charlene. Obstructions occur far more often in males than in females.

It was once thought that too much ash and magnesium in cat food caused bladder crystals, but now it's believed their formation is tied into the pH of the pet food. Talk to your vet about the best diet to feed your cat and which ones to avoid.

Bladder infections can be caused by bacteria, fungus, virus, or can be a result of crystals.

Because of their desert roots, cats don't drink much water. A wild cat gets water from his prey, but cats who eat dry food could have a problem with dehydration. Make sure your cats have fresh, clean water at all times. Water dilutes the concentration of the pee and reduces the chance that crystals will form.

One way to encourage your cats to drink more is with a kitty drinking fountain. The 🐾 **Drinkwell Platinum** is a pet fountain large enough for a multicat home.

Prevention and Home Monitoring

Having a megacat household or even multiple cats can run into big bucks when you start facing vet bills especially if you have to use a shotgun approach to find out who's sick. There are some ways you can cut down on vet bills and improve your cats' quality of care. Home monitoring of urine pH and for the presence of blood may be performed with urine dipsticks after urine has been collected from the litter box.

You can do this by isolating your suspect and replacing the cat litter with aquarium gravel or the perforated strips from computer paper. Because these don't absorb cat pee you can use urine testing papers or granules to check for pH, blood, or glucose. You can do a quick in-home test to check the pee for the presence of blood, crystals, or glucose with 🐾 **KittyCheck**, a litter additive. They're covered in the Shopping Guide.

Diarrhea

Diarrhea is a technical term for watery poop without a specific cause. It's especially a problem for kittens because kittens are so small they become dehydrated very quickly. In adults, it's nasty and stinky, but it's also a sign that something's amiss.

If it lasts for more than a day or two, call your vet and find out if she wants a poo sample or if she wants to see the real deal. Take Kilroy in right away if he's also vomiting, lethargic, or if you see blood in the poop. If he's not eating, that's another clue that you could have something serious in the works. Causes of diarrhea range from the routine (parasites, infection, lack of gut bacteria, poor-quality diet) to life threatening (intestinal blockage or cancer). Your vet will try to read your cat's poo like a fortune teller reads tea leaves. Sometimes those protozoa or worm eggs hide from the microscope, so don't be surprised if your vet can't eyeball them. If he finds a protozoa such as *coccidia* or *giardia*, he'll give your cat some yucky-tasting medicine like Albon. For worms, Strongid or

Panacur often does the trick. Keep reading to learn about the flea preventatives that also fight some internal parasites.

Don't give your cats an over-the-counter diarrhea remedy for humans unless your vet tells you to. Both Pepto-Bismol and Kaopectate contain salicylate, which is the active ingredient in aspirin. Several years ago, the manufacturer of Kaopectate changed its formula, so the older reference books that say it is safe are incorrect.

Hairballs

You've most likely seen the bumper sticker that reads: THE ONLY SELF-CLEANING THING IN MY HOUSE IS THE CAT. Your cats' fastidious nature is one of the reasons you love them, but you probably loathe those seasonal land mines you find with bare feet in the dark.

Your kitties spend most of their day grooming the loose hair from their coats. Once the fur becomes trapped on that barbed tongue, it has to go all the way through the cat's body. As the hair makes its way through the digestive tract, it winds itself into a tight little tube. In small quantities, it causes no problems. If too much hair accumulates, the hairball won't be able to pass through the pyloric sphincter (the valve that controls food leaving the stomach and going into the large intestine). Eventually, the cat vomits the mass and leaves it as a gastronomical land mine.

When you find that disgusting puddle on the floor, your first impulse is to grab a tube of hairball remedy. Distinguishing between hairballs and actual "coughing" or chronic vomiting can be sometimes quite challenging. If you eyeball that tube-shaped wad of hair, it's probably a hairball problem. If your cat vomits repeatedly, pukes up blood, or it's coming out of both ends, take him to the veterinarian.

The most effective and easiest way to control hairballs is to groom your cat frequently. In case you can't keep up with your cat's shedding, petroleum-based hairball remedies are available over the counter for occasional hairball relief. Don't use them to treat persistent vomiting. They hinder the absorption of fat-soluble vitamins, so don't give them to your cats an hour before or after eating.

Human Medications You Should *Never* Give Your Cats

- acetaminophen (Tylenol)
- aspirin
- calcipotriene
- Fleet Enema
- ibuprofen (Advil)
- isopropyl alcohol (skin lotions, hair tonics, aftershave)
- Kaopectate
- ketoprofen (arthritis relief medication)
- topical painkillers; ointments, creams, and sprays with "caine" in the ingredients: lidocaine, benzocaine, dibucaine
- ma huang/pseudoephedrine/ephedrine
- other pain relievers: naproxen, nabumetone, indomethacin, diclofenac, carprofen, piroxicam
- Pepto-Bismol

Isolation

Now that you've determined who is sick, you must decide what to do about it. Sequester cats as soon as you notice sneezing or runny poop. A spare bathroom or bedroom can double as an infirmary. You have no guarantee that the entire herd won't still catch it.

Your central air conditioner may be efficiently circulating those airborne germs before you even realize you have them. But you could reduce some of the particles with a HEPA air filter in the sick room. Also a strict regime of hand washing with antibacterial soap will help prevent the spreading disease to your other cats. Some people also use ultraviolet lights to kill germs.

Dr. Cindy Rigoni says that isolation is like shutting the barn door after the horse has gotten out. As one of the smaller predators, a cat can't appear sick for fear a coyote will get him. So he's busy passing germs back and forth to your healthy cats before he ever shows symptoms. If the kitties are playing footsie under the door you can't win.

REALITY BITES

In a perfect world, you would be able to brush all of your cats' teeth daily. But not everyone has an ideal situation. If you have a cat that won't tolerate handling, you can't find time to brush everyone's teeth, or you manage a feral colony, try water additives. Dr. Bonnie Shope, who runs the dental service at Tufts University of Veterinary Medicine said there have been no scientific studies on their effectiveness, but the benefits have been anecdotal. She said ascorbic acid and zinc are good ingredients, although not as good as brushing. Zinc and ascorbic acid help with healing the gums. The water additives don't work with filtered drinking fountains. If you give dental treats, look to see if the product has the Veterinary Oral Health Council Seal of Acceptance.

With This Ringworm ...

Even though it's called ringworm, it isn't a worm. It's a fungus related to athlete's foot and it's the most common skin condition in cats. It's highly contagious and neither you nor your family are exempt from these circular mementos. You've got to get some effective treatment or everyone in the house could wind up scratching. Treatment must be effective or it will continue to spread.

This pesky skin condition sits on top of the cat's skin and affects only the hair and hair follicle. Cats don't usually show other symptoms except for scaly skin, hair, and itching. Fortunately, this ring is not an "until death do us part" situation. It's a self-limiting infection that takes between one and six weeks after exposure to show up. But within two to four months, healthy cats and kittens should build up an immunity to it. However, there is evidence that some cats (usually Persians) can still carry the disease for five years without symptoms.

You're most likely to find ringworm in multicat homes and shelters, on strays and feral cats, very young kittens, and old and sick cats. Persians, especially Himalayans, seem to be more susceptible to it than other breeds. Your cats can get it directly from another cat, or you can bestow it on them after you've handled an infected animal. You can even get it from your garden, or the roses sent by an admirer because it lives naturally in the dirt.

Lord of the Ringworm.

About half of the cases of ringworm can be detected in a darkened room with the same ultraviolet light that helps you find cat pee. It'll glow bright apple green. Just because it doesn't glow doesn't mean you or your cats are off the hook yet. Some strains don't show up under the black light, so your vet may have to get a skin scraping for a culture. Under ideal conditions, the fungus among us can survive in the house for up to eighteen months. Make sure you wash your hands after handling an infected animal. If your cats have ringworm, vacuum their favorite hangouts and wash bedding with bleach.

An injectable ringworm vaccine is available for treatment and suppression. While it doesn't appear to be highly effective against the disease, the vaccine may be helpful in multicat households where ringworm has been a problem. But the cats can still be asymptomatic carriers. Also ask your vet about treating ringworm with the flea preventative program

Fleas-ing the Cats

The little buggers do more than constantly torment your cats; they'll infect them with tapeworms and can cause anemia, allergic dermatitis, and transmit a number of serious diseases. Let us not forget the fleas that took out a third of the European population in the Middle Ages.

A new generation of products has taken the bite and scratch out of flea control for cats and humans. Easy-to-apply monthly insecticides containing

---

REALITY BITES

Sharing Parasites

Parasites suck. Yes, they do. Some of them suck nutrition directly from cats' intestinal tract. Others suck blood, like a low-level Bela Lugosi. At any given time your poor cats can have countless unwelcome hitchhikers on or in them.

Parasites and fungus are social diseases of sorts. Certainly a solo cat can suffer from any of them. But these bugs are just looking for a free lunch and your cats have "meal" written all over them. Unfortunately, with most parasites and fungi you'll need to treat all your cats because often if one has it, they all have it. Keeping your cats inside will greatly cut down on their passengers.

Fortunately, unlike the old days when you had flea powder, ear mite drops, and several different internal wormers, today we have one-stop bug-icide. Your vet can prescribe topical medications that will take care of fleas, ear mites, and intestinal parasites (except for tapeworms). Some even prevent heartworms if the cat is on the preventive before an infected mosquito bites him.

---

longer-acting insect growth regulators (IGR) kill eggs and larvae and break the reproduction cycle. However, your cat needs constant protection. If you lapse by even twenty-four hours, fleas have a chance to lay more eggs and start the nasty cycle again. Halting continued viable egg production consistently is the key to preventing persistent infestations—and consequently insecticide-resistant fleas, says Dr. Michael Dryden, professor of veterinary parasitology at the College of Veterinary Medicine at Kansas State University. He knows because he's tried them all in controlled and independently financed studies.

Contrary to popular myth, fleas don't spend most of their three-week lifetime in the carpet. They stay on their meals-on-paws full-time to feed, breed, and lay eggs, says Dr. Dryden. After just a few minutes of arriving at their new home, they begin feasting like miniature vampires. Within twenty-four to forty-eight hours, each female will begin laying forty to fifty eggs a day. So by the time you notice fleas on your cat, he has a thriving population of eggs residing in his fur.

An important part of any flea control program is to physically remove eggs and the larvae. So each week wash flea magnets, like such as kitty's bed, blankets, area rugs, and his carrier and cushions after he goes for a ride. Thoroughly vacuum his favorite places. Don't forget to take the cushions off your couch and chairs so you can vacuum the eggs that accumulate underneath. After each use, throw your vacuum cleaner bags into an outside trash can, otherwise the eggs will hatch and you'll spread them through the house as you vacuum. Hard flooring should be mopped because fleas may develop in cracks and crevices.

If you use traditional products without IGRs, you will need to treat the shady areas of your yard. Fleas thrive in dark, moist places, so pick up leaves and clippings. Don't forget to treat areas like the garage or basement if your cat spends time there. Before deciding on a flea treatment, talk to your veterinarian.

REALITY BITES

According to Michael Dryden, several of these new insecticides and IGRs have been shown to be extremely effective in eliminating flea infestations in even the most flea-friendly environment. Studies have demonstrated that regular administration of 🐾 **Frontline, Advantage, Program, Capstar,** and **Revolution** eliminated established flea populations within sixty to ninety days without the need to treat the premises. Most insecticides, including 🐾 **Revolution, Frontline, Advantage,** and **Capstar,** effectively eliminate existing fleas from dogs and cats within four to twenty-four hours after application. These products are effective because they kill the fleas before they can lay eggs or they make the eggs unviable.

😺 **Revolution** (selamectin) is a monthly systemic topical treatment that kills adult flea and eggs. This is one of the most expensive treatments, but it is also labeled to control heartworms, roundworms, ear mites, hookworms, some mange mites, and ticks in cats. Dr. Dryden says Revolution provides the greatest residual adulticidal activity on fleas on cats. It can be used on kittens eight weeks and older. Get it from your vet.

😺 **Advantage Multi for Cats** (imidacloprid and moxidectin) is a monthly topical and systemic flea control that is effective in preventing heartworms, hookworms, roundworms, and ear mites. It kills both adults and flea larvae. It's considered safe for kittens who weigh at least two pounds. In severe infestations talk to your vet about possibly applying it every three weeks. It shouldn't be used on sick or debilitated cats. Bathing *does* compromise the imidacloprid. You can get this from your vet.

😺 **Program** (luferuron), an insect development inhibitor, is an oral liquid suspension that should be given *with food* monthly. It won't kill existing flea infestations or stop your cat from being bitten. Instead it prevents flea eggs from developing, interrupting the reproduction cycle. This is a long-term solution. An adulticide should be used for the first few weeks to provide the cat with immediate relief. All pets in the home must be treated for Program to be effective. According to Dr. Dryden it is two hundred times safer for animals than insecticides. It is also used to treat ringworm.

😺 **Frontline Plus** (fipronil-methoprene) is another spot-on applied monthly between the shoulder blades. It is not systemic, instead it mixes with the oils in your cat's skin and settles into the sebaceous glands. It's labeled for treatment of ticks on cats. It kills all life stages of fleas and brown dog ticks, American dog ticks, lone star ticks, deer ticks, and it kills chewing lice. Some vets also use it for ear mites. Frontline Plus is labeled safe to use on any cat eight weeks and older, as well as on breeding, pregnant, and lactating queens. Frontline Plus is available over the counter.

😺 **Advantage** (imidacloprid) kills both adult fleas and larvae. One treatment prevents infestations for up to four weeks. The product is not systemic, rather it settles in sebaceous glands. Don't use Advantage on kittens under eight weeks of age. Talk to your veterinarian before using Advantage on medicated animals or with other pesticides, and on debilitated, aged, pregnant or nursing animals. This is available over the counter.

REALITY BITES

Monthly flea control for four or fourteen cats can set you back a lot of nickels. An off-label application might help you afford flea and/or heartworm treatment for all of your cats. This is off-label and not recommended by the manufacturers so talk to your vet before you use these products on your kitties. Rather than buying ten packets of individual tubes of Revolution, Frontline, or Advantage, you can purchase packets for large dogs and adjust the doses down for cats. Presently, these are the only three "dog" products that are safe for use on cats. Your vet can give you a medicine bottle to pour the contents into a 1 cc syringe for measuring. Before you start, mark the 0.4 cc and 0.8 cc line in tape because the oil in the solutions will take the numbers right off the plastic. You can treat your herd for a fraction of what the individual cat tubes cost. (*Don't confuse Advantage with the dog-only K-9 Advantix.*) For leftovers: put the top on the medicine bottle and store it in a cool, dry place. You can use it next month.

Revolution:
0.125 cc for cats up to five pounds
0.375 for cats 5.1 to 15 pounds

Advantage:
Under nine pounds, use 0.4 ml between the shoulder blades.

Nine pounds and up, use 0.8 ml

Frontline for the extra-large dog (89 to 132 pounds):
For all cats, use 0.5 ml

Even though these products contain the same ingredients as cat products, don't use them on your cats without first talking to your vet.

⊛ **Capstar** (nitenpyram) is a small pill that starts killing adult fleas within twenty minutes and wipes out the entire population within hours. It won't affect eggs or larvae. But it gives cats almost immediate relief for twenty-four hours. As soon as eggs and larvae emerge, the cycle will start over. Get this from your vet.

It was once thought that cats were just little dogs, and anything that was safe for dogs was also OK for cats. But as an understanding of feline physiology increased, vets learned that thinking was dead wrong. While they do share some commonalities (four legs, whiskers, and usually a tail), to slightly rephrase an old saying, what is good for the dog, may not be good for the feline. This couldn't be truer than for flea control. And even though dogs and cats share Ctenocephalides felis, or the cat flea, sharing canine flea treatment with your cat could be *lethal!*

Before you give your cat any flea treatment, check the label carefully. Never use a flea or tick product on your cat unless it specifically states that it is safe to use on cats. And under no circumstances should you use a dogs-only product on a cat. Some of these products contain permethrin, a synthetic pyrethrum that is highly toxic to cats. Always read and use products according to label directions. Pay attention to warnings about aging, pregnant, or nursing cats and young kittens. As a precaution if you have dogs, give the label a last-minute glance before putting a flea product on your cats. Even a few drops of Fido's flea treatment can be fatal to cats. So if you have a blended home, and especially if your cats and dogs play or sleep together, go an extra step and use cat-safe flea control products on your pooch too. As mistakes do sometimes happen, if you accidentally use the dog's flea remedy on your cat, contact your vet or the ASPCA/APCC at once.

Ticks

If you have cats who explore brushy areas, they may bring home some unwelcome guests. Ticks are more than just bloodsuckers. They harbor a number of serious diseases that threaten not only your cats, but you as well. So it's important to remove them as soon as you find them. Of all the flea treatments Frontline Plus and Revolution are the only topicals labeled to kill ticks on cats.

To remove a tick from your cat, wear gloves and use tweezers. Get the tweezers as close to the cat's skin as you can. Pull straight out slowly, and the mouth should release. Don't twist the tick or the mouth will break off. Don't crush it between your fingers. Ticks can even survive being flushed down the toilet. Drop it in alcohol to kill it.

If you break off the tick's head, you might need to take your cat to the vet because the tick's saliva contains the virulent matter. The site could become infected or he could develop a number of diseases including Lyme disease and Rocky Mountain spotted fever. Wash your hands after handling ticks because you can catch these diseases too.

Ear Mites

If you notice your cats shaking their heads and scratching in their ears, take a quick peek. Black gunk that looks like coffee grounds in the ear usually means he's probably got a healthy crop of ear mites in there.

Ear mites are pencil-point-size parasites that live and breed inside the ear canals primarily of dogs and cats. Your veterinarian can verify the diagnosis by taking a look at the black stuff under a microscope.

Infestation by ear mites is also a social disease. Your cats get them from close contact with other animals, then pass them back and forth between each other. If you have outdoor cats, chances are they associate with other cats. Even a cat fight gives the little beasties an opportunity to jump ship and infect your pets.

A gentle ear cleaning is the first step to making your cats mitey free. If you see a lot of wax or debris, squirt five drops of mineral oil into the ear and massage the base of the ear for fifteen to twenty seconds and then let the cat shake the gunk out of his ears. Wipe out any remaining debris with a cotton ball. Ear mites can't live in oil, but a one-time cleaning won't do the job because it won't affect the eggs. Also putting cat-safe flea powder on the tail helps. The mites get on the tail when the cat curls up to sleep. Untreated cats can develop painful ear infections or even deafness from ear mites. If you notice an odor or drainage coming from the ear, take him to the vet. He has something else going on.

Internal Parasites

In a multicat home cats share litter boxes, food bowls, and even internal parasites. Newer flea treatments can certainly aid with the eradication of worms, but if your cats aren't on those programs, here's some information you'll find helpful.

Measuring Up to Tapeworms

Everyone loves a party and fleas are no exception. After they feast on your cats' blood, they leave uninvited guests like tapeworms behind. A cat grooming himself swallows flea dirt containing tapeworm eggs. In the cat's intestines, the tapeworms hatch and set up housekeeping. At the same time, they're robbing your cat of nourishment. A fat, happy tapeworm can grow up to six inches long or longer. Each of these large worms is actually made of lots of little segments that hold eggs. The segments break off and the cat poops them into the box. Fortunately, cats can't get tapeworms from each other. But you won't be able to get rid of them until you evict their topside buddy, the flea. Unlike other worms, your vet won't need a poo sample. Tapeworms look like dried white or yellow rice clinging to the fur around the cat's bottom. Cats with a severe tape infestation could have weight loss, diarrhea, abdominal pain, and increased appetite.

Parasite control begins with good sanitation procedures. This includes daily removal of poop and washing the litter box with a disinfectant on a regular basis. (Use one cup of chlorine bleach in a gallon of water. Rinse well and allow the box to dry before letting your cat use it.) Steam cleaning also kills organisms on the box. Avoid overcrowded conditions, diets with raw meats, and control intermediate hosts (fleas, ticks, and rodents).

If you're not using Revolution or Multi Advantage, it's not uncommon for parasites (other than tapeworms) to reappear. (These treatments don't affect tapeworms, but they kill fleas and prevent further infestations.) Over-the-counter tapeworm treatments don't work very well. Save yourself some time and get something like 🐾 **Droncit** or 🐾 **Drontal** from your vet and kill those worms.

A Knockout Round with Roundworms

Roundworms are one of the most common internal parasites in cats. Kittens can get them directly from their mum's milk. Adult cats get them from ingesting contaminated poop in the litter box or on the ground. They also come from prey like mice, roaches, earthworms, and birds. Even the family dog's poop could be a carrier. The larvae set up shop in the cat's intestinal tract where they can grow up to five inches long and they lay eggs of their own. The eggs are pooped into the litter box or grass and they infect another animal. The eggs don't have to be eaten today. They can sit in the grass for years. When a cat gets the eggs on his paws, then grooms himself, the cycle starts over. Isn't nature beautiful? This is where it gets gross. When the eggs hatch, the microscopic larvae migrate through the intestines and around the body until they get into the lungs where they're coughed up and swallowed to once again end up in the intestinal tract.

Your vet will want a poop sample. After mixing the poo with a special solution, eggs float to the top where they're visible under a microscope.

She'll give you enough worming medication (called an anthelmintic) for all of your cats. Because the treatment doesn't kill larvae and eggs, you need at least two or three treatments at two- or three-week intervals.

When you've treated all your cats (and the dog), clean the litter boxes with a diluted bleach solution (one cup bleach to a gallon of water). Rinse it well to wash off all the bleach. If you used clumping litter, toss out all the old litter. Clean up all of the outside dog and cat poop, otherwise viable eggs can hang out in your yard for years. You can track the eggs that are on your shoes onto your floor.

Unhooking Hookworms

Roundworms steal your cats' groceries, but hookworms steal his blood. As with fleas and ticks, the nasty little bloodsuckers can almost suck a kitten dry. When their hooklike mouths attach to the intestinal walls, it's open bar and all the blood they can drink—no limit. When one area of the intestine dries up, the hookworm moves leaving behind a couple of tiny holes that bleed. Hookworms can grow no larger than a half inch long. With a life span of up to eight years, they *could* outlive your cat.

Kittens become infected by nursing from their mother's milk. Adults can become infected by larvae that penetrate their skin or possibly by eating infected rodents. Once on the inside, hookworms migrate through the body to the lungs and then to the intestines to develop into adult worms.

These vampires are more than just a hitchhiker. They can cause anemia from blood loss where they hook into the intestines. Infected cats may puke blood. They also suffer from constipation; dark brown, black, or bloody poop; anemia; or weight loss. Bloody poop will actually look black and tarry. Left untreated, even an adult cat can lose enough blood to become anemic and die. The good news is, they're easily diagnosed and treated. Keep litter boxes scooped daily to help control hookworms. *You* can get hookworms by careless poop handling or by walking barefooted in an infected area. Always wear your shoes if you're walking in an area that cats or dogs use as a restroom.

Showing Some Heartworms

Heartworms aren't just for dogs anymore. Heartworms affect cats differently than dogs, but the disease they cause is equally serious. Cats get them from the bite of an infected mosquito. Unfortunately, just because your cats live inside only doesn't mean they aren't at risk. After all, mosquitoes do sneak past an opened door occasionally. In a North Carolina study, 28 percent of the cats diagnosed with heartworm were inside-only cats.

Heartworm disease causes significant lung disease in cats, said Dr. Richards. "Many cats infected with heartworms don't exhibit any signs. Very tragically, the first sign of the disease is that the cat suddenly dies. That can happen with only one heartworm. It is a very serious disease, but also, very preventable."

Mosquitoes pick up larvae when they feed on an infected animal. Later, while the mosquito enjoys a feast of cabernet catus, it injects the heartworm larvae into the cat's blood. Over the next few weeks, the larvae travel to the heart and pulmonary arteries where they cause swelling of the blood vessels. Symptoms can start showing up with the presence of a single heartworm.

They may be call heartworms, but in cats they mostly affect the lungs. Vets frequently mistake the symptoms (coughing, difficulty breathing, exhaustion, puking and loss of appetite) for asthma and other respiratory diseases. Heartworm cats can also experience blood clots in the lungs. New research shows that heartworm larvae at all stages, not just adult worms, can cause serious health problems.

The vet can run an in-office feline heartworm antigen test in just a few minutes. But the test isn't foolproof either, because the antigen must come from a female worm. It won't detect male worms. As with FIP, vets have to look at the big picture to diagnose heartworms in cats.

Heartworm dogs can be given medicine to kill the parasites. When this treatment has been given to cats, the dead heartworms circulating in the blood are deadlier than the infection. While not a cure, vets use steroids to reduce inflammation and asthma inhalers to make breathing easier. This treatment usually allows the heartworms to die naturally in about three years.

As with so many other kitty health issues, prevention is the best treatment. Revolution, Advantage Multi, Heartguard for Cats, all contain heartworm preventive.

Toxoplasmosis and Pregnancy

Toxoplasmosis is an organism that can infect your cat and has been a great concern to pregnant women. Fortunately, the CDC has announced that you don't have to get rid of your cats. Simply practice good hygiene. Bottom line—clean your box daily, and don't eat cat poop. Wash you hands thoroughly after cleaning cat boxes. And take care when handling raw meat. The full truth and nothing but the truth about toxoplasmosis is in the chapter "Everything You Wanted to Know about the Litter Box, But Were Afraid to Ask."

Who Dun It?

Land mines happen. If they happen more than just occasionally, you need to figure out who is doing it and get him to a vet. The state of your cats' health is based largely on the four Ps: poop, pee, puke, and prevention. The fact that someone is feeling poopy may come to light when you step in something squishy.

While those bodily deposits could be nothing more than a seasonal hairball, they could also be yet to be discovered health issues like kidney disease or cancer. Talk to your vet.

If you have two cats it's easy to figure out whose fluid it once was. As you add kitties to the mix, it becomes exponentially more difficult. After all, cats don't leave their signature. Or do they? It's time for CSI–Special Kitty Puke Unit. Often figuring out who's minding their p's and q's is simply knowing your cats. When cats throw up, they may not leave their signature, but they often use the same modus operandi. Of course, it is best to actually witness the crime, but some breeders can tell who's sick just by listening. A keen ear can recognize whether it's Kilroy's or Fluffy's Prelude to the Puke or whatever sounds accompany the Sicktime Serenade. If you hear that telltale yowl or the "ack ack" sound, look while the evidence is warm and nab the perpetrator for a trip to the vet.

For other cat owners, the actual contents provide the identifying clues. Some cats prefer dry food, while others eat canned exclusively. Hairballs leave more obvious clues because you can at least identify the color of the fur. For poop and puke, you can finger the culprit by feeding the cats finely cut-up rubber bands, or shavings from nontoxic crayons with canned food. Keep a log of who gets which color. Regardless of which end it comes out, you'll know who's responsible. Fine, confettilike pieces of rubber bands (about one-fourth inch) will pass through the cats' systems without being digested or harming the cat.

Cats are such creatures of habit that deviations in their everyday patterns are a plea for help. For example, a cat who likes dry food and suddenly starts eating canned or not eating at all could mean his mouth hurts or maybe he's suffering from kidney or liver disease. An outgoing cat who suddenly hides could mean he's in pain; likewise with a cat who starts biting. All of these are symptoms that something's rotten in the state of Kittyland. Or someone starts peeing or pooping outside the litter box. Anytime a cat suddenly withdraws and spends a lot of time alone you need to get him checked out.

When It's Time to Say Good-Bye

Eventually you will have to face that moment that all pet owners dread—that day you must say good-bye to one of your cats. We humans are both blessed and cursed that we can release our pets from a painful life with no hope of recovery. No one wants to play God, but at some point you may have to decide whether to euthanize your pet. Hopefully, he has lived a long and healthy life, but now his quality of life has declined, he's experiencing a great deal of pain, he's stopped eating, he's facing a long period of painful treatment, or you simply can't afford to pay for expensive treatment.

When is it time to intervene and say good-bye? You might want to ask yourself some soul-searching questions. Can kitty get better? Does he have a terminal disease? Can he possibly improve with treatment? Can you afford that treatment? Many diseases are treatable, but do you want to get a second mortgage to pay for it? Most important, is he suffering? If you are looking at a behavior issue, have you tried working with a behaviorist or drug therapy? Can you find him a new home? Are you keeping him alive for him or yourself?

Signs That It May Be Time to Say Good-Bye:

- Your cat is no longer able to control his bladder or bowels.
- He's in pain. He cries when you touch him. (Have the pain meds quit working?)
- He can't hold his head up any longer.
- He is no longer eating.

Talk to your vet. These symptoms could be treatable. For example, he might refuse to eat because he has a cold and can't smell the food. Does the vet agree with your decision?

It's an individual decision. But I have a rule of thumb, or paw, if you will: is he eating?

Your vet can spare your cat a slow, painful passing by literally putting him to sleep with an overdose of anesthesia. Kitty goes to sleep, the breathing ceases, the heart stops, and the brain stops.

If you aren't at the vet's office when you make the decision, call and make an appointment. Do you want to be with your kitty or not? Watching a euthanasia can be very peaceful, but occasionally things happen that you might consider disturbing. He may cry out, or experience a muscle spasm. He might pee or poop on the table. These are all reflexive actions.

When you make the appointment, tell the staff if you want to stay with your cat when he's euthanized. Some clinics simply don't permit it. If they don't, and you want to be with him, then call another vet. You might even be able to ask your vet if she will come to your house. If not find a mobile vet who is willing to put your kitty to sleep at home.

For your kitty's comfort (and your peace of mind) bring his favorite blanket, bed, or a clean towel that at least smells like home). It's time for *you* to take the ✿ **Bach Flower Remedy Cerato**, which will help you with indecisiveness about your cat's treatment or euthanasia. Elm helps with feelings of being overwhelmed after you have put your pet to sleep. Put Walnut on the crown of your cat's head. It is supposed to help with the transition from life. Star of Bethlehem and Rescue Remedy can help you and your other cats handle the grief.

If you decide to bring the body home for burial, let him lie in state for a while. (Check to see if a home burial is legal in your city.) This is the only way you can explain to his housemates what has happened. You will see some stare in shock. But it's been my experience that most of the time they walk by without much emotion.

Because some cats do form strong bonds and friendships with other pets, they may grieve just like you do. So it stands to reason, when one dies or disappears, the close companions he leaves behind will miss him. While you can call a friend or a grief hotline, your kitty can't express his sorrow in words. He might show the same signs of depression that we do: not eating, change in sleeping habits, refuse to play, or listlessness. You might see him wander around the house aimlessly crying for his friend. The pining friend may become clingy with you, or he may avoid you completely.

When our Turkish Van, Winkie, died we placed his body in the middle of the room for the rest of the cats to see as we've always done. In the past when we've left the dead cat on the floor for viewing, they walked past, ignoring them. With Winkie it was a different story. Some cats stared, others hissed. Groucho, who had always been his special buddy, stood there for a long time just look-ing. It was heartbreaking. For months Groucho pined, wandering around the house calling for his absent friend.

If your grieving cat goes on a hunger strike, encourage him to eat. Don't let him go for more than a day without dinner. Longer than that and he could be in danger of developing hepatic lipidosis (fatty liver disease), a potentially fatal liver condition caused by not eating. You may need some help from your vet here.

You can help him by trying to keep his life as stable and stress-free as pos-sible. Feed the herd and clean the boxes on your regular schedule. Don't make any major changes around the house like redecorating or getting new furni-ture. Spend more time with your grieving kitty—cuddle if he wants to. Try to get him interested in new games. Like you, your kitty won't get over his loss overnight. He may mourn for a few weeks, or it could go on for as long as six months.

Try playing some interactive games—just the two of you. Get out 🐾 **Da Bird** or the 🐾 **PURRFect Wispy Close-Up Cat Toy**. Have a catnip party. Slip him special treats like pea-size pieces of chicken or turkey breast. Don't rush out and adopt a new cat. Kitty may see a newcomer as a territorial threat.

You may have noticed that some of your other cats pick up some of the absent cat's preferences like where he sleeps or his favorite toys. There's noth-ing mystical about it. When a higher-ranking cat dies, it leaves a hole in the hierarchy. Prime real estate and possessions are up for grabs. Other kitties may have moved up in the pecking order, inheriting the privileges of rank.

Now it's time to turn your attention toward you. You may feel you have no one you can turn to, no one you can share your feelings with. You may worry that your feelings of loss are unique, maybe even abnormal. If you have no one around who understands, you can, at no charge, borrow a sympathetic ear from pet-loss hotlines sponsored by veterinary universities and animal rescue orga-nizations across the country.

Tufts University offers one such hotline. You can speak with one of the trained staff members for as long as you wish. While the staff can't make your pain or guilt disappear, with their understanding of the special bonds people have with their cats, they can help you work through your grief and help you get through this difficult time.

You can reach the Tufts University Pet Loss Support Hotline Monday through Friday from 6:00 p.m. to 9:00 p.m. EST by calling 1-508-839-7966. Or check out the Web site at www.tufts.edu/vet/petloss.

CHAPTER THIRTEEN

Happy Habitats

A cat toy is anything not nailed down.
—**Unknown**

IT'S HAPPENED TO ALMOST EVERY cat owner: you come home to find the cats wearing an "I ate the hamster" grin. This time the critter still scurries around safely in his cage, but how long will his good fortune last? Let's face it, cats aren't like dogs, who wear their mantle as man's best friend like a crown. For felines, domesticity is a paper-thin veneer. Inside our homes, with no prey to hunt or predators to hide from, cats often suffer from obesity and depression. As with latchkey kids, bored kitties get into trouble by redecorating the furniture with that postwar look, by showing aggressive behavior toward people or other pets, and by spraying. In nature, cats don't need an activity director or a fitness trainer. Although they sleep 70 percent of the time, in their waking hours, they're very busy climbing trees, snoozing in hideaways, stalking prey, hiding in shrubbery, and, finally, the grand finale, killing and eating a mouse. Indoor cats don't usually have mice running around the house or other interesting diversions.

To avoid behavior problems, you want to mimic the opportunities and lifestyles they'd encounter in the wild.

Expanding Territory

A lot of conflict in multicat homes can be avoided by making sure there's enough territory for everyone. Now I realize you can't build a new wing on your house just for the cats. They don't need one. They do need beds, elevated perches, platforms, and nooks where they can hide—basically space and activities in three dimensions. In a multicat home each kitty needs his own personal base set up for his personal taste. You can create vertical territory in your home just by adding a cat tree or two. Additional territory can be as cheap as throwing a grocery sack on the floor or opening a cardboard box. Within a brown paper grocery bag or box, kitty knows he'll only have to look forward for potential enemies.

TAILS FROM THE TRENCHES

Author Linda Kay Hardie has been called the master of territory space. She and her indoor-only cats live in a mobile home in Reno, Nevada, without the usual peeing, marking, and territorial issues because she manages to squeeze every possible inch in the house. She pleads guilty to having too many books, teddy bears, and moving boxes full of stuff. For her cats' amusement, Linda stacks the boxes like large building blocks. The cats enjoy leaping up on them and hiding in the cardboard cubbyholes. Whenever she needs something from a container, she moves the box. Suddenly, the cardboard wall transforms into a brand new shape worthy of exploration anew. Linda throws old blankets and cat beds on top of the boxes so they can snooze at various heights.

With the exception of boxes and paper bags, hidey-hole preference is a matter of individual taste. Older cats may prefer something closer to the ground because of arthritis and a low energy level. Longhaired cats or kitties with thicker coats tend to like things more open so they don't get hot. Likewise, shorthaired kitties may appreciate more closed-in places to help retain warmth.

Petmate makes great little hiding places for cats, such as the ⊛ Cat-A-

Trail cat tunnel, the igloo-shaped 🐾 **Kitty Kat Condo,** and the elaborate 🐾 **Kitty Cat Playhouse.** The Kitty Cat Playhouse has four different sleeping places with two hiding spaces. It's very popular with the Rainbolt Test Kitties because it has enough room for three cats to occupy sleeping spots at the same time.

If you're not into the designer forts, you can buy kitty tents, igloos, and tunnels. You can also use large Rubbermaid stackable containers. Cut holes in them to make your own kitty condo community. You can also make a tent by throwing an old towel over a coffee table or on the seat of a dining room chair .

Up, Up, and Away

In nature, cats climb, lounge on tree limbs, and watch the action below. Explore ways you can make your indoor cat's life more interesting on a three-dimensional level. You can provide your herd with multilevel lounging and exercise space by clearing out part of a bookcase or mounting some shelves at various levels. This is especially important if you have small children or dogs. You can even buy an old bookcase from a thrift store. Assemble the bookcase according to the directions. Then cut holes large enough for a cat to climb through. On each level switch the hole to the opposite side of the case. You can even cut a hole in the top shelf. Turn it into a megacenter with a second bookcase. Connect the cases with boards (or shelves) that double as catwalks.

Put towels, cat beds, fleece pads, or pillows on the shelves or on top to give everyone something to sleep on. Go one step further to keep the territory worthy of investigation with assorted toys. Every now and then move the shelves to different spots.

To create vertical space set up tall cat trees, window perches, window

Fortunately, a Kittyland for cats doesn't have to cost a paw and a tail.

enclosures, and kitty condos. In multicat homes kitties are happier when they can layer themselves. In addition to the bookcase trick, we have a six-foot cat tree that lets our cats hang out on the top of the china cabinet.

I created a couple of inexpensive catwalks along different walls using a series of coatrack knickknack shelves mounted end to end. The shelf needs to be at least eight inches wide so your cat can turn around—even wider would be better. Gluing carpeting to it will give your kitties more traction. If your cats enjoy window watching, set up window perches or window enclosures so they can enjoy their personal portal to the outdoors. Make things more interesting by placing a birdbath or squirrel feeders just outside the window. The window perch will soon become the most popular place in the house.

Inside Out

Now you've increased territory inside your home. You may be able to increase their territory even more and give them the chance to live as cats do in the wild. Don't get me wrong. That's not an invitation to open the door and throw caution and common sense to the wind.

There is a truly happy medium—a compromise you and your cats can agree on that will allow them to enjoy the great outdoors in relative safety. You can open that door, but with conditions. You could get a window enclosure, install a cat fence, or get a freestanding enclosure.

Before you allow your cats access to nature, there are a few preventive steps you need to take first to ensure his safety. You need some kind of containment system to keep him out of harm's way. The cheapest option is an inexpensive netted tent, but there's a huge problem with this. Tents prevent kitty from getting away, but it can't protect them against dogs or other marauding animals. Left unsupervised in tents, your kitties are very vulnerable. Unless you have a secure fence that keeps other animals out, never leave your cats unattended.

Then there's my favorite option: the cat fence. It's not a cheap way out, although it might be less expensive than replacing a house full of carpeting. These fences are designed specifically with cat behavior and physiology in mind. Ultimately our cat fence allowed the Rainbolt Test Kitties to do everything a normal outdoor cat would do without dog or car dangers.

There are two kinds of cat fencing: extension and freestanding. Extension fences are barrier netting secured by brackets mounted near the top of an existing fence. The plastic mesh prevents your cat from grabbing the top of the fence with his front claws then pushing off with his back legs. Your own fence must be sound. The most ingenious cat fence in the world won't hold a kitty if there are holes in the wooden fence where he can squeeze through. Most cat fencing works on chain link, wood, and even stone fences. Some styles keep your cats inside but may still permit stray cats to get into the yard. You can also find free plans on the Internet. Unfortunately, the top-mounted fences haven't been shown to be effective with feral cats.

The 🐾 **Affordable Cat Fence** is the most effective extension fence, and it's the easiest to install. If your fence is not secure, you can install the freestanding 🐾 **Purr...fect Fence**, which doesn't require a chain-link or wood fence to piggyback on. It's the only freestanding cat fence currently on the market. Stakes secure the fence to the ground at the base to keep cats from slipping through the bottom.

A few caveats about cat fencing. Kitties aren't protected from airborne predators like owls, hawks, and eagles or airborne diseases or parasites. If you live in an area with a thriving hawk population, these fences aren't a good choice. Sheds and trees can help some cats make the great escape. Before you broaden their horizons, make certain that your kitties are current on their vaccinations. Since raccoons and bats won't necessarily respect the fence, make sure your cats have had their rabies shots. You'll need to put them on a flea, tick, and heartworm preventive.

After the fence is installed, monitor your cats. Some cats will exploit any weakness they find. It took a couple of months to contain Basil, our former alley cat. He would jump to the small planters, then onto our storage shed, then over our brand new eight-foot fence. When we blocked one escape route he'd figure out another. We finally had to install twelve-foot poles and hang plastic mesh in that corner to finally keep our nomad home.

If the cat fence isn't an option, then consider an enclosure for your cats' amusement. They vary from freestanding construction plans for complicated wooden structures, to powder-coated wire cages or prebuilt wooden units for

Cat inside says to the cat outside: "It comes with everything: a crepe myrtle to climb, a log to scratch and even a mouse cellar."

the architecturally challenged, to soft net cages that spring into place in seconds. You can jazz up the interiors with hammocks, scratchers, cat trees and hiding places, nontoxic plants, logs, or branches—anything a cat might experience in the wild. Properly installed the wooden and metal structures should give your cats security from predators. The mesh enclosures leave your cats vulnerable to animal attack, so don't leave them unattended especially if dogs can enter your yard. Make sure any netting is small and strong enough to keep them in. Also, be sure the enclosure is sturdy enough for your cats to climb the wire without bringing the structure down on top of them.

Finally, you could screen in your porch.

🐾 **Room with a View** is a powder-coated wire enclosure designed specifically for cats. It attaches to the outside of the house and the cats gain access via a window cat door. It can be expanded a little at a time into an intricate labyrinth of tunnels and enclosures.

The less expensive, no-frills powder-coated wire ✿ **Options Plus 3-3-4 Cat Enclosure** is completely freestanding with four sides and a top. It's very versatile; it can be used indoors or outdoors. It's small enough for an apartment patio. It can be expanded, or disassembled if you relocate.

Window enclosures run about the size of a window air conditioner and usually require double-hung window frames. Some window units have Plexiglas construction, others coated wire. The ✿ **Cat Veranda** can give your cats a taste of the outdoors from the safety of your living room should you consider

---

FELINE FACT OR FICTION

A Lily Can Be as Deadly as Antifreeze

True. Never plant or display anything in the lily family where your cat can get to it. Whether it's in your house or a yard your cats enjoy, you should deep six anything in the lily family (including Easter lily, as well as Stargazer, Tiger, Asian, Japanese Show and Casa Blanca lilies) before it deep sixes your cats. APCC says just chewing on a lily leaf will shut down kitty kidneys. They might just as well have a drink of antifreeze on the rocks. Putting off treatment more than 18 hours will result in fatal kidney damage.

And while dogs may puke their innards out if they eat lilies, they won't do much more than Rolf saying "ralph." Lucky dogs! So try remember when you order flowers for your cat-loving loved ones or plant flowers of your own, forget the lilies. Oleander, a cardiotoxin, is another one to avoid. Roses are more romantic and kitties can chew on the petals to your heart's content.

Eating lilies will have your cat pushing up daisies.

one of these window-mounted observation cubes. The open-air patio has a covered roof to protect your cat from sun and rain. Even though our cats are used to going through a cat flap, the more timid cats never got the hang of it. Installation only took seconds.

You can put one or two cats in a ✳ **Feline Funhouse Outdoor**. The Funhouse is a one-piece tent enclosure that sets up instantly with no assembly required. When your cat comes in, simply twist it back into a flat position and store it in its own zippered carrying bag. Because its soft mesh is designed to prevent escape rather than to protect your cats from animal attack, the Feline Funhouse should be used under human supervision at all times.

Whether you're using an enclosure or cat fence make sure your cat has fresh water. He will also need shade, especially if he's white. Like humans, fair-skinned cats run the risk of skin cancer when exposed to sunlight. Keep his food in the house. Even dry food will attract ants and other pests. Since cats like to be high up, provide shelves or logs to allow him to climb up.

You'll also want to make sure that any outside plants are kitty safe. Crepe myrtle and roses are nontoxic and colorful.

Outside In

After many years of exciting, active outdoor living, you've decided to bring your cats inside. I did it. Your mission, should you decide to accept it, is to give them similar activities inside that they found outside. Boredom is the enemy. In their quest for a little excitement, your cats may go for each other's throats, tear up the furniture, or leave the house smelling like a sewer.

First step, alter your cats. Neutered animals don't have the wanderlust that intact kitties have. That should fix 95 percent of your cats' transition problems.

Dr. Jim Richards suggested confining the cat to a single room as you did when you brought new cats into the house. It's best if the room has no absorbent surface (like carpeting) except for a litter box. Use a sandy, unscented litter. Scoop every time you go in there. Visit and play with kitty frequently. When he's using the box regularly, let him out to explore a little. Don't let him out of your sight. As you feel more confident in his litter box habits, you can expand his territory. Give him sunny windowsills and play stalk-and-pounce games before you feed him. Be careful when entering or leaving the house. He might make a dive for the door any time whenever it's opened. Cats usually adapt to being indoors within several weeks.

Outside enclosures and window patios can help your kitty make the transition from outside cat to inside cat with a room with a view. A strategically placed bird feeder can give your kitty hours of entertainment.

Make sure there are plenty of hiding spots around the house, as well as elevated resting places. Provide window perches in several windows throughout the house.

The Rainbolt Test Kitties gave four paws to the 🐾 **Scratch Lounge**, a cardboard scratching pad that doubles as a bed. This pad has three scratching surfaces: the base and two sides.

Exercise your cats. Think about what he'd be doing as an outside cat: hunting, scratching, running, jumping, and climbing. Get out the interactive toys for ten minutes every morning and afternoon. Tease toys are almost impossible for your cats to resist. You might need to experiment to find out what kind your cat enjoys most: feathers on a string or how about some catfishing? Buy a one- to two-foot-long practice fishing rod and reel, attach a kitty toy to the swivel instead of a hook and bait. Take him on a walk. Some cats enjoy going out on a leash. Others loathe it. Don't force a reluctant cat to wear a harness and leash.

Keep changing the beds and toys around so there's always something new to check out and explore. Set out cardboard boxes and paper grocery bags with the handles removed. Dr. Richards suggested the following:

- Kitty entertainment: bird feeder outside a window. Pinwheels in the garden on a windy day are a great distraction.

- Cat Videos: even though there's not much plot, many cats love them. They can watch and listen to the outdoor exploits of fluttering bugs, squirrels, mice, rats, birds, lizards, and even a graceful butterfly or two.

- Provide thirty-inch-tall scratching posts that don't wobble or an angled cardboard scratching pad. Better still, since your cat is used to being outside, try a scratching post made of natural wood with bark. Put the scratcher near his napping spot because cats like to have a good stretch when they wake up. If the cat is scratching the wallpaper, mount a large cork bulletin board over the spot. Cork is a kitty magnet. Keep a broom and dustpan handy; you're going to need it.

- Instead of just free feeding him, put his food in a treat ball.

- Keep the litter box clean. If the box is kept tidy, kitty is more likely to use it. When he was outside, if his bathroom was dirty he moved. He'll do the same inside.

- Give him Bach Flower Remedy Walnut. It's for cats who are transitioning from outside to inside, or are hypersensitive to their environment. It's also good to give before you introduce new animals to each other.

Preying for Something to Do

Your inside cats are like a house full of mischievous kids. If they have nothing to do, they're going to get into trouble. Unfortunately, most indoor kitties have nothing to do but fight with other cats, tear up the furniture, and spray the walls. One way to keep your two-legged children out of trouble is to assign them chores or give them a kid-safe video to watch. A few planned activities will make it more likely when you return home that you'll find the house and the kids relatively intact.

Dr. Dodman gave me some words of wisdom that have proven invaluable with my own cats and my clients' cats: "A tired cat is a good cat." At first I didn't really understand the depth of his statement. But ten minutes of rigorous interactive play, twice a day, depletes a great deal of that predatory energy. Kitty's no longer like a bomb waiting to explode. He has to sleep to recharge his batteries just like his wild counterpart.

Studies have shown that owners who played interactive games with their kitties at least fifteen minutes a day, reported less marking and peeing outside the box. Owners who played almost twenty minutes a day reported no pee problems.

If your kitty needs to shed some of that cat fat, he's going to have to burn more calories than he presently uses. Since you may not have mice that can give your guys some cardiovascular exercise, you're going to have to become a mouse substitute. Cats have preferences when it comes to prey. Some like birdlike prey that flies through the air. Others prefer prey that scurries along the ground. You'll have to experiment to see which style appeals to your cats.

🐾 **Da Bird** is an especially effective toy because it mimics a bird in flight. This bird appeals to all of his senses. Because of its design, the toy flutters through the air, looking and sounding just like a live bird flapping its wings. The cat can snag it in his claws and chew on the feathers. I've had sixteen-year-olds who would join the group to take a swat or two. Everyone stands in single line to play with Da Bird. It's like a community athletic center in a single toy. You wear out long before they do! Da Bird can dash convincingly along the floor too.

It's not just a matter of getting a toy out and dangling it in their faces. You have to convince your cats that you *are* the bird (or the mouse, bug, or lizard). You want them doing what they would do in a hunt—running, leaping, biting, swatting. Practice with it. Make it swoop and fly. Make the cats jump up and down from furniture and climb stairs. When a cat grabs it, the toy should struggle and flutter as any decent (temporarily) live prey would do. Don't make it too easy for him. When he's had the toy in his claws or mouth for a few seconds and he relaxes, it's time for the bird to escape. Give it a gentle yank and the game starts all over. Play and escape, play and escape. Keep it up until he's tired enough to need a nap. When the game is over, give everyone a treat. After all, if they had killed real prey, it would be time to eat and then get some hard-earned rest. Hide the toy inside a closed closet. If you're convincing enough, they'll begin to obsess about how to get to it. There's no operating string toys without a license. And kitties aren't certified as they could swallow the string (causing an intestinal blockage) or strangle.

If you're having aggression problems, set aside two or three, ten- to twenty-minute rigorous play sessions every day. (Cats love routine, so try not to deviate from these times.) Keep it up until your "bad" boy is lying on his side swatting at the toy. Often a more dominant cat will try to monopolize preytime. That's not all bad. After all, he's probably the one who needs it the most. You might want to separate him so the other cats have their chance to play.

Kitties are living oxymorons. They need a predictable schedule, but they thrive on novel experiences—just like they'd have in the wild. You need to give your guys things to explore and investigate around the house. When you exercise them, try to engage all of their senses: sight, sound, smell, taste, and touch. Real prey would. 😸 **Play-N-Squeak** is a little fake fur mouse with a microchip that squeaks when tapped or swatted. 😸 **Play-N-Squeak Fishing Pole** has the squeaking mouse lure on a short rod and reel.

The one thing you don't want to do is use your fingers or toes (or any part of your body as a kitty tease). Your six-week-old kitten nibbling on your finger is cute. The eleven-pounder clamping down is a different story. It's a bad habit that's hard for kitty to unlearn.

Most kitties can't resist laser pointers, and they're easier to use if you have mobility problems that make using Da Bird or other tease toys difficult to animate. Because of the dangers of eye damage, don't point a laser light at anyone's eyes and don't let small kids play with this toy. A lot of cats just love a little agility workout chasing the light by going through tunnels, up and down stairs, and bounding from chair to chair. 😸 **Cat Dancer** is a clever and inexpensive toy—a twist of paper at the end of a piece of spring wire. It mimics insect action. Rotate toys so they always seem new and exciting. Swap out toys during each play session, as well. Any catnip toys keep stored in a plastic bag in the freezer to keep the scent strong.

You can create games the cats will love for almost no cost. A ping-pong ball and a bathtub are all that's needed for bathtub hockey. Cut paw holes in a shoebox and drop a couple of ping-pong balls inside. For close-up action there's the 😸 **PURRfect Wispy Close-Up Cat Toy.**

Rotate their small toys. Hide them throughout the house so the cats can be surprised by their discovery.

Cutting Back on Kitty's Waist Expansion Program

An unfortunate side effect of strictly indoor living is the waist expansion program. Too much food and not enough exercise add to the feline flab factor. They sleep all day, watch Jerry Springer Spaniel on TV, and sneak snacks whenever they can. A cat foraging for his food in the wild doesn't usually get fat. He may have to kill between five and ten mice a day to keep his home fires burning. That's a lot of work. You see, cats are designed to eat a lot of little meals, not chow down from a trough.

Give your kitties something to do while you're away. Remove the dry-food bowl and keep your cats busy with a treasure hunt. Hide treats throughout the house. The cats' job is to go seek out the munchies. Like their wild counterparts, they hunt.

In a different kind of treasure hunt, hide treats among toys in the 🐾 **Peek-A-Prize Toy Box**. It's a square box with paw holes that are slightly larger than a standard cat ball. Stuff the Peek-A-Prize full of different kinds of cat balls and toy mice. Kitty has to fish all the toys out to get to the food. While he's at it, he finds toys he wants to play with. Buy balls made of different materials and textures. A couple of times a day you'll have to gather up the toys and put them back. The Rainbolt Test Kitties never tire of this. And I have the challenge of finding unique toys to fill the box with.

Or, if you free feed, put their rations of dry food in treat balls and scatter them throughout the house. Rather than filling the ball with calorie-packed treats, put his kibble inside. That way, instead of pigging out at his bowl then going and ripping the couch, he has to push the little ball around until a few pellets fall out. He'll eat those and then push it around some more. This keeps his mind occupied, gives him something to do, and helps him use up a few calories working for his food.

Yet another variation is to divide the cats daily ration into six or seven mouse-size portions and place them in tiny sushi soy sauce bowls all over the

TAILS FROM THE TRENCHES

Mary Anne Miller, of Sweet Home, Oregon, drills holes in the plastic capsules that hold vending machine toys. She drills small holes in the plastic, puts a few treats inside, and drops them on the floor. The cats get a meaty treat after batting these around the house for a few minutes.

house—in different rooms, on top of things, under furniture. And the cat is only able to eat one mouse-size portion at a time. Try hiding those little soy bowls with frozen pieces of fish or meat.

You don't have to go out and buy a treat ball. You can make your own food puzzle by taking an empty toilet paper roll and punching a number of holes in the tube. Make the holes large enough to release the kibble. Fill it with kibble and securely tape the ends to contain the food. You may need to show your cat how to roll the tube around in order to get the food. Give your kitties several food puzzles, fill them with their kibble, and set them throughout the house. Finally, he has a job to do. Hopefully this will keep him physically and mentally stimulated. Some cats also enjoy small, frozen, canned cat food balls. Since you have multiples cats, you may want to separate them. You don't want anyone going hungry because they haven't figured out how to get the treat, but another cat has.

Pavlov's Cat is a scratching-post food puzzle that drops a few kibbles into a bowl whenever he uses the scratching post. Naturally there's big payoff for using the scratcher and not the settee.

Buy or build a big scratching post. No matter how tall or sturdy it is, a single cat tree or scratch post isn't enough. Scatter them throughout the house. And remember, individual cats have different scratching preferences. Provide various surfaces: wood with bark, carpet, cardboard, and sisal.

TAILS FROM THE TRENCHES

Kari Winters, an Albuquerque, New Mexico, resident who's involved in Siamese rescue, has a variety of cat toys to keep her personal cat and her foster cats happy. Her kitties like the Cat Dancer, which mimics snakes or lizards, and the laser. She also gives her kitties catnip toys. On occasion she leaves catnip on the carpet so they can roll and play in it. She says that the cat toys her cats like the best usually come from cat shows.

Just as different cats have different tastes in the texture of their cat litter, they also have specific preferences for what they scratch and sleep on. Sisal's a perennial favorite for scratching *and* napping. You might also try chamois, carpet, logs, burlap, fur, fleece, cardboard, and newspapers. Remember they love to sniff things out. Make it more interesting by sprinkling a little catnip around.

With a lot of imagination and some effort you should be able to broaden your cats' horizons and enlarge their world. With activities to stimulate their bodies and their minds, both you and your little herd will enjoy a happier, healthier, and more harmonious life together.

When It Doesn't Work

IN MOST CASES, CATS SHOULD accept each other in three or four weeks. Unfortunately, not every case will end like *The Brady Bunch*, where everyone lives happily ever after. If you have taken the advice I've given in chapter 4, "Family Feud," and throughout the book, and you met with your vet and are still running into trouble, you may need to contact an animal behaviorist. Or, you can give one cat the bedroom and the others the run of the house. In most cases, problems can be worked through.

Sometimes though, despite your best efforts, a new cat doesn't work out. You've made your decision that the chaos can't continue. You must now find the new cat another home.

Most rescue groups and breeders have an escape clause in their contracts that *requires* you to return the animal if for any reason you can no longer keep him. Since many humane societies keep pets in foster homes, give them plenty of time to arrange a place for your cat. In other words, don't call them on Wednesday when you're planning on moving Friday morning.

Even if you adopted a cat from a friend, a kill shelter, or picked him up off the street, you still have an obligation to find him a suitable home.

Of course, the ideal scenario would be if a friend or family member could take him. Or you could call the closest pet supply store to see if humane groups have adopt-a-pets there. When checking out shelters, don't confuse a rescue group with city animal shelters. Some humane groups euthanize unadoptable animals, as do most city shelters, so ask if the humane organization is no-kill. Go down and meet with the cat rescue coordinator. Explain your situation and ask if you can place the cat in the organization's program. Offer to foster the cat until he is adopted. The coordinator will probably require that the cat be neutered, be current on his shots, wormed, and tested for feline leukemia and feline immunodeficiency virus. You'll most likely be expected to bring him to adoption events and pick him up when the event is over if he hasn't found a home.

There are a lot of great animals out there. Do what you can to make your cat stand out. Make him wear a cute jeweled collar or a scarf with a fun phrase, such as, Got Milk? Teach him to shake hands.

If you decide to find a family on your own, you'll have to get the word out and then ask a lot of questions. In the world of animal rescue, it's called *screening* an adopter. Put signs up in places where animal people go: vet clinics, pet stores, and animal shelters. Call your area rescue groups and ask to be put on their referral list. Also, don't rule out other avenues like the bulletin boards at the post office, grocery store, fitness centers, and churches. For cats with socialization or litter box problems, feed stores are good locations to place ads because people need barn cats from time to time. But be selective of the places you post the signs. The more places you advertise the cat, the more calls you'll get, and the more screening you'll need to do.

TAILS FROM THE TRENCHES

Many years ago, a friend of mine rescued a pregnant mom cat and then put an ad in the newspaper offering free kittens to a good home. A family answered her ad and wanted the entire litter. She asked one of the children what she was going to name her new kitties, and the kid responded unenthusiastically that she didn't know. The other children didn't act excited about their new pets either. She got no information from them. Only after they left with all five kittens did she realize that the kittens would probably be fed to large pet snakes or used as bait to train fighting dogs.

Be prepared, there are a lot of crazies out there. Screen the callers carefully. Not everyone has pure intentions.

When people call to inquire about your ad, ask a lot of questions. Be friendly and conversational. You'll get more information that way than if they think you are interrogating them. Go with your gut instinct. You aren't obligated to hand over your cat just because someone shows interest. If the people are vague or evasive with their answers, such as where they live or about other pets they've owned, that's another warning sign. You can even charge an adoption fee of five or ten dollars. Even a small fee like this will ward off snake feeders and dogfight trainers.

While you have your potential adopter on the phone, here are some questions you should ask:

- **Have you ever had pets?** If she had to give a pet up because they moved or there were behavior problems, that's a red flag. If any of their pets died, sympathetically ask what happened. Death by car, dog, or disappearance—more red flags. If the sixteen-year-old died of congestive heart failure, continue the conversation. This is probably a good home.

- **What kind of dogs do you have?** Do the dogs like cats? Does she have a pit bull or a Jack Russell Terrier that might be aggressive? How old are their pets? Are they spayed/neutered? Do they have current shots? Are they inside or outside pets? These are all good indications of how your cat will be treated.

- **Who's your vet?** Call the clinic the adopter uses. The staff may not tell you if the person has been a poor pet owner, but you might be able to glean some information by the tone or hesitation of the person you speak with. If the potential adopter was a responsible cat owner, the office staff would probably be glad to tell you.

- **What is your landlord's pet policy? Have you already paid your pet deposit?** If an adopter hasn't yet paid the landlord a pet deposit, tell him or her to bring you a receipt before you hand over the cat. Humane societies across the country get cats back because adopters get "caught" not paying the deposit. Warn her that you will call the landlord to check before you release the kitty.

- **Do you plan on declawing him?** The answer might affect your decision.

- **If your child becomes allergic, what will you do?** Will the adopter at least make an attempt to keep the cat by vacuuming more often or bathing the cat every week?

- **What happens if you have to move?** This is one of the most common reasons for surrendering a pet to a shelter.

Draw up a contract. Ask to see identification and get a phone number. Legitimate adopters shouldn't mind your caution. Assure them you want to hear from them.

If your kitty is not very sociable toward people, ask the rescue groups about feral cat rescue or barn cat relocation rescue. You can get more information at www.saveacat.org and www.barncats.org.

By following these recommendations, your cat stands a good chance of a happy outcome in his new home.

The Cat Wrangler's Shopping Guide

As you read my book you ran across products that earned the Rainbolt Test Kitties Paw Print of Approval. I have listed most of them below, divided into the following categories: behavior, outdoor entertainment, happy habitats, litter, odor control and cleaning, and health.

I'm also giving you a list of books, services, and Web sites I've found useful.

Oh, Behave!

Comfort Zone with Feliway

Cats seldom spray a location they have head marked. Comfort Zone with Feliway mimics a cat's friendly facial pheromones in order to control urine marking and furniture scratching. It comes in a pump spray (nice little irony) or plug-in diffuser like an air freshener. When you spray Comfort Zone on a wall or other vertical object at about nose height to a kitty, it changes the pee- or paw-marking site to a face-marking site. The diffuser, while more expensive, fills the entire room with the comforting scent of synthetic facial pheromones rather than just limiting it to a small area. Because we humans are nasally challenged, we can't smell Comfort Zone.

Comfort Zone convinces every cat that the calming pheromones are his own personal scent, making him feel like he's among friends rather than among rivals.

A 2000 study conducted by Wayne Hunthausen, DVM, found that out of fifty households, 33 percent enjoyed total elimination of spraying after using Comfort Zone. In other studies in the United States, United Kingdom, France, and Japan, cat owners saw between a 74 percent to 97 percent reduction in spraying. Of course, nothing's 100 percent effective.

First, clean the walls or carpets that have been marked. If you use an odor-removing product, let it dry before using Comfort Zone.

Because habits aren't established in a day, they take a while to break. Once the cats have calmed down—in about three months—you may be able to stop using Comfort Zone. Some people continue to use the product a couple of times a week as reinforcement.

Comfort Zone with Feliway
Central Life Sciences
1-800-234-2269
www.petcomfortzone.com

Flower Remedies

To help your cats deal with emotional issues, such as stress, aggression, and fear, you might want to turn to the natural calming effect of Bach Flower Remedies. Bach Flower Remedies have a formula to treat most specific negative emotions and stress, promoting healing on an emotional level. A cross between homeopathy and aroma therapy, they're considered a safe method of natural healing. Expect to pay $10 to $15 for a single remedy at any health food store.

Massage eight drops into the crown of the cat's head or add a dropperful to his drinking water. Unlike medications, it won't hurt other cats.

Some of the Bach Flower Remedies that you might find helpful are:

- Aspen for fear of unknown things and constant anxiety.
- Beech for cats who can't tolerate other animals or people or changes in their routine.
- Centaury for meek cats who are picked on by other animals.
- Chamomile calms irritable and fractious cats.
- Chicory for manipulative, possessive, or clingy kitties or cats with separation anxiety.

- Crab Apple for overgrooming and compulsive behavior.
- Elm for easily overwhelmed cats, obsessive-compulsive behavior, or for territorial stress.
- Holly for lost status or attention, jealousy, abandonment, or for abused cats.
- Honeysuckle for grief, homesickness, rescued, or shelter cats.
- Impatiens for impatience, nervousness, and irritability.
- Larch for cats who are intimidated by other cats, and for cats who spray.
- Mimulus for coping with identifiable fears, like such as vet trips or fireworks. It's also for timidity, and fear of people or other animals.
- Pine for cats who feel they've done something wrong, for guilt, feeling rejected, abused, or fearful.
- Rescue Remedy for traumas and emergencies. In a stressful situation give it to all your cats and even take some yourself.
- Rose Rock eases terror or panic even if it was in the cat's distant past.
- Star of Bethlehem for any kind of physical or emotional trauma.
- Vine for cats who are control freaks, or cats who are aggressive or bully other cats and people.
- Walnut helps cats who are going through changes (such as divorce or other stressful family situation) and for cats going into a new environment or meeting new animals. It's also for cats who are transitioning from outdoor to inside only.
- Water violet for grief, or for loners or reclusive cats.

Ultimate Peacemaker

This is Dr. Hofve's special combination of essences formulated for conflicts in multicat households.

SpiritEssence

1-720-938-6794

www.spiritessence.com

CatStop

This battery-powered sensor detects movement and then emits an ultrasonic tone at a high decibel level out of the range of your hearing. It's species specific, so people, dogs, and other animals can't hear it.

Contech Electronics Inc.

1-800-767-8658

www.scatmat.com

Scarecrow

This outdoor animal repellent is a sprinkler with a motion detector trigger. When it senses movement, the sprinkler squirts throughout the target area with full garden hose pressure.

Contech Electronics Inc.

1-800-767-8658

www.scatmat.com

Soft Paws Nail Caps for Cats

These vinyl nail covers should be reapplied every four to six weeks. You must be able to clip your cat's nails in order to apply Soft Paws yourself.

Soft Paws Inc.

1-800-522-0800

www.smartpractice.com

Ssscat

This is the ultimate weapon in the human-feline territory dispute. It's an aerosol spray triggered by a battery-activated motion sensor. When it senses movement it shoots off a blast of air that sends cats flying. Cats never get used to it.

Premier Pet Products

1-888-640-8840

http://premierpet.com

Sticky Paws XL/Sticky Paws for Furniture

Sticky Paws is double-sided tape that repels cats because they don't like the feel of sticky surfaces. It can be placed directly on the furniture, drapes, or carpet—any place you don't want your cat to be. Don't use it on leather or wood. (For countertops, stick the sheets to cardboard so you can easily remove them when you need the counter.) It can also be placed on clean carpets to discourage cats from peeing in a place they've been soiling.

Fe-Lines Inc.

1-888-697-2873

www.stickypaws.com

Fun in the Sun Products

Affordable Cat Fence

This is a godsend for the Rainbolt Test Kitties' sanity. One-piece brackets mounted at the top of your fence hold plastic mesh in place. It's easily installed on chain-link, wood, and stone fences. Your fence must be intact with no holes, not even tiny ones that your cats can squeeze through.

Affordable Cat Fence Co.

1-210-736-2287 or 1-888-840-2287

www.catfence.com

Cat Veranda

This is a neat open-air window patio about the size of a window air-conditioner.

PetSafe

1-800-732-2677

www.petsafe.net

Feline Funhouse Outdoor

This one-piece tent springs into shape instantly. Its soft mesh prevents escape, but doesn't protect kitty from animal attacks. It should be used under human supervision at all times.

Wild Whiskers
1-360-647-8868
www.wildwhiskers.com

Options Plus 3-3-4 Cat Enclosure

This cage is an inexpensive and safe outside option. Since there is no window access, you must physically put the cat in the cage. It's small enough for an apartment patio and can be disassembled if you relocate.

Options Plus Inc.
1-800-760-3841 or 1-740-694-9811
cats-on-line.com

Purr...fect Fence

This is the only freestanding cat fence currently on the market. If your present fence has holes, you can place this one on the inside

Benner's Purr...fect Fence
1-888-280-4066
www.purrfectfence.com

Room with a View

Using special crimping pliers and fasteners, this expandable enclosure is surprisingly easy to assemble. You can order optional window adapters with a cat door and tunnels so the cats can come and go as they please.

The Cat's Den
1-866-484-0644
www.thecatsden.net

Products for a Happy Habitat

Animal Food Services

This freeze-dried raw cat food can be moistened with water or served dry.
1-800-743-0322.
www.animalfood.com

Bell Rock Growers Catnip Bouquet, Live Catnip and Pet Grass

The Rainbolt Test Kitties chose the dried and live catnip as their favorite way to spend a catnip party.

Bell Rock Growers
1-888-943-2847
www.bellrockgrowers.com

Busy Pet Toys Treat Dispenser

This two-and-one-half-inch treat ball has two openings and a catnip impregnated bead rattling around inside.

Stelaur Products LLC
www.busypettoys.com

Da Bird

This is the world's best toy. When swung through the air it makes a fluttering sound like beating wings. It engages all of their senses and makes them feel like great hunters. Because it is a string toy, put it in a closet when your play session is over.

Go-Cat Feather Toys
1-800-466-7519
www.go-cat.com

Drinkwell Platinum

This cat fountain holds a gallon-and-a-half of drinking water.

Veterinary Ventures Inc.
1-866-322-2530
www.petfountain.com

Feline Furniture Starter Kit

This is an affordable and expandable modular cat furniture set with lounging areas, hammocks, and a private cubicle. Assembly requires no construction skills or tools except a rubber mallet.

Feline Furniture

1-909-336-9414 or 1-909-337-3474

www.felinefurniture.com

Kitty Cat Loft

This is hardwood loft has an optional penthouse that gives kitty a high place to hide. A spiral staircase provides several different lounging heights for several cats simultaneously. Installation requires some woodworking experience.

Iroquois Innovations

1-216-381-1369

www.iroquoisinnovations.com

Omega Paw Cat Window Seat Deluxe

This window perch requires no assembly.

1-800-222-8269

omegapaw.com

Petmate Cat-A-Trail, Kitty Kat Condo, and Kitty Cat Playhouse

These are great cat hiding places.

1-877-PETMATE

www.petmate.com

Play-N-Squeak Mouse

The fake fur mouse contains a microchip that squeaks whenever the toy is tapped.

Our Pet's Company

1-440-354-6500

www.ourpets.com

PURRFect Wispy Close-Up Toy

Wispy peacock hurl feathers mounted on a rigid wand make this is an irresistible prey substitute.

Vee Enterprises
1-323-938-8304
www.veeenterprises.com

ScratchAway Cat Scratcher

This carpeted arm shield is for cats who insist on scratching furniture arms. Its angled plate slides under the furniture leg. Because it's held in place by the weight of the furniture it's extremely stable. Cats love it and it's under $30.

Birmingham Industries
1-909-886-1355

Scratch Lounge

This cardboard scratching pad is a bed as well as a scratcher. It has the cardboard scratch pad on three surfaces: the base and two sides.

Scratch Lounge
1-213-683-1963
www.scratchlounge.com

SmartyKat SuperScratcher+

This cardboard scratching is stable and wide enough for a cat to sleep on.

WorldWise Inc.
1-800-WORLDWISE
www.worldwise.com

SmartCat Peek-A-Prize Toy Box

This toy box has twenty-eight openings. Hide toys, treats and kibble inside to make your cats "hunt" for their food.

Smart Cat Products
1-866-317-6278
www.esmartcat.com

Starchaser/Turbo Scratcher
The Test Kitties never tired of this trackball toy. It even has an enticing scratch pad.
> Bergan
> 1-877-922-5489
> www.berganexperience.com

Ultimate Scratching Post
This affordably priced scratching post appeals to cats because it's stable and sturdy.
> Smart Cat Products
> 1-866-317-6278
> www.esmartcat.com

Litter-Related Products

Cat Attract Cat Litters
These therapeutic cat litters are manufactured with the sole purpose of getting the cats to use the litter box again. All Cat Attract litters contain an herbal attractant that cats love. Precious Cat Senior is a sandlike silica gel (not crystalline silica). Its very fine texture makes it attractive to cats with sensitive paws (especially declawed cats). This is my first choice for any cat who misses the box. Kitten Attract is a very fine clay clumping litter. Precious Cat Longhair is a larger silica gel granule litter preferred by longhaired kitties with toe and paw tufts.
> Precious Cat Litters
> 1-877-311-2287
> www.preciouscat.com

DuraScoop
This scoop has a large-capacity shovel made of one-piece cast aircraft-grade aluminum alloy. But it's light and comfortable to hold. It's also dishwasher safe.

Sweet Home Industries
1-630-879-3579
www.sweethomeindustries.com

Litter-Lifter

This large ABS plastic scoop makes fast work of litter boxes but still manages to catch the tiny pieces of broken clumps. The design also cuts down on dust and is dishwasher safe.

Preferred Merchandizing, Inc.
1-888-548-8375
www.litter-lifter.com

LitterMaid Elite Mega—Advanced Self-Cleaning Litter Box

The LitterMaid is a great option for cats who insist on a pristine litter box.

1-800-LITMAID
www.littermaid.com

Marchioro Deluxe Enclosed Litter Pan with Door

This is the largest covered litter box I've found. Once I removed the door, the box became one of their favorite privies. If you feel you need a covered box, get this one.

Marchioro USA Inc.
1-866-365-2260
www.marchiorousa.com

Petmate Giant Litter Box

Most cats want a large, open litter box. Although not attractive, this box is designed with the cats' needs in mind. This *is* their favorite.

Petmate
1-877-738-6283
www.petmate.com

World's Best Cat Litter

This hard-clumping, fast-clumping crumbled corn cat litter is the only natural litter that can be used with electronic litter boxes. It's flushable, which makes it perfect for travel.

GPC Pet Products

1-877-367-9225

www.worldsbestcatlitter.com

Best Odor Control and Cleaning Products

EnzymD

This product showed the best results when I tested enzyme/bacteria odor removers. The carpet must stay moist until the odor is removed, usually about twenty-four hours.

Big D Industries

1-800-654-4752

www.bigdind.com

Fabulon

Fabulon gives your wood flooring a protective finish similar to the varnish used in bowling alleys. It prevents pee from damaging wood floors.

Pratt & Lambert Paints

800-289-7728

www.prattandlambert.com

Handi-Brush

This is my favorite hair removal product for furniture. It gets even the most embedded hair from carpet and upholstery. It also has a sister product for carpets.

Groom Industries Inc.

1-800-397-3759

www.groomindustries.com

Magnet Broom

This broom has a foam broom head that attracts fur and dust and holds on to them.

Casabella

1-800-841-4140

www.casabella.com

Pet Hair Eliminator

Both a cat brush and a hair remover for furniture or carpet, this brush has a V shape that is very effective in removing fur from corners.

Solutia Inc.

1-800-325-4330

www.astroturfmats.com

StickySheets

These will get the hair off your clothes and furniture fast. They're expensive, but you can remove the hair in just seconds with the giant adhesive sheets.

StickySheets Unlimited LLC

1-888-878-4259

www.stickysheets.com

Stink-Free Stink-Finder Ultra-Violet Light and Flashlight

This ultraviolet light/flashlight combination simplifies your hunt for yellow graffiti because you don't have to carry around a flashlight.

Stink Free Stink-Finder

1-800-TAILEND

www.stinkfree.com

Tuff Oxi for Pets

Tuff Oxi is a pet-safe oxygen-based powder concentrate that's highly effective on pee and poop stains and incredible for cutting grease in the kitchen and for mopping floors. Color test your carpet before you use any product on it. The manufacturer warns that it can damage wood flooring.

Tuff Oxi for Pets

1-866-269-1953 or 1-310-574-3252

Urine-Erase

The most affective enzyme product is the two-step Urine Erase system. An enzyme powder is mixed with water and allowed to sit before applying to the stain. The enzyme breaks down the bacteria and the oxygenation action finishes the job and prevents mildew.

Urine-Erase

Reidell Chemicals Ltd.

1-519-285-2083 (Canada)

www.reidell.com

Zero Odor

This molecular odor eliminator is my very favorite product for removing pet odors. When other products failed, Zero Odor removed old cat pee from a 60-year-old felt hat without damaging it. It can be used on any water-safe surface, but the manufacturer warns that the product could damage hardwood flooring.

Zero Odor, LLC

1-800-526-2967

www.zeroodorpet.com

Litter Mats

Cat Large Litter Box Mat™

This fabric litter mat has a waterproof (pee-proof) backing. You can machine wash it on the cool and gentle cycle. It stays put on carpeting and hard flooring.

RPM Inc.

1-800-872-8201

www.drymate.com

Litter Welcome Mat

This mat actually traps litter inside a tray covered by a comfortable grill.

GroupOne Pet Products

1-989-269-7949

www.grouponepetproducts.com

OxyMagic's Natures Way

This is a pet-safe carpet cleaning company.

www.oxymagiconline.com

Vacuum Micro Attachments

This vacuum attachment kit is designed to pull dust out of a computer keyboard.

Ziotek

1-800-327-6703

www.ziotek.com

Health-Related Products

KittyCheck

Sprinkle this indicating paper additive over your cat's litter and they change color if there are any abnormalities in the urine.

Systems Complete LLC.

1-800-773-2060

www.kittycheck.com

Other Valuable Services

ASPCA/Animal Poison Control Center

1-888-426-4435

www.aspca.org/site/PageServer?pagename=pro_apcc

Humane Society of the United States

http://hsus.org

International Association of Animal Behavior Consultants
www.iaabc.org

Kathryn M. Kollmeyer
Animal Issues Attorney
www.lawyers.com/kollmeyerlaw/firmoverview.jsp
1-214-638-7900
National Association of Professional Pet Sitters
1-800-296-PET
www.petsitters.org

PETFAX
Tufts University Cummings School of Veterinary Medicine Behavior
Clinic offers PETFAX for remote behavior consultations. The service
costs around $200. You can reach Petfax at 1-508-887-4640.

Pet Sitters International
1-336-983-9222
www.petsit.com

Tufts University Pet Loss Support Hotline
Monday through Friday from 6:00 p.m. to 9:00 p.m. EST
1-508-839-7966
www.tufts.edu/vet/petloss

Suggested Reading

Adelman, Beth. *Every Cat's Survival Guide to Living with a Neurotic Owner.* New
York. Main Street Books: 2003.

Aslett, Don. *Pet Clean-Up Made Easy.* 2nd ed. Avon, MA: Adams Media, 2005.

Christensen, Wendy. *Outwitting Cats.* Guilford, CT: Lyons Press, 2004.

Catnip: A Newsletter for Caring Cat Owners. Cummings School of Veterinary
Medicine at Tufts University. Subscribe by calling 800-829-5116 or online
at www.tufts.edu/vet/publications/catnip/index.html .

Graham, Helen, and Gregory Vlamis. *Bach Flower Remedies for Animals.* Forres, Scotland: Findhorn Press, 1999.

Johnson-Bennett, Pam. *Cat vs. Cat.* New York: Penguin, 2004.

Rainbolt, Dusty. *Kittens for Dummies.* New York: Wiley, 2003.

Walker, Bob, and Frances Mooney. *The Cats' House.* Kansas City, MO: Andrews McMeel Publishing. 1996.

———. *Cats into Everything.* Kansas City, MO: Andrews McMeel Publishing, 1999.

Web Sites

www.spiritessence.com

www.maxshouse.com

www.Indoorcat.org

Alley Cat Rescue: www.saveacat.org

www.barncats.org

American Veterinary Medical Association. "Vaccine-Associated Feline Sarcoma Task Force. Feline Vaccines: Benefits and Risks." www.avma.org/vafstf/rbbroch.asp (accessed April 19, 2007).

Animal Management in Disasters. "The Public and Animal Health Consequences of Pet Ownership in Disasters," September 23, 2005. www.animaldisasters.com/Pet%20Owners.htm (accessed May 5, 2007).

Aslett, Don. *Pet Clean-Up Made Easy.* 2nd ed. Avon, MA: Adams Media, 2005.

Beata, Claude. "Understanding Feline Behavior," World Small Animal Veterinary Association World Congress, Vancouver, Canada, August 8–11, 2001. www.vin.com/VINDBPub/SearchPB/Proceedings/PR05000/PR00025.htm. (This Web site is accessible by subscription only to licensed veterinarians. If you would like to read it, ask your vet.)

Brooks, Wendy C. "Feline House Soiling," January 1, 2001. www.veterinarypartner.com/Content.plx?P=A&A=633&S=&EVetID=0.

———. "Feline Immunodeficiency Virus (FIV)," May 11, 2002. www.veterinarypartner.com/Content.plx?P=A&A=1313.

Business Trend Analysis, Inc. "Cat Litter Market Trends," 2005–2006 U.S. Outlook Report. www.bta-ler.com/lan/CatLitter2005.asp.

Buzhardt, Lynn. "Medically Managing Multi-Cat Households." *DVM.* May 1, 2002.

Commings, Karen. "Cat Fight: How to Handle Feline Aggression." www.catwatchnewsletter.com/sample/fights.html.

Cornell University College of Veterinary Medicine. "Feline Vaccines: Benefits and Risks." www.vet.cornell.edu/fhc/brochures/vaccbr.html.

Cruden, Diana. A Winn Feline Foundation Report on Early Spay/Neuter in the Cat. www.cfa.org/articles/health/early-neuter.html.

———. "Gastrointestinal Parasites of Cats." www.vet.cornell.edu/fhc/brochures/parasite.html.

Dodman, Nicholas, and Alice Moon-Fanelli. "Inter-Cat Aggression." www.petplace.com/cats/inter-cat-aggression/page1.aspx.

Ewing, Tom. "On the Lookout for FIV," March 29, 2006. www.vet.cornell.edu/fhc/news/fiv.htm.

"Feline Infectious Peritonitis (FIP)." http://petplace.netscape.com/articles/artShow.asp?artID=150.

Gilmer, Maureen. "Herbs Through the Ages." www.hgtv.com/hgtv/gl_herbs/article/0,1785,HGTV_3595_1395883,00.htm.

Graham, Helen, and Gregory Vlamis. Bach Flower Remedies for Animals. Forres, Scotland: Findhorn Press, 1999.

Hartwell, Sarah. "Cat Communication," 2002. www.messybeast.com/cat_talk2.htm 2002.

———. "The Unsociable Cat—Are Cats Really Unsociable?" 1994. www.messybeast.com/soc_cat.htm.

———. "When Cats Grieve," 2004. www.messybeast.com/cat-grief.htm.

Hofve, Jean. "Flower Essences for Animal," 2002. www.littlebigcat.com/index.php?action=library&act=show&item=floweressencesforanimals.

Hoskins, Johnny D. "Pharmacologic Studies Help DVMs Dispel Commonly Held Myths." DVM, December 1, 2006. www.dvmnews.com/dvm/article/articleDetail.jsp?id=392866.

Hunthausen, Wayne. "Fighting Tooth and Nail: A Look at Some Common Types of Feline Aggression." westwoodanimalhospital.com/BhvArticles/ cat_behavior_articles.htm.

Jensen, O. C., and I. Petersen. "Occupational Asthma Caused by Scented Gravel in Cat Litter Boxes." *Ugeskr Laeger*, 153, no. 13 (March 25, 1991): 939–40. www.ncbi.nlm.nih.gov/sites/entrez?cmd=Retrieve&db=PubMed &list_uids=2024303&dopt=Abstract.

Johnson-Bennett, Pam. *Cat vs. Cat*. New York: Penguin, 2004.

Kalstone, Shirlee, and John Martin. *Good Cat!: A Proven Guide to Successful Litter Box Use and Problem Solving*. New York: Howell Book House, 2004.

Kingstown Cat Clinic. "Protocol for Redirected Aggression in Cats." www.kingstownecatclinic.com/Redirected%20Aggression.htm.

Kipling, Rudyard. *Barrack-Room Ballads & Other Poems*. Mount Vernon, NY, Peter Pauper Press, 1963.

Knowheartworms. Cover Letter. www.knowheartworms.org.

Lang, Susan. "Diagnosis: Feline Infectious Peritonitis," March 29, 2006. www.vet.cornell.edu/fhc/news/FIP.htm.

Leatherneck. "The Legends of 'Kilroy Was Here.'" www.leatherneck.com/ forums/archive/index.php/t-3057.html.

Lienhard, John N. "Cats in Ancient Cyprus." www.uh.edu/engines/epi1906.htm.

Little, Susan. "A Practical Approach to Feline Housesoiling," 1996. www .priory.com/vet/catlit01.htm.

———. "Early Age Altering," 2006. www.winnfelinehealth.org/Pages/ Early_Age_Altering_Web.pdf.

———. "Establishing Vaccination Protocols for Catteries." *Cat Fanciers' Almanac*, 15, no. 2 (June 1998). www.cfa.org/articles/health/vaccination- protocol-catteries.html.

———. "Feline Immunodeficiency Virus." www.cfa.org/articles/health /FIV.html.

Max's House. "Bringing the Outdoors In." www.maxshouse.com/out-door_risks.htm.

———. "Outdoor Risks." maxshouse.com/outdoor_risks.htm.

McConnell, Patricia B. *The Fastidious Feline*. Black Earth, WI: Dog's Best Friend, Ltd. McConnell Publishing, 1998.

"Meows Mean More to Cat Lovers," May 21, 2002. www.channel3000.com/news/1472741/detail.html.

Montenegro, Alvaro, Adauto Araujo, Michael Eby, Luiz Fernando Ferreira, Renée Hetherington, and Andrew J. Weaver. "Parasites, Paleoclimate, and the Peopling of the Americas." *Current Anthropology* 47, no. 1 (February 2006). www.journals.uchicago.edu/CA/journal/issues/v47n1/200027/200027.html.

Moriello, Karen A. "Feline Dermatophytosis: Topical and Systemic Treatment Recommendations." www.dermapet.com/articles/Feline_Dermatophytosis.html.

"National Studies Reveal Why Pet Owners Take Animals to Shelters and How Many Find New Homes; Statistics Point to Epidemic." Colorado State University Science Blog, 1998. www.scienceblog.com/community/older/1998/A/199800939.html.

Natural History Museum of Los Angeles County. "Egypt and Domestication." Cats! Wild to Mild. www.nhm.org/cats.

Ontario Veterinary Medical Association. "Feline Infectious Peritonitis (FIP)." www.ovma.org/pet_owners/cats/fip.html.

———. "Is Your Cat Safe from Feline Distemper?" 2007. www.ovma.org/pet_owners/cats/feline_distemper.html.

Orion Foundation. "Cattery Management." www.orionfoundation.com/Information.htm.

———. "For Cat Owners: What to Do If Your Cat Is Diagnosed with FIP." www.orionfoundation.com/petowners.htm.

Overall, Karen L. "Cat Signaling: Learn the Behavior Dance to Help Patients." *DVM*, September 1, 2005. www.dvmnews.com/dvm/article/article Detail.jsp?id=181037.

———. "Feline Communication: Listen to the Tail's Tale." *DVM*.

———. "How to Deal with Anxiety and Distress Responses: Cats and Elimination, and Cats and Aggression." Atlantic Coast Veterinary Conference 2001. October 9–11, 2001. Atlantic City, New Jersey. www.vin.com/VIN DBPub/SearchPB/Proceedings/PR05000/PR00381.htm. (This Web site is accessible by subscription only to licensed veterinarians.)

PACT Humane Society. "Medications in Transdermal Gel Form Offer Relief to Caregivers & Their Companion Animals." www.pacthumanesociety .org/Transdermal.htm.

Pedersen, Neils. *Feline Husbandry Diseases and Management in the Multiple-Cat Environment*. Goleta, CA: American Veterinary Publications, 1991.

Perry, Denise. "In the Society of Cats." *Animals* 128 (May 1, 1995): 12.

Peterson, Nancy. "Find Cat-Friendly Landlords." *Catnip*. Vol. 11, No. 10, October 2003.

Peterson, N. C., and C. A. Tony Buffington. "The Effects of Active Playing on the Inappropriate Behavior of Singly Housed Indoor Cats." www.vin .com/Members/Proceedings/Proceedings.plx?CID=acvim2003&PID=pr 04196&O=VIN. (This web site is accessible by subscription only to licensed veterinarians.)

Pierson, Lisa A. "The Litter Box from Your Cat's Point of View," August 2005. www.catinfo.org/litterbox.htm#Top_reasons_for_a_cat_to_stop_ using_his_litter_box.

Plotnick, Arnold. "Vaccinating Fluffy in the 21st Century." *ASPCA Animal Watch*, Spring 2000. http://content.petfinder.com/journal/index.cgi? article=453.

Pounds, Sue. "Information and Facts on FIV," 2000. www.dcn.davis.ca.us/ vme/DrSue/letter.html.

Quality Cat Resources. "Multi Cat Behavior Problems," http://qualitycat resources.com/multi-cat-behavior-problems-2007-04-14.

Rainbolt, Dusty. *Kittens for Dummies.* New York: Wiley, 2003.

Segelken, Roger. "It's the Cat's Meow." *Cornell News* press release. May 20, 2002. www.news.cornell.edu/releases/May02/cat_talk.hrs.html.

"Semaphore." www.reference.com/browse/wiki/Semaphore.

Shea, Lisa. "Cats and Ticks: Removing a Tick from a Cat." www.lisashea.com/petinfo/articles/cat_tick.html

Shojai, Amy D. *The Purina Encyclopedia of Cat Care.* New York: Ballantine, 1998.

Siegal, Mordecai. *The Cornell Book of Cats.* 2nd ed. New York: Villard, 1997.

Simmons, Rebecca. "Cool It! Summer's Heat Can Be Deadly for Your Pet." www.hsus.org/pets/pet_care/cool_it_summers_heat_can_be_deadly_for _your_pet.html.

Springer, Ilene. "Soothe Your Cat's Grief," *CatWatch,* Vol. 7, no. 3, March 2003.

University of California Davis. "UC Davis VMTH Canine and Feline Vaccination Guidelines." www.vmth.ucdavis.edu/vmth/clientinfo/info/genmed/vaccinproto.html.

VetCentric. "Urine Marking." www.vetcentric.com/reference/encycEntry.cfm? ENTRY=16&COLLECTION=EncycIllness&MODE=full.

Virga, Vint. "Environmental Enrichment for Indoor Cats." Proceedings from the Western Veterinary Conference 2003. Feb. 17-20. Las Vegas.www .vin.com/Members/Proceedings/Proceedings.plx?CID=wvc2003&PID=p r03090&O=VIN. (This web site is accessible by subscription only to licensed veterinarians.)

Yahoo! Pets. "Keeping Your Cat Happy When You're Away." http://pets.yahoo .com/pets/cats/bt/keeping_your_cat_happy_when_youare_away.

Zimmer Foundation. "Cat Retirement Communities." http://tlconline.org/art/0018.html.

Index

Dusty Rainbolt is product editor for *Catnip*, and the author of *Kittens for Dummies* and *Ghost Cats*. She has won various awards from Iams, the ASPCA, HSUS, and the Cat Writers' Association for her books and articles on cat and kitten care. She and her houseful of cats live in north Texas.